SET UP & SOLD OUT

Find Out What Green Really Means

Holly Swanson

Updated - Third Edition

Published by

CIN Publishing

PO Box 2645

White City, OR 97503

CIN Publishing, P.O. Box 2645, White City, OR. 97503

Copyright © 1995, 1998, 2003 by Holly Swanson
First Printing 1995
Second Printing 1998, Updated Second Edition
Third Printing 2001
Fourth Printing 2003, Updated Third Edition

Swanson, Holly.
    Set up and sold out : find out what green really means / Holly Swanson.
    p.cm.
    Includes bibliographical references and index.
    Preassigned LCCN: 2003101255
    ISBN 0-9645108-2-0

1. Green movement--United States--Political aspects. 2. Environmentalism--United States--Economic aspects. 3. Sustainability. I. Title.

JA75.8.S93 2003   322.4'4
                         QBI95-20388

Manufactured in the United States of America

Books are available in quantity for promotional or premium use. Write Special Sales, CIN Publishing, PO Box 2645, White City, OR 97503, for information on discounts and terms or call 541/830-1446.

Set Up & Sold Out

Chapter 1

Chapter 2

Chapter 3

Chapter 4

Chapter 5

Chapter 6

Chapter 7

Chapter 8

1

SET UP

Every American shares a fundamental concern for and sincere appreciation of the beauty of our natural environment. We can all identify with the special feelings that automatically arise as we experience the wonder of nature; warm summer nights, crisp fall mornings or dark, cloudy, windy days. From creatures in the wild to a box full of puppies, even the scent of a freshly mown lawn stirs our senses. There is no question, Americans care about the environment, animals and nature.

Americans support environmental protection and taking the necessary steps to correct environmental problems. The dilemma we face is different than either of these points. The problem is, the environmental cause is being used to conceal the implementation of a specific political agenda most Americans are not aware of.

Our immediate challenge involves making more and better distinctions about the answers to environmental questions. We need to begin making distinctions between productive steps toward a healthy environment and steps to implement a political agenda under the guise of environmental protection.

Set Up & Sold Out is a revealing look into the secret side of environmental politics. Americans must understand there is a subversive motivation behind the push for drastic change and rigid environmental regulations. We are all involved. This is not a liberal vs. conservative or a Republican vs. Democrat issue. This situation transcends all others. No one is exempt.

Before better distinctions can be made, a general grasp of the situation is required. What does Green really mean? To most Americans, green still means the color. Many people now associate the color green with the environmental cause. Most Americans do not realize the word green is now defined in political terms.

The overall environmental cause is commonly referred to as the Green movement or simply the Greens. The Green movement represents a multifaceted political arm. It represents multiple special interest politics, concealed under the political umbrella of environmental protection. The Greens, or Green political party is also part of that group. The problem is, Americans do not understand how their concern for environmental protection is being used by the Greens to advance the Green political agenda, an agenda most Americans would totally disagree with. The Greens use deceptive tactics to advance their goals, such as:

- lying to the American people
- using entertainment to mold public opinion
- taking advantage of children

Why should Green politics concern every American? The American people have been set-up to believe Green means good for the environment and good for the American people. One does not equal the other. Green politics and environmental protection are two completely different issues. American's support for environmental protection does not equal support for the hidden political agenda of the Green movement.

The Greens are advancing their political plans disguised as progressive solutions to environmental protection. Greens plan to use fear of environmental doom to pass laws that will:

- control individual opportunities and actions
- control business
- end private property rights

This is only the tip of the 'Green iceberg'. Americans need to fully understand the political goals and manipulative tactics of the Green movement. What appears to be a spontaneous effort to help us find the path to a healthy environmental future is more like being led down the garden path.

The Greens are manipulating environmental issues to force massive social change on unsuspecting Americans. We are not talking about reduce, reuse and recycle. The Green plan calls for a complete social transformation that will erase our culture. The issue is, do we need to change everything about America to protect the environment for future generations?

There is a tremendous amount of good that can result from the universal awareness of environmental issues. Recognizing the oppressive and negative aspects of the Green political agenda will not prevent America from continuing to take positive steps toward our goal of environmental excellence. It will only ensure we make intelligent and informed decisions regarding the future of our country. We do not need to eliminate efforts to protect and clean up the environment. We need to make careful distinctions between ideas that are good for America and the environment and subversive efforts by the Greens to use different issues to advance their political agenda.

We are all willing to do our share. The question is, how far do we need to go to achieve our goals? Before we can determine if the Green political plan reflects the kind of future we see for America, we need to look at the kind of America the Greens envision.

Jonathan Porritt is a well-known author, political activist and a leader in the Green movement. Porritt's book, *Save the Earth* provides a look into the Green future and reveals an insider's perspective of the political goals of the Greens.

Porritt describes the future as a 'Green World Order' that means more than achieving the goal of world government. The Green future includes specific laws to regulate what people can do and how people will live.

Porritt defines this future lifestyle as 'compulsory Green living'. 'Compulsory Green living' means obeying the Green's rules will be mandatory. Porritt suggests this Green lifestyle will be forced on citizens by their government, from the top down.

The Green rules Porritt described included:

- rationed foods (lentils)
- one washing machine per 20 people
- lights out by 10:00 p.m.
- mandatory tree-hugging every Sunday

Porritt offers us another snapshot of the Green future. Porritt describes a World Order where the Green flag replaces the Red flag and where Green Dictators rule.

'Compulsory Green living' sounds like Green Communism. Would transforming America to match Porritt's vision solve our environmental problems? The Greens are not out to save the earth. The Greens are using the environmental cause to advance their hidden political agenda.

The Russian dictator, Nikita Krushchev seemed to share Porritt's dream of seeing his Red flag fly over America. On June 19, 1962 he predicted that:

> *"The United States will eventually fly the Communist Red Flag. The American people will hoist it themselves."*

Porritt indicates the Green flag is a replacement for the Red flag. One can be substituted for the other because they are interchangeable. If Americans accept the Green plan for our future, we will have, in essence, hoisted the Red Communist flag ourselves.

Green politics and ideology parallel the Socialism to Communism political process. Socialism is the first step, but Communism is the goal. The Greens are using the environmental cause to camouflage their efforts to move Americans toward Socialism, then force us into Communism.

Porritt suggests this is just a Green dream and that people would only live this way because they want to save the earth. The alternative to being forced into Communism is for citizens to volunteer, as Krushchev predicted.

Excusing this plan as a Green dream is a standard tactic used by Communists. Communists say what they mean, then say, they didn't mean what they said. This is how Communists can openly communicate with comrades. They say what they mean then quickly dismiss it as a joke or dream so others will also quickly dismiss it and disregard its political significance.

The Green slogan, 'Think Globally Act Locally' takes on a whole new meaning when you realize the goal is still world Communism.

Mr. Porritt is Green. This does not mean everyone involved with the environmental effort is a Green Communist. It means the political ideas and tactics of the Green movement mirror Communism and Communist strategies. The environmental cause offers Green Communists abundant circumstances to use our emotions and our political system to put themselves in a position to seize power.

This is a calculated political effort based on using the fate of mankind to justify massive changes in our society. It involves justifying more and more government control over American citizens by using fear of pending environmental disaster to gain public support to pass major environmental protection laws. The Green objective is to 'make control possible by making control legal'.

Could we end up in a Green future? We could, if we continue to let the Greens use the environment and other Green causes to dominate American politics. Political leaders and citizens cannot continue to let emotions be their guide. From Earth Day to politically correct speech, the Green movement is not what America thinks it is.

Whittaker Chambers was a member of the Communist Party. Chambers defected from the Communist Party for moral reasons and wrote the book, *Witness* in 1952 to warn the American people of the Communist's long term plans to take over America in the 20th century. Chambers states:

> "...*the nation, too, wanted peace above all things, and it simply could not grasp or believe that a conspiracy on the scale of Communism was possible or that it had already made so deep a penetration into their lives...*"
>
> *Witness*
> Whittaker Chambers

Information in the following chapters will confirm the political direction the Green movement is taking fits with the long-term plans of the Communists to overthrow our government and take over America.

Throughout this book, all references to the Green movement or the Greens refer to the Communist faction within the Green movement that is manipulating our concern for the environment and other issues, to advance Communist goals. Reference to the Greens is used in a general sense to identify those who are Communist and those who may not be Communist, but promote a similar political philosophy.

Communism in America

Communists never stop promoting their political program. It is a lifetime commitment. The language of Communism hasn't changed. Communists introduce their ideas as new and progressive but the buzzwords and political goals are consistent. The message, the goals and the methods remain the same.

The language among Communists is also consistent. From the early books warning Americans to beware of Communism to the most recent environmental publications, the term *fellow traveler* is used. *Fellow travelers* are those involved in the Communist struggle for revolution in America. The only difference between *fellow travelers* and Communists is official membership in the Communist party. Their goals and political philosophies are the same. Comrade is another term the Greens and the Communists use. The Democratic Socialists of America use the term comrade in their Red-Green literature.

The Communists preach the concept of 'true democracy' and use the term 'progressive' because it appeals to intellectuals. They seek the political support of intellectuals because intellectuals pride themselves in being on the cutting edge of social thought. This offers Communists fertile ground to cultivate their ideas and get intellectuals to present them as new and creative solutions to existing problems. Communists also con well-known people into promoting their ideas because it encourages others to follow.

Before embracing progressive ideas, those who consider themselves intellectuals ought to take a tip from Hitler on the role they play in political mass movements. They are used like anyone else to enlist the support of others. To illustrate his point, Hitler quotes Hans Sachs:

> "Despise not your master craftsmen. But the great masses of those who call themselves the 'educated' are the superficial intellectual demimonde, conceited and arrogant incompetents who are not even aware of the ridiculous figures they cut as they dabble."
>
> Adolf Hitler
> *Hitler--Memoirs of a Confidant*
> Henry Turner

Communists also target the middle class and the poor to con them into believing their lives will be radically improved if they help do away with Capitalism. Once Communists seize power, promises disappear. Force and fear become the tools to control the people. Equality under Communism means the masses work as slaves and live under the same conditions. Communism does not end oppression, it makes it universal.

Greens promise equality and social justice. They guarantee people a job, food, shelter and health care. The Green objective is to convince the American masses the only way to achieve these goals and save the environment is to abandon Capitalism and let the government take control of their lives.

Green Communism

"the environmental movement promises to bring greater numbers into our orbit than the peace movement ever did"
Carl Bloice
McAlvany Intelligence Advisor-March 1995

Carl Bloice is a leading U.S. Communist. Bloice was the Associate Editor and Moscow correspondent for the '*People's Daily World*'. He is reported to be close to Mikhail Gorbachev. This statement by Bloice makes it easier to understand why Communists, like Gorbachev have become involved in the environmental cause. Gorbachev is currently the President of an international environmental organization, called Green Cross International, with a chapter in the United States called, Global Green.

Communists target all radical or popular movements where they can weave their political ideas into the cause and con the masses into thinking those ideas are new and progressive. Communists operate like criminals. They don't plan to get caught in the act. They plan to get the job done without being noticed. Green Communists planned to have all their snowballs in a row before the cat got out of the bag.

The environmental cause was identified in its infancy to serve as a front for Communists and to be the catalyst to promote Socialism and set-us-up for Communism. Communists planned to be the organizers and the leaders in the U.S. environmental movement a long time ago. They identified fear as a key element to convince Americans that Capitalism threatens our survival.

Who is Gus Hall? Why should we care?

Americans need to understand this attack on our nation isn't new. It began years ago and it has never stopped. We have been deliberately misled to believe Communism is no longer a threat to our nation so the Greens can carry out their calculated political plan to take over our nation.

> "*The key factor will be the leadership of the struggle of the working class...Masses who after all are the power of any revolution...This is true in the struggle to save the environment. What is new, is that the knowledge of the point of no return gives this struggle an unusual urgency. Those of us who know that capitalism cannot basically be reformed, must work with and for people who have not yet come to that conclusion. We must be the organizers, the leaders of these movements*"
>
> *Ecology -- 1972*
> Gus Hall
> Bold Emphasis Added)

To understand how dedicated Communists are to achieving their long-term political goals, it is important to review a court case involving a group of Communist conspirators. Twelve members of the Communist Party of the United States were indicted by a Federal Grand Jury in July, 1948 and charged with conspiracy. Albert Kahn, author of, *High Treason*, stated:

> "*The indictment accused the Communist leaders of plotting to subvert the Government by:*
>
> *...organizing a political party dedicated to the principles of Marxism-Leninism*
>
> *...Arranging to publish and circulate...books, magazines and newspapers advocating the principles of Marxism-Leninism*

...establishing schools and classes for the study of the principles of Marxism-Leninism, in which would be taught and advocated the duty and necessity of overthrowing and destroying the Government of the United States by force and violence."

Two of the men named in the indictment were: Henry Winston and Gus Hall. They were both found guilty and sentenced. Sentences ranged from 30 days to five-year prison terms and one of the twelve also received a $10,000 fine.

Gus Hall has been a leader in the CPUSA, the Communist Party of the United States of America, for decades. Hall and others in the U.S. Communist Party convicted of conspiring to overthrow our government in 1948 have continued their efforts. Hall was still at it 50 years later. Hall wrote the book, *Ecology* in 1972. He outlined strategies and explained how the environmental cause could be used to advance Communism in America. Hall was the National Chairman of the CPUSA.

The CPUSA receives substantial financial support from the Soviet Union. According to an article in *Harper's*, June 1992, the Communist Party of the Soviet Union has been contributing $2 million dollars per year to the Communist Party of the United States. This information surfaced when a letter from Gus Hall was discovered in the 'personal files' of Mikhail Gorbachev.

The letter was sent to Soviet leaders requesting an additional $2 million dollars to cover expenses from election campaigns and increased operating costs. The letter was written to Soviet leaders in January 1987; Hall indicates the Soviets financial investment in America's political campaigns had been successful.

Hall made the following statement in that letter:

"we went all out in the 1986 congressional elections, which, in my opinion paid off very well...we were influential, and even the deciding factor, in the defeat of some of the extreme Reaganite candidates."

The article points out:

"Two months after the letter was sent, Hall received $2 million from a KGB courier."

Hall received money from the Soviet Union to finance their fight against Capitalism, influence our elections, elect communist sympathizers and defeat American candidates by spreading communist propaganda. In May 1995, Bruce Fellman, documents this in the article "What Secret Soviet Files Reveal", featured in the May, 1995 edition of *Yale's Alumni magazine* and the *Sacramento Bee* newspaper. In the article Fellman refers to the book, *The Secret World of American Communism*. This book is based on new information from the Soviet archives about the activities of the Communist Party USA Fellman states the authors of the book:

"demolish what they call 'the predominant view among scholars' that the C.P.U.S.A was simply a political alternative to the Republicans and Democrats, and not an arm of a Soviet government bent on toppling the U.S. government."

"As the documents in this volume show the authors note, the C.P.U.S.A. was in fact a 'conspiracy' financed by a hostile foreign power that recruited members for clandestine work, developed an elaborate underground apparatus and used that apparatus to collaborate with espionage services..."

Gus Hall regularly wrote for *Political Affairs* magazine.

Henry Winston led the party until his death in the late 1980's. *Political Affairs* is affiliated with the Communist Party. The June 1994 edition of *Political Affairs* featured excerpts from a speech Hall made at the Advanced Young Communists League (YCL). Hall's comments included:

> *"The key to what we have to do in a popular way is what the Communist Manifesto did over a hundred years ago...expose Capitalism, develop class consciousness...and find creativeways to present socialism USA.*
>
> *"Only our party can provide the organization, the tactics, the strategy and perspective of struggle, change and revolution*
>
> *"... only political party capable of leading the working class to revolution and socialism."*

Hall emphasized a goal of the Communist Party and the YCL was to use the anger and militancy of American youth to recruit members and organize acts of rebellion.

> *"the young people...when they meet us on the street or in action, they see the YCL and party as an organization that will help them protest, fight and win"*
>
> *Political Affairs - June 1994*
> Gus Hall

Hall indicated Communist clubs would be used to offer a place for young people to go, so they can learn, plan and participate in militant actions. This would be a new social life for young people. The Greens are using any opportunity to present Socialism as the alternative to Capitalism. They are targeting young people, promoting national health care and abusing environmental issues. The plan is to reform our system and con Americans into believing the only solution is more government control of our lives.

Communist Rules for Revolution

These 9 rules were seized in a 1919 raid in Dusseldorf Germany. Files were marked, *Communist Rules for Revolution.*

1. Corrupt the young; get them away from religion. Get them interested in sex. Make them superficial; destroy their ruggedness.

2. Get control of all means of publicity. Get peoples' minds off their government by focusing their attention on athletics, sexy books, plays and other trivialities.

3. Divide people into hostile groups by constantly harping on controversial matters of no importance.

4. Destroy the peoples' faith in their natural leaders by holding the latter up to contempt, ridicule and obloquy.

5. Always preach 'true democracy' but seize power as last and as ruthlessly as possible.

6. By encouraging government extravagance, destroy its credit; produce fear of inflation, rising prices and general discontent.

7. Foment strikes in vital industries; encourage civil disorders and foster a lenient and soft attitude on the part of government toward these disorders.

8. By special argument cause a breakdown of the old moral virtues; honesty, sobriety, continence, faith in the pledged word, ruggedness.

9. Cause the registration of all firearms on some pretext with a view of confiscation of them and leaving the population helpless.

Is there evidence to indicate any of these rules may have been applied to disrupt our society, reform our system of government or change our constitutional rights? It is important to remember that Communists are dedicated to their political beliefs and spend a lifetime devoted to the advancement of Communism. The Soviets paid Hall to sabotage our electoral process. Hall has spent fifty years working to change America. It is most likely these rules have been followed. Review the list of rules and think about a few of the issues Americans are now dealing with:

- government extravagance
- gun control
- moral decay
- manufactured divisions within society

It is hard to ignore the long-range goals of the Communist party when they match the emergence of the Greens in America. At this time, Greens and Communist leaders are calling for mass Party building. Recruiting plans include targeting these unsuspecting Americans: the poor, jobless, young people, minorities, the homeless and the illiterate. These Americans are key political targets because they are the most vulnerable to the promise of Socialism.

We are in a political fight for our lives. If we ignore this fact, we will probably end up in a Green future. If we plan to avoid, 'compulsory Green living', we must instantly become more committed to preserving our freedom than the Greens are to taking it away from us.

> *"Human society cannot basically stop the destruction of the environment under capitalism. Socialism is the only structure that makes it possible."*
>
> Ecology 1972
> Gus Hall
> National Chairman CPUSA

Just Like Termites

While most Americans haven't even heard of the Greens, the Greens have been working away for years, just like termites, to weaken the foundation of our nation. Our nation is like our home. Our safety and comfort depend on a strong foundation. Last time we looked, our foundation was in decent shape. We felt safe. We had the time to focus our attention on other things.

Now there is a visible crack in the foundation. If we want to be safe, we need to repair the areas where damage has been done. A house with a weak foundation can collapse. The Green strategy is to change key elements within our society until piece-by-piece the America we know falls apart.

The Greens liken their vision to what appeared to be the overnight collapse of the Soviet Union. The only difference between the collapse of the two superpowers will be the result. The Green goal for a massive transformation in America promises to establish Communism.

Hide and Seek

We have seen it. We have felt it. We just haven't been able to put our finger on where all the push, push, push, for change, change, change was coming from.

A great deal of our current social unrest stems from subversive Green activism. What appear to be random, isolated incidents are actually coordinated efforts to challenge long-standing American policies and traditions.

The Greens have set the stage. Each group has a role to play in creating conflict within our society. Green activists are dedicated to the goal of revolution and routinely perform assigned political tasks such as:

- Handing out propaganda
- Building coalitions with like minded groups
- Infiltrating various groups to advance party goals
- Organizing political events
- Staging protests and demonstrations
- Recruiting new members, including youth
- Moving as needed to organize support in key areas

Staged public demonstrations have political value. It's much easier to convince politicians to vote for special interest laws if they are set up to believe citizen unrest is real and political action is necessary. At one Green meeting, the speaker indicated that 'if they couldn't get the vote, they would import the vote'. Whether the Greens stage demonstrations or import votes, we all lose an incremental piece of our freedom each time the Greens are successful in forcing an end to another American tradition or slaughtering another American value.

The founding fathers knew, from personal experience, too much political power was dangerous. Our government was founded on a system of checks and balances to prevent one political force from dominating government. If one interest group gained too much political power it would eliminate equal representation and put our political system out of balance and at risk.

Americans have responded to the environmental cause by joining environmental groups and offering generous financial contributions. This show of support translates into too much political power. The Greens are pushing for changes in public policies at an unprecedented rate without the scrutiny that is typical of our check and balance system.

Throughout history, revolutionaries have lied to people to gain power. Revolutionaries operate on the 'end justifies the means' plan. Deception is part of the revolutionary process.

> *"I hate deception, even where the imagination only is concerned"*
>
> George Washington
> Letter to Dr. Cochran, Aug 16, 1779

Is the environmental situation as bad as we have been lead to believe or is our love of nature being used to manipulate us into accepting Green politics?

> *"The great masses of people will more easily fall victims to a great lie than to a small one."*
>
> Adolf Hitler

Vladimir Lenin, leader of the Russian Revolution created the Bolshevik party and lied to the Russian people to persuade them to try his political ideas. Hitler created the Nazi Party and lied to the German people to persuade them to try his political ideas. Both political movements were based on ideas or ideology. After Hitler and Lenin seized power, they made their ideas law. After they were in power it was too late for people to ask questions or offer suggestions. The time to ask questions is now, before all the Green's political ideas become law.

The Green movement is also based on ideas. The Greens are directly and indirectly lying to the American people to convince us Socialism is better for the environment. Revolutions are fueled by emotionally charged causes. Trusting people fall prey to political ideas based on feelings, not facts. Emotions are manipulated and ideas become laws.

Can you tell, Hitler or Lenin?

- Public ownership of the Land, abolish private property
- Public ownership of the Healthcare industry
- Public ownership of the Energy industry
- Public ownership of the Auto industry
- Public ownership of the Railroad industry
- Public ownership of the Banking industry
- Public ownership of the Insurance industry
- Public ownership of the Natural Resources
- Public control of the Economy and Small Business

Do the above political ideas represent Hitler's political program for Nazi Germany or Lenin's Communist Party program? Neither, these are the primary goals of the Greens.

Public ownership of all resources includes:

- Land, Water, Mineral, Forest, Plants and Animals
- Electromagnetic, the airwaves, all communication systems including cable and computer networks

The current push to police the Internet, or the information super highway, also fits the Green goal to control everything from the airwaves to the individual.

The Greens are convincing Americans to support Green politics by developing multiple emotional messages that appeal to people in every segment of our society.

It is interesting that in America, we normally refer to a series of political positions or ideas as a *political platform*. Communists refer to their political ideas as a *program*. The Greens use *program* to define their political positions.

More Green Goals on the National Agenda

- 75% Reduction in the Military Budget
- National Healthcare
- US to ratify the Biodiversity Treaty
- Limit multiple use of Public Lands, grazing, etc.
- Gay Rights
- Gun Control

Even though most Americans haven't heard of Green politics, Green politics are evident in many ideas and issues being promoted in America and pushed on the American people.

The Green Party seems like an obscure little band of radicals who are not a threat to this nation. Their ideas appear to receive little or no national attention. Hitler also paraded around, leading his little band of radicals. At first, no one paid much attention. That was a critical error in judgment.

The Greens are successfully incorporating their political ideas into mainstream America. Until we understand the Greens political objectives they will continue to be successful. Green successes include:

- Federal control of timber harvest
- Clinton's call for 50-75% reduction in the U.S. Military
- Gays in the military

Until we recognize when and how the Greens are imposing their political program on America, it will continue. The Green agenda includes working toward crippling and eventually eliminating these industries:

- Cattle industry
- Timber industry
- Agriculture industry
- Fishing industry

- Sport hunting and fishing industries
- Recreationist, off- road vehicles
- Gun and weapons industry

Greens also intend to use our emotions and Animal Rights issues to eliminate these American traditions:

- Rodeos
- Circuses
- Commercial animal breeding
- Animals in entertainment
- Horse racing
- Dog racing
- Zoos
- Aquariums

More Green Goals from the Green Party Program

- Transform society using 'sustainability' as the vehicle
- Reduce United States border defense
- Abolish arms markets and sales in the United States
- Eliminate the use of all pesticides and herbicides
- Phase out gasoline and other fossil fuels
- Alternatives to use of pharmaceuticals
- Work for World or Global Government
- Transform food system: from meat to vegetarian
- Cancel third world debt, debt for nature swaps
- End government tax benefits to gain control of:
  - airline industry
  - nuclear, energy corporations (utilities)
  - virgin paper
- Establish a system of nonviolent civilian defense
- Support for International Law, World Court and International Treaties such as the U. N. Convention on the Rights of a Child.

According to an article by Phyllis Schlafly, this treaty, if passed, could result in losing control over how our children are raised to a world panel. The treaty offers no guarantee an American would serve on the international decision-making panel. Congressman Thomas J. Bliley warned Americans the UN 'Convention on the Rights of the Child' would eliminate the Ninth and Tenth amendments to the Constitution and that it posed a threat to our government.

Another Green goal:

- Abolish the CIA and covert operations agencies

December, 1993, Jane Fonda spoke at the United Nations as part of the Eminent Citizens Committee and suggested the United States should cut our CIA budget and spend the extra money to help develop Third World countries. Eliminating part of the CIA budget would cut investigations of covert and foreign government activities regarding the national security of the United States. It is not a good idea to hinder the agency that protects our national security when Communists are already in the United States and using the environmental cause to camouflage their activities.

It appears both Jane Fonda and her former husband, Ted Turner, support the Green movement. Porritt's book, *Save the Earth*, was published by Turner Publishing, Inc, a subsidiary of Turner Broadcasting System, Inc. Why was Jane Fonda suggesting to the United Nations what America ought to do with our CIA funding?

The political objectives of the Green movement include; abolishing the CIA and redistributing American's wealth to Third World countries. Do Ted and Jane understand the Green wealth inventory will include their mega-millions?

Like A Thief In The Night, Greens Plan To Steal

"The chic upper-class ecologists, with their hot-tubs, their quarter-million-dollar homes, their designer clothes, and their Mercedes Benzes, had best realize that their calls for clean air must be accompanied by meaningful actions that will lead to a redistribution of their own unwarranted economic abundance. If they do not voluntarily begin to make this economic adjustment, then others will make it for them."

Entropy – 1980
Jeremy Rifkin

Jeremy Rifkin is an active leader in the Green movement. The above statement is from the 1980 edition of his book, *Entropy*. It is interesting that in the 1989 reprint of the book the above statement was omitted. Wonder why?

Could it be, now that the environmental cause has been made so popular, Rifkin does not want anyone to notice part of the Green plan involves redistributing the wealth of 'upper-class ecologists' and if Americans don't agree to this, 'then others will do it for them'? Was this paragraph left out to cover-up the Greens plan to steal American's wealth, using force if necessary? This sounds like Porritt's implied idea that we can either volunteer for Communism or be forced into it.

Would Americans continue to offer their financial support to environmental groups if they realized this was part of the Green plan? Doubtful. Americans would probably stop donating millions of dollars to finance the Greens and funding their own demise. The Greens need to keep the money coming in to finance their political efforts to change America.

"Foreign policies should further encourage an equitable global distribution of wealth"

Green Party Program

The Greens call for the redistribution of the wealth earned by all American citizens. This is not just about Americans with abundant wealth. All different kinds of people with all different kinds of income would be subject to converting to 'compulsory Green living'. Rich, poor and in-between, it comes down to limiting every Americans ability to choose what they want and the opportunity to pursue their dreams.

Others have called for the redistribution of citizen's wealth using similar justifications. Hitler convinced people to support the Nazi's confiscation of the property and wealth of the Jewish people. Hitler's speeches and writings show the propaganda ideas he used to manipulate the masses.

> *"We see that the primary cause for the existing tensions lies in the unfair distribution of the riches of the earth."*
> *My New Order*

> *"Against the infection of materialism, against the Jewish pestilence we must hold aloft a flaming idea."*
> *The Speeches of Adolf Hitler*

> *"The Jews are a people under whose parasitism the whole of honest humanity is suffering, today more than ever."*
> *Mein Kampf*

> *"Jewish parasites...plundered the nation without pity."*
> *The Speeches of Adolf Hitler*

Hitler played on people's fears. Hitler set people up to actually believe the Jewish people were irresponsible, evil materialists (capitalists) who had raped Germany and stolen wealth from the German people. Hitler convinced normal people to seek revenge against the Jews, the people he decided to hold responsible for Germany's problems. The Greens have duplicated many of Hitler's emotional ploys. This time the scapegoat is the American people. Americans are portrayed as materialistic capitalists who rape the earth, steal its riches and are to blame for causing environmental problems around the world. Hitler suggested redistributing Jewish wealth to protect the sacred soil.

The Greens imply redistribution of American's wealth will save the earth. The Greens blame Americans, Capitalism and materialism for environmental problems. Hitler blamed the Jewish people for Germany's problems. The environment instead of race is the issue this decade. Is there any significant difference in the propaganda message?

- problem caused by unfair distribution of wealth
- against infection of materialism
- causing the rest of honest humanity to suffer
- plunder the nation without pity

Hitler knew if you repeat a lie often enough, people would begin to believe it. Hitler blamed the Jews. The Greens blame Americans. If we look at the list of Americans on the Green hate list of environmental crimes we can see how the Greens have used Hitler's simplistic methods to shape the opinion of the masses.

The Greens shape public opinion by labeling Americans who question Green politics, 'anti-environmentalist'. Hitler was successful using labels and his tactic appears to be working well the second time around. We all need to understand, the only difference between self-proclaimed environmentalists and anti-environmentalists is the label the Greens put on them. As in Nazi Germany, the only difference between the Jews and other people was the label they were forced to wear.

Hitler used that label to create division and promote intolerance towards the Jews. The Greens are using labels to create intolerance towards certain Americans. Hitler labeled the entire Jewish population as sub-human and people accepted it. The Greens have labeled any American concerned with Green politics as anti-environmentalists and have convinced some Americans to believe it without reason or fact.

Hitler did the same thing. He presented one group as good and another as bad, so the public would pick the pre-designated correct side to be on. This tactic discourages citizens from thinking or asking questions because the politically correct opinion has been provided in advance. Have the Greens been successful using the Hitler approach? Does it work? Read the following list of political issues.

Ranchers	or	Wolves
Dolphins	or	Fishermen
Recreationist	or	Turtles
Delhi Sands Flies	or	Developers
Spotted Owls	or	Loggers
Farmers	or	Wetlands
Animal Rights	or	Citizen Rights

Which is the politically correct side? What is this political opinion based on?

- Knowledge from an in-depth study of the issue
- A ten second sound byte on the evening news
- Newspaper headlines
- Green political messages on television and in movies
- Green propaganda from environmental organizations

We need to remember as we form political opinions, that these issues are multifaceted. Real people, just like us, are attached to these issues. Their families and their futures are involved.

"There are people who eagerly accept their own freedom but do not respect the freedom of others...They would do well to look at what has happened in societies without moral foundations. Accepting no laws but the laws of force, these societies have been ruled by totalitarian ideologies like Nazism, fascism, and communism, which do not spring from the general populace, but are imposed on it by intellectual elites."

Margaret Thatcher
Prime Minister of Britain -1979-1990
IMPRIMIS - March 1995
Journal of Hillsdale College

Our futures are involved also. It is irresponsible for us to accept unqualified, simplistic information that impacts the lives of our fellow citizens and determines the future of our country.

The key to the Greens successful manipulation of the American people to date, stems from copying the political ideas and tactics of both Adolf Hitler and Vladimir Lenin.

BIG MISTAKE

How did Hitler convince a nation to go along with his ideas? Many Germans jumped on the Nazi bandwagon but others didn't take Hitler seriously or consider the Nazis a threat. Citizens did not believe the Nazis could gain enough political power to force their ideas on the German people. They stopped paying attention to the politics of the Nazi movement and went on with their lives. Big mistake!

Meanwhile, Hitler and his little band of Nazis continued to have parades and sell Nazi trinkets to promote their cause. What started out as a small but solid band of fanatics grew into the Nazi movement. The Nazi parades were similar to the Greens Earth Day events. It wasn't a good idea for big business to help finance the Nazi movement and it isn't a good idea for big business to finance the Green movement.

Hitler convinced thousands upon thousands to join the Nazi movement by using emotional ploys, political fanfare, clever propaganda, hate and terrorism. He promised all things to all people. He even persuaded German parents to involve their children in the Nazi movement. Hitler lied all the time and manipulated himself into power, lie by lie. Hitler began his political career by finding people he felt comfortable with and superior to. He surrounded himself with other derelicts, perverts and a few ambitious politicians who felt he was on the right track. Slowly but surely, Hitler built a coalition of militant, intolerant outcasts.

Hitler planned for the future. He knew what he was doing when he involved children in national politics. He formed the famous Hitler Youth groups so he could grow a loyal Nazi army. Germany's children were molded into pledging their allegiance to Hitler and no one else.

Children were taught to believe Hitler was God. They were loyal to Hitler over friends and family. Germany's children grew into murderers because they were trained to be Nazi terrorists and political activists as young children. We cannot blame the children. It was their parents who initially allowed them to participate in national politics as children. Nazi leaders taught them Hitler's ideology. How could the children know it was wrong? They could not. They were sacrificed to the Nazi movement.

Tolerance from most citizens and aggressive support from others gave Hitler the time he needed to set up the right political opportunity to put him in the position to attain absolute power over Germany. Hitler made control possible by making control legal.

The American people are making the same mistake about the Green movement the German people made about the Nazi movement. Americans are buying into the Green movement based on emotional ploys, political fanfare, clever propaganda, hate, lies, terrorism and the promise of all things to all people. American parents are allowing their children to be involved in the national politics of the Green movement.

Many Americans have jumped into the Green movement without fully understanding the scope of the movement. Other Americans are too busy to pay attention or are looking the other way because they don't understand how this affects them. Many Americans do not believe the Greens can gain enough political power to force their ideas on the American people. Big mistake!

There are so many aspects of Green copy-cat politics. Even the color is significant. Anne Frank noted, it was the Green Police who came to arrest her. The Greens also want to establish a Green Police force or Green Helmet forces to enforce ecological laws. The Green Party, like the Nazis, originated in Germany. The symbol of the Green Party is the sunflower. The sunflower was a Nazi symbol of honor. Sunflowers were used by the Nazis to pay tribute to fallen soldiers. Sunflowers were planted on soldier's graves. When they bloomed, the cemetery became a field of bright yellow and a striking memorial to the Nazi cause.

Subliminal Green political messages are prominent in numerous television programs, movies and advertisements. The sunflower emerged a few years ago. It can now be seen on display everywhere. The sunflower is more than a fashion statement. It's a political symbol that is being promoted for a reason. The plan is to get us to identify with this symbol and get attached to it. The plan is, if we like the symbol we will support the politics that go with it.

S.S.D.D. Same Stuff Different Decade

Green political ideas and propaganda messages mirror the psychological and emotional ploys Hitler used to successfully manipulate a nation.

Nazi Movement	Green Movement
Used Nature	Using Nature
Save the Fatherland	Save Mother Earth
Earth is a living organism	Earth is a living being – Gaia
Used animal rights	Using animal rights
Green police - SS men	Green police - Eco Cops
Sunflower was symbol	Sunflower is symbol
One people, one nation	One people, one planet
Used women	Using women
Fascination with wolves	Fascination with wolves
Religion - Hitler was God	Religion - Earth-based, atheist
Myth, Pagan, Goddess	Myth, Pagan, Goddess
Nazi - High Holy Days	Greens - Earth Day
Nazis - mostly teachers	Greens - mostly teachers
Children taught Nazism	Children taught to be Green
Hitler stressed community	Greens stress community
Hitler stressed activism	Greens stress activism
Jews root of all evil	Americans root of all evil
Nazi Party began Germany	Green Party began Germany
Scapegoat - Capitalist	Scapegoat - Capitalist

The Greens are using Hitler's ideas because he successfully convinced thousands of reasonable people to support political insanity. Nazism in Germany seemed to happen spontaneously, but there were certain factors that helped

Hitler. The Greens have recreated some of those same factors by introducing alternative ideas that enticed the German masses to abandon their traditions and morals. The same alternative ideas that prompted the people to become Nazis are prompting Americans to go Green.

> *"at the turn of the century, there was a rising tide of materialism in Germany and Austria, with a countervailing reaction that yearned for a more harmonious and spiritual past. Many of Germany's youth became known as 'the birds of passage' with vegetarianism, herbal healing, communal living, nudism, and meditation becoming fashionable... and in every major city, cults devoted to spiritualism, astrology, magic and the occult formed."*
> Now is the Dawning of the New Age New World Order
> Dr. Dennis Cuddy

Obviously, similar circumstances can produce similar results. That is what we must avoid. There is nothing wrong with herbal healing or vegetarianism. We need to understand it was the combination of all the new, alternative ideas that led to the broader acceptance of Hitler's fanatical blend of spirituality and politics. Once the German people started dabbling in alternative ideas, it was easier to justify changing traditions and accepting the Nazi's political and spiritual ideas. Americans must understand our acceptance of this combination of alternative ideas can lead to a broader acceptance of Green ideas on spirituality and politics.

Talking Points

The Greens even use the same language and arguments Hitler used to justify his actions. Hitler persuaded a nation to support theft and murder in the name of saving the sacred soil of the Fatherland, sometimes referred to as the Motherland.

Hitler convinced a nation of intelligent people to try his blend of spiritual politics that included aggressive and intolerant political opinions combined with a fierce commitment to:

- protect the sacred soil
- preserve the German species
- animal rights above human rights
- see the earth as a living organism
- identify with the earth as their Mother

Greens are convincing intelligent Americans to accept copy-cat spiritual politics. Green politics include aggressive and intolerant political opinions combined with a commitment to:

- protect the sacred soil
- animal rights above human rights
- see the earth as a living organism, or Gaia
- have a spiritual connection with the earth
- identify with the earth as our Mother

Hitler preyed on emotions to create a fanatical political following dedicated to protecting the sacred soil of the Fatherland. The Greens are preying on emotions to create the same type of political loyalty based on the same kind of spiritual relationship with the earth. It wasn't a healthy or normal mentality then and it isn't a healthy or normal mentality now.

The Greens justify their actions in the name of environmental protection. The Greens are using Hitler's reasons to promote and justify their actions. Hitler used the following ideas:

- the earth does not belong to us, it is not given as a gift
- earth belongs to those who take control and preserve it
- not wrong to take property in name of cause
- preserve it for future generations

The Greens also use Hitler's method of controlling opposition.

- divert public attention by attacking character of enemy
- avoid public disclosure and measures to be taken
- blame current political actions on injustices of the past

After he achieved power, Hitler operated by the 'comply or die' rule to maintain government control of citizens.

Eliminating the opposition was a key factor in the success of the Nazi movement. Gun control was a priority. Hitler rendered the people defenseless by seizing all the weapons. Then it was easy to eliminate anyone who opposed him. Hitler accomplished this by force and by promoting the idea that Nazi troops would protect citizens so they did not need guns. Americans are supporting parts of the Green movement without realizing the political ramifications.

Consider the politically correct position that gun control will prevent crime in America. Same stuff, different decade. Gun control in Germany did not keep citizens safe. It rendered them helpless and vulnerable to escalating Nazi terrorism and excessive government control. Americans must protect their right to bear arms. Hitler successfully conned the German people into trying his Nazi ideas, but they didn't have the blaring historical example of the Holocaust to refer to. We do.

Germans and others watched as their neighbors lost their freedom and did not realize it was connected to their own. The German people were upset. Their country was in economic ruin. Hitler presented a political alternative and they tried it.

The Greens have set Americans up to make the same error in judgment, to take leave of our senses and try the Green political experiment. We can be guinea pigs or we can learn from the mistakes of others. Had citizens taken *Hitler* seriously, had the Jewish people not been so accommodating and tolerant of Nazi demands, things could have been different. How different, we'll never know. One thing we can safely assume is those poor people would have had a chance.

> *"Perhaps in a hundred years another genius will take up my ideas and National Socialism, like a Phoenix will arise again from the ashes."*
>
> *Psychopathic God*
> Adolf Hitler

Review the following quotations. Note the same goal to transform public life. Note the same goal to reorganize society around a political cause. Note the same idea to set public policy based around a political cause. Note the same level of commitment to the ideals of the political cause.

> *"the new Green vision places the environment at the center of public life, making it the context for both the formulation of economic policies and political decisions"*
>
> *Voting Green-The Framework for Politics*
> Jeremy Rifkin and Carol Grunewald-Rifkin

> *"The task of saving the earth's environment must and will become the central organizing principle of the post-Cold War world"*
>
> *Putting People First*
> Senator Al Gore

> *"No compromise in the name of Mother Earth"*
> Earth First!

> *"Our ideology is intolerant ... and peremptorily demands ... the complete transformation of public life to its ideas"*
>
> *Psychopathic God*
> Adolf Hitler

More Copy-Cat Politics

The Greens aren't taking any chances, they not only have borrowed from Adolf Hitler's bag of political tricks, they have borrowed most of the ideas Lenin used to force the Russian Revolution and establish Communism.

Lenin glorified his utopian vision in the minds of citizens. The world the Bolsheviks described sounded like heaven. Writers helped promote Lenin's ideas to the public and targeted the working class to gain support for the party.

Lenin made it sound wonderful, but it was a lie. Communism and total oppression were not what the Russian people expected to see at the end of Lenin's rainbow. Lenin conned the Russian citizens into trying his ideas instead of sticking to Capitalism. The Greens have updated the terms to make the ideas sound new but the following ideas are basically the ideas Lenin used to get Russian citizens to try Communism.

Lenin	Greens	Political Promises
Social	Public	Control of the economy
Societies	Bioregions	Form small communities
Talents	Abilities	People to do socially useful work
Trade	Barter	No money needed
Share	Redistribute	Wealth, promise of equality
Bolshevik	Green	Politics equal a true democracy
Utopian	Ecological	Society is better than the rat race
Riches	Wealth	Put people before profits
Shorter	Shorter	Work week will free the people
Bottom-up	Bottom-up	People will control government

Lenin stressed, before he could take power, he had to build a well-organized alternative political party. Lenin spent 17 years working behind the scenes to develop the Bolshevik Party as an alternative to the existing Russian order.

Both Lenin and Hitler's plans for revolution included the need for the people to help eliminate an obstacle before the perfect society could be formed. Lenin set up Capitalism and Capitalists as the obstacle Russians had to eliminate to establish utopia. Hitler set up the Jewish Capitalists as the obstacle that had to be eliminated before he could create his version of paradise. The Greens are offering Americans an alternative to our political system. The Greens are setting us up to believe Capitalism must be abandoned and our society transformed to save the earth. This must occur before the Green version of a perfect society can be formed.

Changing all our values, abandoning Capitalism, agreeing to Socialism or submitting to Communism will not create a perfect society nor will it save the environment.

Lack of awareness of the political goals of the Greens is at the root of Americans inability to understand what is happening in our country and why it is happening. Americans are not supposed to discover that beyond the headlines of environmental disaster lies a network of radical Green groups whose goal is not just change, it's revolution.

Some Green concepts are reasonable, some are unreasonable but most are extremely, extreme. Americans need to remember the politics and propaganda of Lenin's Communism and Hitler's National Socialism before falling for Green politics and propaganda. To avoid revolution, we must be able to recognize when and how we are being manipulated.

The Greens propaganda tactics look like a combination of both Lenin and Hitler's 'politics of persuasion'. How do Green political ideas match the ideas of the master manipulators?

	LENIN	HITLER	GREENS
Created crisis-level mentality	x	x	x
Promised all things to all people	x	x	x
Used children as political pawns	x	x	x
Capitalism, Capitalists root of all evil	x	x	x
Goal to transform society	x	x	x
Public control production/distribution	x	x	x
Bottom-up not top-down rule	x		x
Vision to create a perfect society	x	x	x
Violent beginnings, people terrorized	x	x	x
Classless society over hierarchy	x	x	x
Public to share wealth equally	x		x
Seized, sequestered private property	x	x	x
Intolerant, end justified the means	x	x	x
Individuality must submit to cause	x	x	x
Render public helpless, seize guns	x	x	x
Deplete financial assets of enemy	x	x	x
Dehumanized life and death issues	x	x	x
Keep real agenda out of public eye	x	x	x
Political ideology form of religion	x	x	x
Plans to relocate part of population	x	x	x
Plans to reduce the population		x	x
Political objective rule the world	x	x	x

So far only two out of three revolutions have ended in dictatorship and mass suffering.

The politics of Lenin, Hitler and the Greens are like the story of *Hansel and Gretel*. It's the same concept on a larger scale. The candy on the outside of the witch's house was put there to entice children to come closer. Like a snake in the grass, as soon as the children came close enough, the witch struck. She lied to get the children into the house. Then she lied to get the children to look in the oven so she could shove them inside and slam the door. Like the Greens, the witch knew it was easier for her if the children came along willingly until she was in a position to take control.

"Just because all the rest of the children stick their heads in the oven, does that mean you ought to do the same thing?"
Grandma Hacker
Teaching us to think – 1960

Lenin, Hitler, the Greens and the witch have something in common. What you see is not what you get. Hitler preached the Jewish people had to be eliminated. At first, both the Jews and the Germans thought that meant the Jews would be relocated to work farms. It was not originally common knowledge that Hitler meant extermination.

Lenin promised peace, land and bread for all. He promised people would be happier and that the people would share the wealth and governing power. Utopia didn't turn out that way. Lenin abolished private property ownership, took control of the banks, police and the army. Russia quickly became a dictatorship sustained by slave labor.

The Greens are making similar promises and blaming the evils of Capitalism for environmental damage. Sharing and equality means different things to different people. Russia's social elite benefited and the general public lost it all.

Generous People or Selfish Pigs?

Capitalistic Americans are the most generous people in the world. When there is a crisis, where do the eyes of the world turn? Who helps? If we were selfish, as the Greens imply, we would not be willing to share our resources with those in need. Before we allow ourselves to get conned into accepting Socialism or Communism is better for the environment, we ought to revisit the value of Capitalism.

> *"The moral foundations of a society do not extend only to its political system; they must extend to its economic system as well. America's commitment to capitalism is unquestionably the best example of this principle. Capitalism is not, contrary to what those on the Left have tried to argue, an amoral system based on selfishness, greed and exploitation. It is a moral system based on a Biblical ethic. There is no other comparable system that has raised the standard of living of millions of people, created vast new wealth and resources, or inspired so many beneficial innovations and technologies. The wonderful thing about capitalism is that it does not discriminate against the poor, as has been so often charged; indeed, it is the only economic system that raises the poor out of poverty."*
>
> *Margaret Thatcher*
> IMPRIMIS - March 1995
> Journal of Hillsdale College

Capitalism and freedom promote generosity, increase business opportunities and offer different choices to people in different situations. This includes the freedom to develop environmentally friendly products. We can change our lives to better protect our environment, but only if we are free to do so.

Recycling isn't new, although you'd think the Greens invented it. The Red Cross, Goodwill Industries, Salvation Army and church groups prove recycling has been a part of our culture for a long time. Over the years, generous donations to these organizations by thoughtful Americans have helped thousands of individuals and families all over the world.

Americans constantly volunteer to lend their support to charity, telethons and other events intended to help those in need. The January 31, 1994 edition of, *Newsweek*, featured the article, *Here's Some Good News, America*, by Robert Samuelson. Samuelson reported 10 good news items. Number nine on the list was:

> *"We remain remarkably generous with our time and money. About a fifth of adults do volunteer work. Of these, 37 percent work for churches and religious groups, while 15 percent work in schools. In 1991, we gave $125 billion to charities. Most ($103 billion) came from individuals. Americans now give more of their disposable income to charity than in 1970."*

Samuelson also reported that:

> *"Most children still live with both natural parents and the divorce rate may be stabilizing."*

American families are a unique and intricate part of how our system promotes recycling and family fun. Americans love to explore second-hand stores, garage sales and swap meets. One man's trash is another man's treasure! What's the ultimate form of recycling in America? Americans have made the antique business an art form. We collect special pieces of our history and restore them or sell the piece for someone else to enjoy. We know how to save, reuse and recycle. As a nation, we went through a depression. We understand the difference between want and need.

Another old idea being introduced as if it were new is the idea that Americans need encouragement to '*commit random acts of kindness.*' The phrase is a nice reminder, but kindness is not a new value to the people of this nation. Americans have earned the reputation for 'giving other's the shirt off their back'. It's another tradition we can be proud of.

America is a kind nation with few exceptions. Americans always drop what they are doing to help someone in need. This attitude has always been a part of being an American. Caring is part of what makes our society work.

The purpose of reinventing America's time-honored traditions is to discredit our past and make Green ideas feel comfortable and non-threatening. Greens present their ideas as progressive but use familiar-sounding concepts to cloud the political goals.

Communism may sound enticing to those who would prefer not to take responsibility for their own lives. The grass is always greener on the other side of the fence. In this case, it's really Green. Life under Communism would be like slavery or living as indentured servants. The government has total control. Citizens trade work time for products. Communism offers citizens little freedom, few rights and limited opportunities to improve their status in life.

There is a gap between *have's* and *have-not's* in America, but there are many degrees of wealth within our economic structure. Communism operates under a different premise; the *have's* live in luxury and *have-not's* live in poverty. Life in our country spreads the wealth around. Everyone has the opportunity to excel. This is why we have millions of 'rags to riches' stories. From Abraham Lincoln to Elvis, those who start out with little can become millionaires in America.

Americans have set up ways to assist those in need. We share our wealth voluntarily. The dollars to finance assistance programs come out of our paychecks. We have never refused to help others. The Greens condemn Capitalism, but it would be wise for them, and for us all, to remember, Capitalism and the generosity of caring Americans helped finance their cause.

Turning Up the Heat

The frog in the pan story is a good example of how the Greens have and are executing their political agenda. If a frog is placed in a pan of warm water and the heat is turned up gradually, the frog doesn't notice the gradual change in temperature. The frog doesn't sense the slight changes in temperature as being life threatening so it will sit there and gradually expire.

If you placed a frog in a pan of boiling water the frog instantly senses the temperature of the water is dangerous to its health and will leap out of the pan to save itself.

This story parallels Green politics in America. The Greens have been turning up the heat gradually so the American people will not notice slight social changes or connect the shifts in public policies to Socialism and indirect steps toward Communism.

We are not expected to protest Green calls for social change because we have been set up to believe the Green movement is good for America. Like the frog, if we don't sense the 'Green heat' is dangerous to our health, we won't jump out of the pan and save ourselves.

The Green plan is to turn-up the political heat and legally force change after change until life as we know it gradually expires. Many Americans have not yet sensed danger because the heat of choice is the environmental cause. Exposing the Green political agenda now is like placing the American people in a pot of boiling water. How will the American people respond?

Free Speech or Treason?

People in America have the right to free speech and recruiting support for their ideas. What words and deeds are considered treason? Openly running for office as a Communist, or discussing the merits of Communism, is different than abusing our system by running as an independent, with the intent to advance the goals of the Communist party. When does the Communist plan to overthrow our government become an issue of treason and national security?

We have to pay close attention to those planning to impose Socialism or Communism. Our government operates on the premise, we are free to challenge and change. People must be free to think and speak. How do we define the difference between the freedom to promote political change, and the point a group becomes a threat to our national security? Greens call for revolution at meetings and in the alternative press, but that does not translate into public awareness.

> *"What's public is propaganda, what's secret is serious."*
> Charles Bohlen
> U.S. Ambassador -- to U.S.S.R 1969

Treason describes citizens who are disloyal to a nation and who are considered untrustworthy. The difference between free speech and treason seems to hinge on whether or not terms like force and violence are used to describe how the traitors are planning to execute their plan. Another difference is whether or not the general public understands the agenda and has an opportunity to accept or reject it vs. the revolutionary's tactic to keep the agenda out of the public eye.

We have learned that the Communist Party USA:

- works with the Soviet Union (like agents do)
- are paid by the Soviet Union (like agents are)
- are 'using our system to break down our system'
- is not just an alternative to the two party system
- lied to Americans about secretly working for the Soviets
- plan to overthrow our government (like enemies do)
- planned to use the environmental cause to hide behind
- have indicated the takeover may not be peaceful

What is the difference between the activities and objectives of the members of the CPUSA and Soviet paid KGB agents? Aren't Communist agents, bent on destroying our government, still considered a threat to our national security?

Facts show the CPUSA is an extension of the Communist Party of the Soviet Union. That makes the CPUSA and those who support the same goals, enemies of this nation. The activities of the CPUSA, the long-range goals of the Soviets, and the goals of the Greens match. This combination is a serious threat to our nation. This is not a free speech issue. Political leaders are supposed to be our first line of defense, guardians of our nation. As the following quote indicates, we can't trust everyone. We must be more responsible.

> "*The important point about the Washington apparatuses is that, in the 1930's, the revolutionary mood had become so acute throughout the world that the Communist Party could recruit its agents, not here and there, but by scores within the Government of the United States. And they were precisely among the most literate, intellectually eager and energetic young men in a nation...*"
>
> Witness
> Whittaker Chambers

Chambers was working for the Communist Party at that time.

Unfortunately, some politicians are not in politics to serve the people of this nation. If they aren't acting in our best interests they are there for the wrong reasons.

The political objectives of the Green movement must be evaluated by the American people. We must demand accountability of our political leaders. We must support those who are dedicated to the principles of the Constitution of the United States. We ought to remove from office those who do not understand the job description.

We do not need to abandon our goal of environmental excellence. We need to recognize how the environmental cause is being used to advance Green Communism in America. We must make more and better distinctions about environmental issues and legislation. We ought to insist that environmental decisions and laws be based on scientific facts and common sense, not Hitler-like Green spiritual politics and pseudo-science.

When making distinctions about environmental issues, we ought to keep in mind, nature is an ever changing, dramatic and unpredictable force. It can be gentle. It can be violent. It can nurture. It can destroy. We cannot predict, completely protect, or expect to control nature.

> *"Nature has no mercy at all. Nature says, I'm going to snow. If you have on a bikini and no snowshoes, that's tough. I am going to snow anyway."*
> Maya Angelou
> 1974

Nature controls nature. We ought to be able to use, not abuse our natural resources. We ought to be able to strike a fair and reasonable accord by discouraging extremism, and supporting moderation. We need to protect our country and the environment. One doesn't do us much good without the other. The Greens, like the Nazi movement, believe the sacred soil, or the environment, comes above all else. We need to respond, not react, to Green claims and political demands. The Greens are using most of the ideas Hitler used to convince people to join the Nazi movement. The Greens hope Americans will continue to fall victim to the temptation and join the Green movement.

When people finally figured out Hitler was insane, it was too late, they had no power. The Green call for us to accept the earth as our Mother, a living being, is not a Green original. It was the idea Hitler used to get the German people to abandon their traditional beliefs. Hitler's message:

> *"I address myself to all those, who detached from their mother country...now, with poignant emotion, long for the hour which will permit them to **return to the heart of their faithful mother.**"*
>
>

Hitler's Ideology - Mein Kampf
Adolf Hitler
(Bold Emphasis Added)

The Greens are copying Hitler's ideas because they worked. The end justifies the means when the goal is political power. Green Communists are working behind our backs to foster revolution. This is indecent, insulting and ought to be considered treason.

We are being 'Set-Up' by the Greens abuse of environmental issues and 'Sold-Out' one step at a time due to the false perception   our political leaders and others have that the Greens speak for the American people. What other Hitler ideas are on the Greens political agenda hidden under the guise of environmental protection?

Hitler's political program included these points:

- We demand colonies for settling our surplus population
- All citizens shall enjoy equal rights and duties
- First duty of a citizen is to work for the common good
- We demand that the State take over large businesses
- We demand profit sharing in large concerns
- We demand land reform
- We demand a ruthless struggle against profiteers
- We demand our whole system of education be revised
- State must provide for the improvement of public health

Hitler and Nazism
Louis Snyder

Every one of these demands is included in the Greens political agenda. Learn from the witch in the forest, if Green promises sound too good to be true, run the other way. The choice is still ours. We do not have to accept being Sold-Out. We can stand-up for reason, use our personal power and work within our political system to push the pendulum back to center.

The Green assault on America has nothing to do with environmental protection. This is about power and Green Communists seizing control of America. Americans are not accustomed to being told what to do or how to raise our children. Are we ready to be told how to live? All these things, and more are integrated into the Green agenda.

The only Americans Green politics won't affect, are dead. Americans are famous for an irrepressible, independent streak. There may be a few Americans who won't mind a Green government controlling their lives; then there are the rest of us.

"Forgive your enemies, but never forget their names."

President John F. Kennedy

2

Subvert The Dominant Paradigm

*"In an effort to assess the most significant environmental events of the year, Earth Journal independently polled 19 environmental and special interest groups, together known as **the Green Group**. The CEOs of each group meet roughly once a year to discuss issues that impact them. The participating groups believe **the Green Group Alliance** makes them more effective and gives them additional lobbying power. Listed below are the members of the Green Group."*

- Children's Defense Fund
- Defenders of Wildlife
- Environmental Defense Fund
- Friends of the Earth
- Izaak Walton League of America
- National Audubon Society
- National Parks & Conservation Association
- National Toxins Campaign
- National Wildlife Federation
- Native American Rights Fund
- Planned Parenthood
- Population Crisis Committee
- Sierra Club
- Sierra Club Legal Defense Fund
- Union of Concerned Scientists
- Wilderness Society
- World Wildlife Fund
- Zero Population Growth

1993 Earth Journal

It's A Numbers Game

What matters in Washington is who shows up. Since most of the largest environmental organizations and associated Green groups have headquarters in Washington, D.C., they can show up every day. Americans who live outside the beltway can't physically show up everyday. American's support for any part of the Green movement can be used to show support for other Green political goals. Here's how

Several different Green groups show up to lobby in favor of the same bill. Each group has (x) number of members they represent. Because of the total number of members the Greens can hold up, the perception is the bill has as much voter support as the groups combined membership. Big numbers get attention and bills get passed. It doesn't matter if Americans or members of these groups have a different opinion. If we don't show up or share our opinion with our political leaders our opinion doesn't count. The Greens are over $2.5 billion dollars strong with a political lobby that knows how to play the game in Washington D.C. According to the authors of *Trashing the Economy*, the $2.5 billion figure is based on a 1991 estimate by *Money* magazine. The Greens separate their calls for change so politicians and the public won't see they are part of one political movement. John Rensenbrink, spokesman for the Greens puts it this way:

> *"all the parts of the movement need to be interrelated ... to have the opportunity to align their strategies with one another. Alignment of strategies is the creative way forward, not the integration of strategies. In this way maximum pressure is applied to the prevailing system dominated by the oligarchs. It is maximum because it comes from a variety of sources: the many parts of the movement."*
> *The Greens and the Politics of Transformation*

This allows the Greens to promote change in multiple areas. Many little changes are the Green's way to quietly force a shift to Socialism. It is a step-by-step process. The Greens are not flamboyant about their victories or associates. It is better for them to work behind the scenes, sneaking their political ideas into legislation here and there. The Greens want to keep America's focus on progressive ideas and environmental doom so we will not recognize Green Socialism. This is the Green way to make control possible by making control legal.

Green Quicksand

The Greens pretend the push for social change is coming out of the blue due to America's concern for the environment. When discussing the emergence of Green legislation or Green legislators, the Greens create the impression Green politics are just now evolving. They pretend the political goals of the Green Party are not part of the environmental movement. This allows the Greens to use the environmental cause to advance their political goals. John Rensenbrink, national spokesperson for the Greens or Green Committees of Correspondence (GCOC) describes their strategy:

> *"Green party organizing committees (and in some cases, full blown party structures) are forming side by side with the movement-centered GCOC. Some say this is a good thing, meaning that party and movement should be strictly separate. Others argue that the two are essentially one and should be treated that way."*
>
> (Bold Emphasis Added)

Most Americans are not aware of the political goals of the Green party or that the goals of the party and the Green movement are one. Americans have been deliberately left out of the loop. This way, the Greens can move their political program forward unchallenged. This prevents Americans from knowing how, when and who is promoting Green politics. This movement is like quicksand. What you see is not what you get. It looks safe but it is not. It is a dangerous trap.

> *"Green strategy should include at least three elements; steady alliance-building on the basis of an evolving holistic program that stresses the interconnection of all the issues: grassroots organizing which fosters a Green community in as many locales as possible: **and a working distinction between party and movement."***

> John Rensenbrink
> (Bold Emphasis Added)

The Greens have built a broad political coalition with a variety of special-interest groups. American's support for environmental protection may inadvertently be showing support for any or all of these parts of the Green movement:

- Environmental organizations, Green groups
- Eco-Socialists
- Democratic Socialists of America
- Gay and Lesbian Members/Supporters
- Gun Control Advocates
- Eco-Terrorist, Monkeywrenchers
- American Indian Rights Groups
- Animal Rights Groups
- Feminist, Eco-Feminist Movements
- Peace Groups
- War Resisters, Amnesty Activists
- Green Teachers, Radical Education Groups
- Holistic Health and Holistic Education
- Anarchists
- Deep Ecologists, Earth worship, Spiritual Politics
- Mother Earth, Gaia, Goddess spirituality
- Witches, Pagans, Atheist
- Vegetarian Activists
- Population Control Groups/Activists

This is a quick study and does not represent all allied groups. The list reveals some of the emotional traps the Greens are using to get political support from different segments of our society. We need to recognize that all of these interest areas are being targeted to promote different parts of the Green political program.

> *"The Communists never do anything in their own name that they can do in someone else's."*
>
> Red Blueprint for the World
> John Drakeford

Gil Green is a well-known U.S. Communist who joined the party in 1924. Since that time he's served in a variety of leadership positions for the Communist Party. During an interview for the 1993 book, *New Studies in the Politics and Culture of U.S. Communism,* Green indicates that several communist districts split off of the party to:

> *"form **Committees of Correspondence** as a transition form to something new"*

The United States Green Party has gone by the name, Green Committees of Correspondence for years. The party just changed its name to the U.S. Greens or Greens.

Green political power is generated by Green propaganda. In addition to lobbying in Washington the Greens increase local and regional influence using the following methods:

- establishing and funding activist groups nationwide
- working together to achieve goals, locally and nationally
- using environmental conferences to brainwash attendees
- using media to spread propaganda
- getting Green political messages into entertainment
- sponsoring State initiatives, ballot measures

Most of the Green political agenda can be camouflaged as environmental legislation. The Greens are using any subject that can be stretched into an environmental issue to present socialist and communist ideas as the solution.

A key factor in the success of Green Communists involves changing America by 'planting ideas' and setting us up to 'think Green' years before they make their move. Another key to the Greens success is their strategy. The Greens pick a target and then hit it with their combined political power. This is one of the reasons Americans are in trouble.

The Greens frame their public image as, 'local environmental group fights industry'. That is what Americans hear on the evening news. What gets deliberately lost in this propaganda is that the big Green groups and their hired guns run the show. What is also conveniently left out is that the Greens are not attacking an entire industry. They are attacking the individual business people that make up the industry. The little guy, the individual American, cannot stand up to the Green onslaught alone.

The Communists targeted the environmental cause years ago and have spent the last 20 plus years developing the best ways to con the American people into accepting Socialism. The Greens are twisting the issues to hide a massive land grab. Environmental ruin is the excuse to gain control of our land base by gradually giving control of individual properties (i.e. how they can be used) to the federal government.

We do not know to what extent the Communists have infiltrated environmental groups. We do not know how many agents are working in key positions within our government. We do not know to what extent environmental issues have been exploited to advance the Communist's objectives.

The Greens have spent time and money (yours) to present their argument on an emotional level. Business and industry organizations attempt to defend themselves from Green accusations by explaining facts. Green Communists do not focus on facts. They use emotional arguments. The American people do not understand the way Greens think or that they are being used.

Inner circle slogans, popular among allied Green activists and other progressives within the Green movement are revealing. Many Americans are not privy to these Green thoughts and feelings. America's support for environmental protection, including financial, may be advancing these political ideas:

- **Die Yuppie Scum**
- Question Authority
- **Go Reds, Smash State**
- **Recycle or Die**
- **Eat the Rich**
- No Compromise in Defense of Mother Earth
- **Sure, I'm a Marxist**
- Stop Treating Our Soil Like Dirt
- No Cows
- **Visualize Industrial Collapse**
- Born Again Pagan
- **Ban People for a Safe Future**
- Pregnancy: Just Another Deadly Sexually Transmitted Disease
- Think Globally, Act Locally
- Earth Police, One Planet, One Precinct
- **Alternative: The Greens**
- **Subvert the Dominant Paradigm**

Subvert the Dominant Paradigm? What does that mean? Words that mean the same as, Subvert, Dominant and Paradigm are listed below each word:

Subvert	Dominant	Paradigm
Overthrow	Governing	Model
Destroy	Common	Standard
Ruin	Controlling	Example

Apply the Green slogan, Subvert the Dominant Paradigm to the Green Communists call for revolution. The political objective remains the same: overthrow the United States government and destroy the American way of life.

- Overthrow the Governing Model
- Destroy the Common Standard
- Ruin the Controlling Example

Overthrow the Governing Model sounds like a plan, not a suggestion. The Greens present themselves as peace loving but consistently use aggressive language, hint of violence and call for revolution. Peaceful coexistence is not the objective.

Subvert the Dominant Paradigm also sounds like the 1948 Communist attempt to subvert the government of the United States. That subversive effort led to the arrest and imprisonment of Gus Hall and his comrades.

The priorities of Mikhail Gorbachev's environmental organization, Green Cross International include creating a new paradigm for a global civilization. The term Communists use, including Gorbachev, when referring to their system of government, is the term 'model'.

Too Close For Comfort

Many Americans currently involved in the environmental cause may not know about the Green party or understand the overall objectives of the Green movement. Other people know exactly what they are doing. There is no excuse for those people, political leaders included, who understand the Green agenda and are using their power to put it in place. Our politicians took an oath and they ought to keep it.

America's national security is threatened because some Greens are positioned within our political system now. Many Greens will run for office as Greens. Most will run as Democrats or Independents with a strong environmental focus. This is dangerous because the American people will not realize they are voting for a Green Communist. The newly elected Greens have joined existing Green legislators whose political ideas have enjoyed the political clout of:

- most members of the Clinton Administration
- some Democrats already in office
- some of the largest environmental groups
- some in media and entertainment

We need to bring the Greens and the environmental issues out in the open and get the facts to the American people. We need to know who supports what and why.

Green Politicians

Green politicians have been identified by *Voting Green, Your complete environmental guide to making political choices in the 1990's* by Jeremy Rifkin and Carol Grunewald Rifkin. *Voting Green* identifies the following politicians as the: "Green Leadership for the '90s."

SENATE

Albert Gore	D-TN*
John Kerry	D-MA
Joseph Lieberman	D-CT
Claiborne Pell	D-RI
Alan Cranston	D-CA*
Timothy Wirth	D-CO*
Patrick Leahy	D-VT
Harry Reid	D-NV
Brock Adams	D-WA*
Daniel Moynihan	D-NY

HOUSE

Barbara Boxer	D-CA
Ted Weiss	D-NY
Ronald Dellums	D-CA
James Scheuer	D-NY
Nancy Pelosi	D-CA
Edolphus Towns	D-NY
Major Owens	D-NY
Cardiss Collins	D-IL
John Lewis	D-GA
Peter DeFazio	D-OR
Wayne Owens	D-UT

THE 'A' LIST   (Combined 101st and 102nd Congresses)

Gary Ackerman	D-NY	Edward Markey	D-MA
Chester Atkins	D-MA	Christopher Shays	D-CT
F. (Pete) Stark	D-CA	Barney Frank	D-MA
Peter Kostmayer	D-PA	Robert Mrazek	D-NY
George Brown	D-CA	Thomas Foglietta	D-PA
Howard Wolpe	D-MI	Frank Pallone	D-NJ
Samuel Gejdenson	D-CT	Arthur Ravenel	R-SC
Bernard Dwyer	D-NJ	Gerry Sikorski	D-MN
Charles Bennett	D-FL	Jim McDermott	D-WA
James Jontz	D-IN	Mervyn Dymally	D-CA
Gerry Studds	D-MA	Don Edwards	D-CA
G.Hochbrueckner	D-NY	Andrew Jacobs	D-IN
Mel Levine	D-CA	Norman Mineta	D-CA
Anthony Beilenson	D-CA	Jolene Unsoeld	D-WA

Voting Green * Retiring

The Clinton administration filled key positions with well-known members of the Green Team. These individuals stepped away from leadership positions in some of the largest environmental organizations to take a government position. Many Greens have been elected to office. Identifying Green leaders, Green followers and Green ideology is an important part of protecting our country and ourselves.

This book is not about people. It is about people's politics. It is about the duties and responsibilities of those involved in politics and other positions of pubic trust. People who choose a career in politics have a responsibility to let those they represent understand their political position. We cannot decide whom to vote for without these basic facts.

Are these Americans unaware of the Green political agenda or is their personal philosophy clouding fair judgment? Is it political irresponsibility or dereliction of duty? We pay the salaries. We need to know the answers.

The following quotations help us better understand how the Green political agenda was promoted by members of the Clinton administration.

> *"We believe the concept of national security must be re-examined to include health, education, economics and the health of the natural environment, rather than the present focus on military hardware"*
>
> Greens

> *President Clinton and I are broadening our definition of security in the post-cold war world. Security means having a stable, good-paying job; having clean air to breathe and clean water to drink; raising our families without fear of crime and violence; and preventing conflict in the global community that can result from over population, environmental degradation and famine"*

> *"we must reinvent environmental protection to protect public health and natural resources"*
>
> *Earth Times, June, 1994*
> Vice President Gore

The Greens are promoting the idea that environmental health and public health are the same issues. The reason for linking all environmental issues with public health issues is to give the Greens a universal excuse to completely transform our culture. The point is to mold public opinion to accept that when the Greens insist on rapid changes in the name of public health, Americans will not question the need. Hitler also justified his actions in the name of public health.

It is not wise to give the Greens a blank check. We cannot trust one interest group with the future of our nation. Anything, from the right to smoke, eat beef, own private property, drive a car or have a child could fall into the category of a public health issue. Linking environmental issues to public health issues is a political power play. It is not about environmental health and it is not about public health. It is about making control possible by making control legal.

Greens also linking equality, national security and having a job to environmental health. Communists believe all citizens ought to be guaranteed the basics: food, job, healthcare and housing. All these issues come to the forefront in American politics. These ideas were evident in Vice President Gore's statements. This idea was also evident in legislation proposed by Congressman Ron Dellums D-CA. in July 1995. Congressman Dellums introduced H.R. 1050, "A Living Wage, Jobs-for-All Act" The opening sentence of the bill reads:

> "To establish a living wage, jobs-for-all policy for the United States in order to reduce poverty, inequality, and the undue concentration of income, wealth, and power in the United States and for other purposes."

This jobs-for-all policy is supposed to reduce poverty and inequality by guaranteeing a job and income for all. Beyond the fact that Communism guarantees all citizens a job, healthcare, and set income, how did Dellums propose this could be financed? Congressman Dellums explains:

"this proposal would mandate the transformation of the entire U.S. budget of more than $1.5 trillion into a jobs-for-all budget."

To change our society into a jobs-for-all society; Dellums indicated we must change the:

"concentration of income, wealth and power in the United States"

Dellum's bill mandated we transform our entire budget and use over $1.5 trillion to finance this idea by diffusing the concentration of wealth and power in America. Before the government could redistribute or spread America's wealth around, the government would need access to citizen's wealth. Unless Americans volunteer to give all their money to the government, the government would have to acquire or seize control of citizen's wealth. The following items were addressed in Dellum's bill.

- distribution of income and wealth
- a wealth inventory
- wealth inventory includes personal wealth
- wages and benefits: urban, suburban and rural

The final statement in the bill reads:

"There are hereby authorized to be appropriated such sums as may be necessary to implement the policies, programs and projects set forth in accordance with this Act."

If our representatives passed this bill, industries and individuals across the nation would have given the government access to their business and personal bank accounts. The last sentence can be interpreted to give the government permission to find and allocate whatever dollars they deem necessary to achieve the objectives listed in this bill. If this bill passed, the result would be the Green goal of economic conversion and more government control of people's lives. The Basic Rights promoted in the bill included the right to:

- earn a living, do a useful job
- adequate income
- adequate medical services
- environmental rights
- quality of life information
- personal security
- shorter work week, work year
- stronger rights for employees to organize
- farmers to produce and sell goods at living wage
- business to trade without unfair competition
- business to trade without domination by monopolies
- every family to have a decent home
- protection from fears of old age, sickness, accidents
- good education

These rights apply to adult Americans who are able and willing to earn a living. Does that mean Americans who are able but not willing to work, are entitled to these rights? Dellums described the purpose of the act:

> *"One of the basic needs in our lives is a job which will pay us a living wage...It is unrealistic to expect that corporations which are only market oriented will take responsibility for a healthy, national economy"*

Taking a closer look at the idea of Socialism, Congressman Dellums was proposing that a job ought to be guaranteed. No one disagrees people need jobs. Communism guarantees jobs. Dellums attacked American corporations for being market oriented and inferred, if corporations were responsible, his bill would not be necessary. Capitalism is to blame. It is the reason our government needs to pass a law that guarantees everyone a job and a living wage. What Congressman

Dellums seemed to be saying, is our society puts profits before people, and he wanted the government to legally put people before profits. Lenin, the leader of the Russian revolution, who successfully established Communism, used the same idea and slogan, 'People not Profit'. The Greens use the same idea and slogan, 'People Before Profit'.

> *"Today our economy entails nearly total domination by 'for profit' corporate enterprise. The corporate sector has failed to meet human needs and has consistently abused the environment. Therefore, **we will work to promote alternative economic structures that put human need ahead of profits** and that are accountable to the communities in which they function."*
>
> Greens

Dellum's bill had all the characteristics of Green Communism. The May 1995 summary of this bill states:

> *"This is a policy measure designed to help nurture an activist movement based on high ideals of democratic human rights and responsibilities."*

This movement is part of the Green movement. It's no wonder the Greens are secretive. Most people in the United States would consider their ideas un-American. Green politics are not what most Americans imagine or accept.

Five of the fifteen co-sponsors for Congressman Dellums, "A Living Wage, Jobs-for-All Act" were identified by the Rifkins as Green legislators, including Congressman Dellums. The other Green co-sponsors were:

- Nancy Pelosi   D-CA
- Edolphus Towns   D-NY
- Major Owens   D-NY
- Jim McDermott   D-WA

Congressman Dellums also launched the '*Campaign Against Poverty*' and worked with a coalition of groups, to hold hearings across America, to draw attention to America's 'Economic Insecurity' and gain public support for this bill. The coalition included the Democratic Socialists of America and Americans for Democratic Action.

The focus on helping to end or reduce poverty in America hits anyone in the heart. It can also blind Americans to the magnitude of the ramifications of this bill. Beyond the political objective to access and redistribute citizen's wealth, this bill would serve to help transform our society.

Democratic Socialists

The Democratic Socialists of America (DSA) have been working to build a broad social coalition that includes the Greens. DSA goals include turning America's economy away from Capitalism toward a public controlled economy with a focus on environmental issues. DSA's objective is to overturn the current way America operates. The following quotations are from the *DSA brochure*:

> "*We're Greens, and we're Socialists too*"

> **"We stand in the traditions of the earliest anti-capitalists rebellions"**

> **"the Green agenda cannot be achieved without a broad social movement that challenges the ideology of profit and free enterprise head-on"**

To gain the power to execute the 'Green agenda', DSA indicates a broad social movement that challenges free enterprise head-on will be necessary. DSA indicates this movement will emerge in one of two ways, by:

"a revived Democratic party, or through the splitting off of the left-wing Democrats to join a popular mass movement."

The Green Party is the left-wing split off. The environmental movement is the popular mass movement of choice. The Green Party program is the blueprint, the check-off list which is being implemented one step at a time.

"I think of myself as a hired hit man up against those right-wing'ers."

The Progressive-- January 1995
Barbara Ehrenreich

It is hard to understand why those who call for peace have such a violent attitude towards those with different political ideas. Barbara Ehrenreich is a DSA Honorary Chair, serves on the DSA Environmental Commission Advisory Board and is a socialist writer with a regular column in *Time* magazine.

DSA's talking points are like Lenin's and the Green's. DSA's political goals include:

- economic conversion
- demilitarization
- cooperatives
- community planning
- worker ownership
- decentralization
- shorter work week
- socially useful work
- bottom up, not top down government

Congressman Dellums "Living Wage Jobs-for-All" bill included most of the above points and if passed, would have advanced the goals of the Greens; the Democratic Socialists, the CPUSA and the liberal Democrats.

DSA's political priorities include:

- anti-Capitalism
- education
- Earth Day
- industrial conversion
- environmental policy
- post-Communist society
- multi-culturalism
- foreign policy
- eco-spirituality
- national health care
- third party politics
- ecology politics

The *EcoSocialist Review* is the newsletter of the environmental commission of the Democratic Socialists of America, DSA. The following articles were in the Summer, 1990 issue.

- **Building Eco-Socialism in the 90's**
- Prison Notebooks on Earth Day at Wall Street
- Critique of Commodity Consumerism
- **Tools for Watermelon Activists**

Upcoming events listed in this newsletter included highlights of the upcoming Midwest Academy Retreat sponsored by the Democratic Socialists. Participants and speakers listed for the three-day retreat included:

- **Ron Dellums**
- David Dinkins
- **Barbara Mikulski**
- **Pat Schroeder**
- **Jesse Jackson**
- **Al Gore**
- **Edward Kennedy**
- Ruben Zamora
- **John Sweeney**
- **Jane Fonda**

Unless there are multiple people with these names, it appears the participants were some of our elected representatives:

Ron Dellums	Congressman	D-CA
Pat Schroeder	Congressman	D-CO
Al Gore	Senator	D-TN
Barbara Mikulski	Senator	D-MD
Edward Kennedy	Senator	D-MA

Then Senator, now former Vice President Gore participated in that Democratic Socialist Retreat? Were our tax dollars used to pay for these representatives to participate? Ron Dellums, and Major Owens are members of the Democratic Socialist of America. Congressman Dellums promotes DSA and appears in the DSA brochure. Dellums ran on the Democratic ticket but refers to himself as a Socialist. Congressman Dellums was also the Chairman of the Armed Services Committee that oversees America's military establishment. Dellums has a curious reputation. When the military budget came up for the final vote, he voted against it. The reason given for this Jekel and Hyde performance is, he believes in less military funding. It seems that would stagnate our political process and further the Green objective of downsizing our military.

It was reported, that in 1982, Congressman Ron Dellums, Patricia Schroeder and other Congressional representatives were connected to a Communist-front organization, the World Peace Council. According to the report, House Intelligence Committee Chairman at the time, Edward Boland, attempted to modify the report to hide this information.

What are Watermelon Activists?

> "*watermelon describes those whose politics are green on the outside and red on the inside, though some add that there are anarchist black seeds scattered throughout.*"
> *EcoSocialist Review*
> Summer 1991

Other items on the DSA conference agenda included national health care, a radical teacher's conference and a DSA youth conference.

The Spring 1994 edition of the *Eco-Socialist Review* featured a letter from the Sierra Club Legal Defense Fund. The letter attacked private property rights advocates for being concerned about the ramifications of the Endangered Species Act on private property. The Sierra Club called these groups anti-environmentalists and accused them of trying to destroy all environmental laws.

The letter takes the usual approach of blanket condemnation without qualification. It ignores the issue of why citizens are concerned. The Sierra Club Legal Defense Fund letter takes citizen concern and sensationalizes it as an effort to destroy all environmental laws. The allegation is absurd. The exaggeration generates fear or dislike for citizens who are legitimately concerned about the language and legal interpretation of some environmental laws. Citizens have good reason to be concerned. The letter from the Sierra Club Legal Defense Fund closes with this statement:

> "*Environmentalists argue that the protection offered by strong, effective environmental law is pro-property rights. Restrictions on individual behavior, not only environmental restrictions but also those regarding health, safety, civil rights and consumer affairs ensure that powerful property and business owners may not ignore the rights, including the property rights of others. If the so-called property rights or takings movement succeeds, it will be too expensive to implement environmental laws.*"
>
> Sierra Club Legal Defense Fund
> (Bold Emphasis Added)

The Green goal is to control our land base. One way to do that is to control individual property owners. The Sierra Club Legal Defense Fund is looking for ways to set legal precedents to force government control of private land. That is Socialism. The issues outlined by the Sierra Club Legal Defense Fund includes; health, safety, civil rights and consumer affairs. These additional issue areas are not about environmental protection. These issues are tossed in to ensure there are more than enough excuses to justify gaining legal control of private property. Make control possible by making control legal.

The political sentiments of the Sierra Club Legal Defense Fund are obvious from the publication their letter appears in. Eco-Socialist is the same as environmental socialist. The Sierra Club Legal Defense Fund, a mainstream environmental group, is working with the Democratic Socialists.

Democratic Socialist, Eco-Socialist

Review these quotes from the *Democratic Socialist brochure.*

> *"Socialism doesn't mean the government ownership of everything, down to and including the corner store. It does mean social control of such areas of the economy as banking and credit, monopoly industries and natural resources, with decisions being made democratically from the bottom up rather than handed down from on high"*

> *"We are working to build a new American left that goes beyond traditional liberalism by embracing radical democratic reforms*

> *"Through a meaningful social wage, we can collectively guarantee everyone economic survival and dignity ...*

> *...traditional liberalism is also inadequate for the task of altering the status quo. It fails to recognize the need to challenge the maldistribution of power and wealth in America and the way key economic decisions are made."*

Compare DSA's ideas to these political opinions:

"I have news for the forces of greed and the defenders of the status quo: your time has come and gone. It's time for a change in America."

Governor Bill Clinton
Democratic National Convention -- July 1992

"It is time to radically change the way government operates - to shift from top-down bureaucracy to entrepreneurial government that empowers citizens from the bottom up. We must reward the people and ideas that work and get rid of those that don't."

Revolution in Government
Putting People First
Governor Bill Clinton - Senator Al Gore

Compare these statements to Green Party ideas:

"The old politics based on top-down organization and leaders and followers simply doesn't work... Our strategyis to build a grassroots democracy from the bottom up... Green politics calls for a fundamental restructuring of our political and economic institutions."

Building a Green Movement in America
Greens

Compare all of the above to Lenin's ideas. He too promised:

"Rule from below, not from above"
The Sealed Train

"The Bolsheviks were proclaiming the only program that the masses could support: peace, land, and bread, and all power to the Soviets"

Journey Into Revolution

Lenin's Bolshevik party promised peace, bread and land for all. He promised to transfer ruling power from the Capitalists and give decision-making power to the people. Lenin promised people rule from below not from above. He lied.

Lenin professed the end of Capitalism was the only way to solve the people's problems. Lenin, shared these ideas for public control in his *April Theses:*

- public control of production and distribution
- dismantling the army and bureaucracy
- confiscation of all private lands for shared ownership
- rule from below, not from above
- public control of banking
- no support for the existing government

The Greens are using the same ideas to trick the American people into believing our environmental future depends on abandoning our culture, changing our government and overthrowing Capitalism.

Is it just a coincidence that the language and ideas of Lenin, the Greens, the Democratic Socialist and some former members of the Clinton administration are exactly the same? Shouldn't we ask?

The Mexican Bail Out

We need leaders who are committed to upholding Constitutional principles. Until that becomes the norm, we need to take politics personally and pay close attention to what is being considered. From environmental issues to economics, we can't complain, if we don't get involved. Political decisions impact our lives and our pocketbook. If we don't want to spend more money, we have to say so. We can't hold our political leaders accountable if we don't make sure they know exactly what we agree and disagree with.

Consider Clinton's $20 Billion dollar loan to Mexico.

The February 13, 1995, edition of *Time* magazine carried the headline:

"*Clinton rescues the Mexican economy - and finds a bold new way to circumvent Congress.*"

President Clinton used the power of executive order to guarantee Mexico's $20 Billion dollar loan. Regarding the use of executive order, the authors of the article Bob Cohn and Bill Turque point out this about President Clinton's action:

"*But as the Mexican bailout suggest, he is looking for a different way to govern, flexing what executive muscle the office provides.*"

Executive orders are not new. Presidents use them. If executive orders are used as, a 'new way to govern', then we have a problem. The people of the United States sent new representatives to Washington for a reason. They wanted change. If President Clinton did not get agreement from those representatives on this massive financial commitment, then he ignored the people of this nation and dictated policy.

Time included another article on the Mexican bail out: "Why the Mexican Crisis Matters". Author Michael Elliott states:

"*the Mexican mess is an example of the kind of economic crisis that will increasingly become the focus of U.S. foreign policy in the post-cold-war era.*"

If we are expected to pay for bail-outs in the future we ought to be part of the decision making process. Continued financial extravagance could force this nation into poverty.

Number 6 in the '*Communist Rules for Revolution*' is:

'*encouraging government extravagance to destroy its credit*'

According to a March 1995 news brief, former President Clinton signed an executive order preventing companies from replacing striking workers permanently. This means workers have a right to strike without fear of losing their jobs.

"The right to strike must be treated as an inherent right"
Communist Party of the United States-1969

Without regard for the public interest or America's national security, workers 'rights' are to be the first concern. Basically, this executive order treats striking as an inherent right.

"We cannot put people first and create jobs and economic growth without a revolution in government."
A Revolution in Government -
Putting People First
Governor Bill Clinton - Senator Al Gore

There is a difference between using terms like reinvent and revolution and meaning them.

"The line and policies presented in this resolution are a guide to the day-to-day work of our Party. In applying these policies, we should never lose sight of our strategic and ultimate goals. They are intertwined elements, and both are present at all stages as the struggle for social progress moves inevitably on the path toward socialism and communism."
Communist Party of The United States

The long-term Communist's goal is to carefully and quietly move Americans toward Socialism. The first step to Communism is Socialism. It is critical to understand how the Communists use Socialism to achieve Communism. There are a couple of ways to get the job done.

John Drakeford, author of *Red Blueprint for the World*, describes two kinds of Socialism. This author summarized Drakeford's explanation to clarify how Communists use

Socialism to manipulate citizens into a position to force them into Communism.

According to Drakeford, Utopian Socialism occurs when all private property becomes public property and the profits generated from the property are shared equally among the people. Drakeford defines the next form is Scientific Socialism. Drakeford indicates Scientific Socialism occurs during the shift from one government system to the other.

If the United States shifted from a capitalist system with a republic form of government to a socialist system, a temporary, centralized, government would have to be formed to handle government affairs until the transition to the new government system was complete. The transition period is when members of the oppressed masses believe they will start to control their government and their lives.

At this time, when the government would be disorganized, the nation would be weak and the masses would be struggling to adjust, the Communists use force and violence to seize power. Scientific Socialism is only a brief, interim stage followed directly by the Communist dictatorship. Communist dictatorships don't have laws to protect people from brutal government actions. Once in power, all actions carried out by the dictatorship, from food rationing to mass murder are justified for the greater good. For the greater good, people are forced to:

- do what the government dictates they do
- live how the government dictates they live
- earn what the government thinks they are worth

Scientific Socialism includes the idea that people who produce more, can have more. This makes Scientific Socialism sound and feel like Capitalism so it will appeal to Capitalists. The Green version of Scientific Socialism is being promoted in the alternative press. It's called, *ParEcon*, short for *Participatory Economics*. The basic ideas of *ParEcon* are:

> *"...an equitable and viable economy designed to minimize self-advancement that is socially counter productive...*
>
> *...ensure that people who live better than others do so only by having undergone personal sacrifice...*
>
> *...there are participatory councils of workers and consumers at various levels, work is divided among balanced job complexes..*
>
> *...One is paid according to one's effort not according to one's output or one's control of the means of production...*
>
> *...economic justice requires that no one be 'free' to appropriate more goods and services than warranted by their personal sacrifice."*
>
> Common Future
Peter Crawford

Karl Marx, shares a similar idea in the *Communist Manifesto*, he states:

> ***"In a higher phase of communist society** ..only then can the narrow horizon of bourgeois right be fully left behind and society inscribe on its banners: **from each according to his ability, to each according to his needs**."*

Bourgeois means Capitalists. The Communist's goal is to destroy Capitalism. Communism operates on the idea; people work to their best ability and in return receive what has been determined they need. *ParEcon*, promotes the same concept. People would be compensated based on their effort but someone else would determine what their compensation would be. With *ParEcon*, no citizen is free to acquire more than is determined they have earned. *ParEcon* also fits with the Green idea to do socially useful work. *ParEcon* stresses working for the good of the people not for personal profit. Socially useful work is what communist workers do.

Another way the Greens are advancing some of these same goals is through the idea of sustainable development.

How does the communist promise to empower the people of a nation lead to the Communists taking control of the people and the nation? Communists use a *'bait and switch'* strategy. The Communists *bait* people with promises and *switch* the rules when they are ready to take power.

The first phase of a Communist revolution involves mentally preparing the people to believe Socialism is the best and only solution to their problems. This is exactly what the Greens are doing using environmental doom as the hot button.

The Set Up, Advance Propaganda

Communists promote Socialism by degrading Capitalism in every way, shape and form. To prove that change is necessary, Communists must devalue Capitalism in the eyes of the people. Capitalism and Capitalists are portrayed as the enemy. Communists magnify anything negative about Capitalism. They use some of the following tactics to mentally prepare the masses to think Socialism is better. Communists attack society from all angles by:

- criticizing traditional values
- creating social conflicts to disrupt society
- helping masses feel sorry for themselves, victims
- directing citizen anger toward system of government
- promising Socialism will give the masses a better life
- introducing socialist ideas as only solution

The Bait

After the Communists have deliberately created citizen unrest they will start to promote the following ideas and promise to take care of the frustrated masses:

- public control of economy and government
- equality, no more class distinctions, share the wealth
- the basics; food, shelter, job, income and healthcare

Citizens buy into these ideas because the current system appears to be falling apart (due to negative propaganda and disruptions). The Communists set the masses up to think:

- they want or need to be taken care of
- a new government system will be for the greater good
- present government system is to blame for all problems

Communists create discontent and blame the capitalist system to lure the masses into Socialism. The Greens plan to keep Americans uptight and misinformed until they are ready to emerge as our political salvation.

> *"The Greens have built carefully for years. They've been busy laying the foundations of a strong social movement...*
>
> *...They are now in a position to build rapidly for transformation*
>
> *They can decisively assist a society in search of answers to overwhelming problems of ecology, democracy, and justice."*
>
> The Greens and the Politics of Transformation
> John Rensenbrink
> Greens National Spokesperson, 1992

The Switch

Communists lie to the masses. Communists promise citizens complete equality. What the Communists forget to mention is that freedom gets lost in the translation. Equality under Communism means all slaves are created equal.

The Green Bait

A key obstacle for the Communists was how to approach, justify and promote an economic conversion in the United States. Even with all the attack strategies outlined in the *Communist Rules for Revolution*, the Communists had to find some other compelling reason for Americans to consider Socialism. What kind of a scam could work in a country where independence is king? A scam that would:

- not be suspected or recognized as Socialism
- direct anger toward fellow Americans
- justify more government control
- hit us in the heart
- appeal to our sense of duty, to right a wrong

Protecting the environment and saving the earth for future generations fits the bill. This is the Green *bait*. It is a compelling reason to consider an economic conversion from Capitalism to Socialism. The Greens are playing off the fear of environmental ruin to persuade Americans that only drastic change will save the earth.

Many Americans have accepted the idea. This is not because Americans are ignorant. It is because Americans are being manipulated. The emotional hooks the Greens are using are powerful, not factual. We need to make more, better and constant distinctions between environmental protection and efforts to impose the Green agenda. The multiple calls for drastic change in America can be traced back to the Green Party program.

The environmental movement offers Green Communists many opportunities to quietly weave socialist ideas into America's public policies. The Greens are using every opportunity to magnify anything negative about Capitalism, our way of life, individual freedom and independent thinking to diminish American values. Some basic rights now under attack by the Greens are:

- property rights
- food choices
- right to bear arms

The Greens have created compelling reasons for the American people to consider major changes. The hook is survival. It is the reason many Americans are going along with Green ideas without qualifying the information. The Greens are tying environmental protection to public health issues to change our values. Private property is a key American value. The Greens are linking human survival to environmental protection to change our independent attitude about property ownership. Greens are using 'fear of extinction' because it is the path of least resistance. The Greens need Americans to 'accept' socialist land-use policies will be better for the environment. The Greens are using '*Chicken Little*' messages to scare Americans into Socialism.

The Green Switch

The Green *switch* will occur if Americans allow the Greens to warp our judgment to believe Socialism is the only way to avoid alleged environmental disaster. If we allowed that to happen, a transition from our current government and economic system would need to occur. Then, Americans would be at the Scientific Socialism point and the Communists would be in position to seize power.

The Greens are aggressively working to convince Americans to replace our value of private property with the Green socialist values of property ownership. The Green excuse to end private property ownership is that placing all lands under government control will ensure environmental excellence. That is Socialism and a major step toward Green Communism. To generate an urgency to change our values, the Greens are using environmental doom and repeating messages like:

- Americans can't be trusted to own property, too much risk
- Americans don't care and are destroying the environment
- the public (government) must protect the land
- survival depends on abolishing private property

Americans are well known for fierce pride of ownership and for placing a high value on private property rights. The above statements are absurd, but they fit *the sky is falling* Green way to mold public opinion. Fear of environmental disaster coupled with promises of a utopian wonderland is the Green way to persuade Americans we must change our values and accept government control of our lands for the greater good. This is what happened with the Spotted Owl issue. It was used to gain control of the timber industry.

Why are the Greens really attacking private property ownership instead of focusing on pressing environmental issues? If we put our emotions on hold, we see survival is not really the Greens objective. It is the Greens excuse.

> *"The theory of Communists may be summed up in the single sentence: Abolition of private property."*
> Karl Marx

A critical difference between Capitalism and Communism is the right to own private property. Karl Marx is the author of the *Communist Manifesto*, a book likened to the Communist's bible. Marx makes the political motivation behind the Green attack on private property very clear.

Keeping our emotions on hold; consider how the Greens are using issues like Endangered Species, Wetlands and Ecosystem Management to set Americans up to accept the end of private property. Americans need to realize this is the top priority for the Greens. We are in serious trouble because the Green movement is also a powerful political lobby. They are pushing hard to increase the power of government (public) control and decrease the rights of individual Americans. We have reached a distress point and we must start protecting each other's property rights.

How are the Greens successfully manipulating environmental issues to abolish private property rights? The Green call to protect and manage entire ecosystems is a good example. We need to look at the Green term, ecosystem. What does it mean? A rough definition of an ecosystem is, everything that lives within a given geographical area and how each piece of the system interacts with other pieces. An ecosystem means everything, living or dead. It includes all species, insect, animal, vegetation, the air, soil and water.

Author Jeremy Rifkin; a well-known leader in the Green movement, explains the Green position on ecosystems and land ownership in his book *Bioshpere Politics*. Rifkin states:

"The very idea of private ownership of part or all of an ecosystem is inimical to biospheric political thinking."

Inimical means adverse, hostile or opposite. That means, private property ownership conflicts or is the opposite of Green biosphere politics. The opposite of private is public.

"Only by placing ecosystems in public trusts will it be possible to reverse the process of rampant short term exploitation of the environment"

Greens like Rifkin are using environmental protection as the excuse to switch from private ownership to public ownership of land in America. Rifkin's biosphere politics, Green politics and Communist politics all share that political objective. Public ownership is 'inimical' or opposite to our American tradition. Rifkin uses many interesting terms throughout his book; like *fellow traveler* and *bourgeoisie*. *Fellow traveler* is the phrase Communists use when referring to comrades who travel the same political path. Rifkin also uses *bourgeoisie* to define American Capitalists. Karl Marx used *bourgeoisie* to define Capitalists in the *Communist Manifesto*.

Ecosystem management is the Greens priority because it creates the opportunity to justify the government (public) taking control of large areas of land for vast habitat and other protected areas. Private property rights will be downplayed. Ecosystem management allows the Greens to:

- designate any area, anywhere as critical habitat
- justify 'taking' private property
- play the 'survival card' over and over again
- make control possible by making control legal
- take major steps towards transforming our society
- eliminate private property rights

Americans need to take Green ideas seriously.

"We must promote the preservation and extension of wildlife habitat by creating and preserving large continuous tracts of open space (complete ecosystems)"
Green Party Program

"adopt ecosystem management as a comprehensive, than have several agencies operating."

Earth Times - June 1994
Vice President Al Gore

The idea of ecosystem management had the support of the former Clinton Administration, Vice President Gore and the Greens. Ecosystem management involves basing all decisions, from political to economic around one view of nature. The Greens plan to use ecosystem management to justify forming one government agency to handle all environmental issues.

"Remove the U.S. Forest Service from under the Agriculture Department, place USFS, the Bureau of Land Management, and the Fish and Wildlife Service under the Environmental Protection Agency."

Earth Island Survey – 1991
Environmental Groups

Coordinating environmental efforts would eliminate the checks and balances that come from the shared power and the different viewpoints of multiple agencies. This is not a good idea. It would create a Green environmental dictatorship with the authority of the federal government. This would be a huge mistake. Too much power corrupts.

Private property ownership is a key distinction between Communism and Capitalism. Independence vs. dependence, freedom vs. slavery and opportunity vs. poverty are also key distinctions between the two systems. The Greens are aggressively working to give the government more control over property owners by increasing the scope of the Endangered Species Act. This act already offers the Greens multiple ways to erode property rights. Fortifying this act would create unlimited excuses to destroy urban and rural property rights. Greens advocate no private ownership local, national, or international. This sounds like global Green Communism.

> *"Green communities are supported by the implementation of land trusts, intentional communities, shared ownership, and other alternatives to traditional individual land and property ownership."*
>
> Green Party Program

Are the Greens successfully eroding private property rights? Yes, absolutely, no doubt about it. An example is the Supreme Court case decision of Babbitt, et.al. v. Sweet Home Chapter of Communities for a Great Oregon. The Summary Judgment of July 7, 1995, by William Perry Pendley, President and Chief Legal Officer of the Mountain States Legal Foundation stated:

> *"the Court had decided, by a vote of 6-3, that federal regulations, which interpret the word 'harm' in the Endangered Species Act as prohibiting 'habitat modification' on private property, are 'reasonable' and therefore legal."*

Pendley explained the ramifications of this decision:

> *"I think what the Supreme Court did was say to the property owners of America who have land on which endangered species might be found, Mr. Babbitt, Secretary of the Interior, is now your landlord."*

What does that mean? According to Pendley, it means:

> *"The Supreme Court's ruling **gives the federal government power over the two-thirds of the country that is privately owned.** Now the U.S. Fish and Wildlife Service will move aggressively to enforce **regulations that define 'harm' as habitat modification', a definition that includes actions that impair essential biological patterns...**" As if this weren't vague enough, **the landowner need only intend to perform the act (plow the field, cut the trees) not intend to harm the species, to be criminally liable."**

These rulings affect every American in one way or another. We foot the bill. These are the kinds of rulings that make control possible by making control legal. This is not to say we don't need to protect wildlife habitat. The Greens are using the Endangered Species Act to achieve their goal to end private property ownership by ending private property rights.

An article in the February 1995 edition of the *San Joaquin County Citizens Land Alliance* illustrates the impact of the Endangered Species Act or ESA. The article reads:

> **ESA Cost: $413,774 Per Fly**
> *The Endangered Species Act (ESA) as applied to the construction of the San Bernadino County Medical Center resulted in an expenditure of $3,310,199 to mitigate for the presence of eight (8) Delhi Sands Flower-Loving Flies. The effort as negotiated with the U.S. Fish and Wildlife Service and California Department of Fish and Game resulted in moving and redesigning the facility to provide 1.92 acres of protected habitat for eight flies **believed to occupy the site.** Cost per fly amounted to $413,774.25 and resulted in a one year construction delay. This cost is equivalent to the average cost of treatment of 494 inpatients or 23,644 outpatients*
>
> California Forest Today-December 1994
> (Bold Emphasis Added)

The use of the phrase 'believed to occupy the site' ought to indicate to us that all this was done without absolute proof. Is this stewardship or deliberate sabotage of the project? We need to examine all the pieces of the ESA puzzle. Does this species exist or flourish in other parts of the United States? How many were there? How many are left?

The Greens focus on one species (like the eight flies) at a time because it is costly and disruptive, not because they care about the flies. Imagine the ripple effect of the Supreme Court ruling regarding the meaning of 'harm' in the Endangered

Species Act. Heaven forbid we should swat or even think about swatting a fly before checking to see if it is a Delhi Sands Flower-Loving Fly.

What if the Greens said eight flies were 'believed to occupy' your backyard? What if federal regulations prevented further use of that area? Imagine, no more family barbecues or mowing the lawn because it might disturb the flies. It might be a good excuse to let the yard go for a while but would it be reasonable in the long term? No, it would make life difficult. People and flies have been coexisting for years. This illustrates no one is exempt. All landowners can be impacted by extreme Green regulations. Pendley made it clear in his summary judgment on the Supreme Court ruling, he stated:

> "...the landowner need only intend to perform the act (plow the field, cut the trees), not intend to harm the species, to be criminally liable."

Everyone who owns property or plans to own property could be in the same position as a farmer who can't plan to plow, let alone, plow their field. We must realize, before it is too late, the Greens intend to end private property ownership. This is not about environmental health. This is about controlling the American people and taking control of the land base. The ESA is just one way the Greens are making control possible by making control legal. Why are extreme interpretations of the law finding support? One reason is the Greening of the Judges. The Environmental Law Institute began holding law conferences in 1991. An article in E *magazine*, "First, Green the Judges" outlined the organization's plan to educate judges on.

- Wetlands identification
- Scientific topics
- Retroactive liability
- New laws
- Legal land use issues
- Basic geology
- New scientific concepts

This amounts to programming judges to render Green judgments on environmental issues. It is not equal representation if the judges have received their instructions in advance from a biased political group. Judgments are supposed to be rendered after evaluating facts and circumstances presented by both sides in the dispute.

The Greens are using our legal system as a political hammer. Teaching judges how to correctly interpret the law to advance Green politics ought to be illegal. Isn't fixing a court case the same as fixing a horse race? If the Greens know how the Judge will rule in advance, isn't that the same as knowing how the race will turn out? The Judge's integrity is not the question. The Greens have set them up and can con them as easily as the next guy.

> *"Lobbying is the art of forcing a specific change in attitude, legislation or government policy. This can be done on the streets and through the media in campaigns aimed at creating the climate where a decision-maker has no choice but to make the decision you're lobbying for. Or it can be done through the courts and no-one does it better than the Natural Resources Defense Council (NRDC), widely considered the most effective lobby and litigating group on US environmental issues."*
> State of the Ark

The founding fathers studied other governments before they crafted our government. They designed a check and balance system to give citizens the power to protect their freedom. They also understood people who wanted to live free would have to protect their rights and defend the land they love.

> *"You are now the guardians of your own liberties"*
> Samuel Adams
> Philadelphia – 1776

Personal freedom offers individuals hope and potential. The right of privacy, the ability to own property and the chance to prosper fosters pride, security and creativity. People who are free to speak and think are also free to be innovative.

People who operate on the ethic of working together are more courteous to others. Good people, freedom and our system of government are the reasons America grew into a great nation and a superpower. America still stands as the beacon of hope to people around the globe. If we intend to preserve freedom for our children and keep America intact, we the people, need to become a stronger voice in Washington, D. C.

Save the Earth, by Jonathon Porritt is a series of worldwide environmental issues and stories. It includes multiple inspirational environmental quotations by influential people such as; Ted Turner (who published the book), Senator Al Gore, Robert Redford, Carl Sagan, Petra Kelly (former Green Party Leader), the Prince of Wales and Jeremy Rifkin. Rifkin's quotation explains the new Green vision that the Earth is a living organism and what that means politically. He states:

> "*The new politics envisions the Earth as a living organism and the human species as a partner and participant, dependent on the proper functioning of the biosphere...the transition to the biospheric culture will spell the end to the nation state as the dominant political institution and the end of the multi-national corporation as the primary economic institution. The biospheric era will spawn political and economic arrangements more in keeping with our new ecological understanding of the Earth as a living organism.*"
>
> (Bold Emphasis Added)

Getting Americans to accept the earth is a living organism or living being is critical to the Greens. Relating to the earth as a living being with human like qualities is the Green way to alter and change our beliefs by blending environmental protection and Green spiritual politics. The strategy has worked before.

Compare Rifkin's political ideas to the following political ideas.

> *"In place of ...the State ...must be set the living organism ...of the people"*
> *"Economics...is a living process, one of the functions of that body which is the people"*
>
> *"From a dead mechanism (the state) there must be formed a living organism"*
>
> *"Our movement alone was capable of creating a national organism "*
>
> *"The task...was to build up the entire administration...until it became a close organic whole, pulsing with life"*

Although the above ideas sound Green, all these statements were made by Adolf Hitler. He created the idea that the people, Nazism and the sacred soil of Germany were all part of a living organism. The Greens are selling the same brand of 'snake oil'. Hitler transformed public life and government to reflect his ideas. The Greens plan to do the same thing. The book, *Hitler's Ideology,* by Richard Koenigsberg, outlines these and many other phrases Hitler used. The above quotes are from *The Speeches of Adolf Hitler* and *Mein Kamf*

Hitler's idea to build a government system around the earth as a living organism is very similar to former Vice President Gore's call for the environment to become the *central organizing principle* of government policies and public life.

> *"The task of saving the earth's environment must and will become the central organizing principle of the post-Cold War world"*
>
>
>
> Putting People First
> Senator Al Gore
>
>

Hitler used the idea of the earth as a living organism to justify his political ideas from the death of the state to a new economics. Green leaders, like Rifkin, are also using the idea that the earth is a living organism to justify the end of the nation state, a new economics and to gain support for Green spiritual politics. S.S.D.D, same stuff, different decade. We need to remember Hitler was a psychopath.

Transforming American Society

Greens are using ideas like ending 'affluenza', the disease of affluence and 'consumerism' to shame us into thinking we must transform our society. Is banning CFC's about products, the environment or the economy? Some products that contain or use CFC's when manufactured are listed below:

- Bronchial-inhalant
- Contact lenses
- Heat pumps
- Telephones
- Radios
- Washer/dryers

- Calculators
- Dishwashers
- Freezers
- Televisions
- VCR's
- Cameras

- Vending machines
- Eyeglass lenses
- Microwaves
- Copy machines
- Smoke alarms
- Tobacco-low tar

We are all willing to make sacrifices. Most of us can live without these items. Some Americans can't. Before these products are banned, shouldn't we have some additional information? Which of these products produce the most CFC's and which ones produce the least? What are the latest findings? How many scientists believe we have an ozone problem and why? How many scientists disagree and why?

Before our political leaders take any drastic steps based on Green propaganda, the American people have a right to full disclosure. They deserve the facts and the answers to these basic questions.

More Green goals to transform our society include:

- **eliminate private automobiles**
- terminate trucking
- **shut down most airports**
- **eliminate the military establishment**
- end chemical production
- **abolish the arms industry**
- **reduce meat consumption**
- **organize communities around communes**
- **limit production and distribution of goods to local area**
- limit services to local areas

Are these the best and only ways to effectively address our environmental problems? We need to answer this question before we accept any of these steps or that these businesses must be eliminated. The Greens are pushing the panic button to get people and politicians to take steps toward achieving these goals without question.

A good example of how Green politics work is the push to control the trucking industry. We have been deluged with media reports presenting negative images of trucking practices and truck drivers. From running triples to drug abuse and rear trailer design; the trucking industry is another industry on the Green hot-seat. The question is, are these reports accurate? Is the intent to improve safety or to justify controlling truckers and interstate commerce?

Green goals advanced by these negative reports are to use public health, safety and the environment to generate public concern. This helps justify more government regulations that can cripple the industry and achieve limited control of production and distribution. If truckers can't haul and deliver goods across this nation, the Greens move closer to limiting production and distribution to local areas.

Greens are using the threat of environmental collapse to scare us into agreeing that we will all be better off if we let the government play a bigger role in our lives. Our current government system is not the problem. The Greens want to change our government system. Review the following simple definitions.

Communism: Government control of production and distribution
Socialism: Public control of production and distribution
Capitalism: Individual control of production and distribution

Who decides what American businesses are acceptable? The free market usually determines the success or failure of a business in America. The Greens are using the environment as an excuse to change the process. Here are two examples:

> *"The Federal Government is the largest purchaser of goods and services in the world, and we are committed to using that massive purchasing power to spur markets for environmental technologies, save taxpayer's money and lead by example."*
> *Earth Times, June 1994*
> Vice President Al Gore

> *"boycotting socially and ecologically destructive businesses."*
> Green Party Program

Choosing to buy from one business and not to buy from another has the same effect as boycotting a business. Is our government now deciding what is and is not an acceptable business? Are our tax dollars being used to put some Americans out of business?

Using the power of government to boycott business owners is not new. Hitler used his power to separate the Jews from the rest of society by boycotting Jewish businesses. Nazi soldiers were used to prevent patrons from entering Jewish shops. Government boycotts of certain businesses are not a good idea.

Tolerance Or Intolerance?

How did Hitler train his army to assault innocent people? It all started in the name of the Nazi cause. Nasty remarks led to vandalism. Rocks through shop windows led to beatings. Beatings led to more brutality and threats to kill people. The injustices escalated from there.

Isolated incidents became a regular part of German life until terrorism became the norm. Terrorism is not a good thing to condone. In the name of Nazi cause, saving the sacred soil, Nazi terrorism grew into control without conscience.

Hitler started out by promoting the idea that Jews were different than other Germans. He kept adding lies to that idea until he successfully labeled the Jews sub-human. Soon, normal people began to treat the Jews like they were sub-human. He separated the Jews from the rest of society, first mentally, then physically. Hitler gave people permission to be aggressive and mean.

The Holocaust was not only the result of Hitler's ideas; it was the result of the people who followed his ideas. If no one followed, he would not have had the power to carry out his ideas.

The people of that nation allowed their standards to be eroded. They allowed themselves to ignore senseless acts committed against their fellow citizens. They allowed themselves to become barbaric, uncivilized animals. They followed the politically correct behavior of the day. Normal people became ruthless political activists who justified what they were doing was necessary.

Most Americans are familiar with the David Koresh incident and the Randy Weaver episode. What many Americans don't realize is that other Americans are also under siege.

Some individuals, who were hired to serve and protect the American people, are operating outside of the law. Perhaps they feel what they are doing is right, but it cannot continue to go unchecked. We need to pay attention to hostile actions against innocent people.

The following report was featured in the June, 1995 issue of the *San Joaquin County Citizens Land Alliance:*

> *"Last May, A Bureau of Alcohol, Tobacco and Firearms (BATF) squad showed up at the home of gun-show promoters Harry and Theresa Lamplugh When Mr. Lamplugh asked the BATF agent (most of whom did not wear identifying vests) if they had a search warrant, an agent stuck an MP-5 submachine gun in his face and told him, "Shut the f---up, motherf----r. Do you want more trouble than you already have?*
>
> *During the six-hour search, BATF agents refused to allow the Lamplughs to get dressed. The search squad held a pizza party in the middle of the search, stomped a housecat to death, spilled Mr. Lamplugh's cancer medicine on the floor, and seized 61 guns, along with the Lamplugh's birth certificates, marriage certificate, medical records, business contact lists and personal mail.*
>
> *The Lamplughs have not been charged with any crime, or even told that they are suspected of any crime, but the Federal Government has refused to return their property."*
>
> National Review
> March 1995

This doesn't sound like something we expect to hear about in the United States of America. It sounds like illegal use of government force. How many Americans has this happened to? Where do we draw the line? Who is responsible?

According to the article: "Yeltsin's eyes and ears", featured in the August 7, 1995 edition of *U.S. News & World Report*, Russia's KGB or Secret Police have regained their authority to:

'arrest and interrogate suspects for days or weeks without bringing a formal charge...the rejuvenation of the secret police occurred in the name of fighting crime and corruption.'

The BATF agents are not alone in stepping over the line. Other government agencies are arming their agents with semi-automatic weapons to question or arrest unarmed, normally law abiding citizens. The justifications for this extreme display of force are environmental accusations or disputes. Not all BATF or other government agents are hostile individuals. These agencies need to reevaluate the need for such aggressive actions against innocent people.

The Greens are using the environmental cause as an excuse to ruin Americans financially, terrorize people and cause others to lose their way of life and their property. Animal rights issues are another Green excuse to gain control over the private lives of Americans. One poor old gentleman was fined for killing a sewer rat in his back yard. The Humane Society cited him for murdering the rat in an inhumane fashion.

These are the same kind of absurdities people ignored in Germany. Green ideology is not flexible or reasonable. It is to the point of beyond ridiculous. Why are we putting up with this? If we do not bring the Greens under control, it will only continue to get worse.

All legislation; from the crime bill to the Endangered Species Act, that will give the Greens or government agencies more power to control our lives or nullify our rights ought to be brought before the people. We can't afford to allow our political leaders to let Green legislation slide by under the guise of environmental protection. We are at a pivotal point. The Greens, like Hitler, intend to make control possible, by making control legal. We must all get personally involved to stop that from happening. Our government system is not the problem. Human error is to blame for the challenges facing the American people. It is the politics of the people we have allowed to gain positions of power and influence that are to blame. We, the people, must take responsibility for our future by taking responsibility for the future of this country.

> **"We a civilized, humane people, had allowed ourselves to become indifferent to brutality committed by our own government on our own citizens. At best, that seemed to make us cowards, at worst brutes ourselves."**
> *A Child of Hitler*
> Alfons Heck

He was a leader in the Hitler Youth. Alfons describes his life in his book, *A Child of Hitler*. He shares his despair that people did not try and stop Hitler. He blames the people for allowing themselves to be taken in by Hitler's lies. He blames parents for sacrificing their children to the Nazi movement. He blames teachers who worked with Hitler and lied to the children about the Jewish people. He blames the people for not protecting the children.

The Hitler Youth were taught Nazism was a new order for a new age. Greens refer to our future in similar terms; calling for a New World Order and branding the 21st Century as our New Age. Hitler said, 'One People, One Nation'. Greens say 'One People, One Planet.' Same stuff, different decade.

Why didn't the people stop Adolf Hitler? History reminds us; the fate of a nation depends on the strength and will of its people. We have enjoyed the benefits of freedom and we share the duty to pass that legacy on to the next generation and they, the next. We have nothing to lose by challenging the Green movement. We have everything to lose by closing our eyes and ignoring the Greens.

There is safety in numbers. At first, there were more regular citizens than there were Nazis. The Germans did not take advantage of the opportunity to stop Hitler. If the majority of the American people stand up and stand together, the Green minority will be forced to listen.

Eco-Terrorism

The Greens have another approach to crippling businesses and affecting the economy of this nation. It's called Eco-terrorism and it's on the rise in America. The Nazis used terrorism to intimidate people and destroy Jewish businesses, all in the name of the Nazi cause. It became routine.

The Greens profess to be nonviolent, but they don't condemn monkeywrenching or Eco-Terrorism. Both these terms define actions of sabotage or terrorism committed against citizens in the name of the environmental cause.

Recreation is another industry under attack by the Greens. From snowmobilers' to horseback riders, the Greens want to control these industries by controlling the individuals who enjoy the sport. The Greens are working all the angles, from limiting access to recreation areas where these Americans go to relax to committing acts of violence and terrorism.

If the Greens decide Americans should not be allowed to use certain outdoor areas they invent ways to terrorize those who enjoy that recreational activity. For instance, one monkeywrenching tactic involves stringing piano wire across mountain trails to trip horses and discourage riders from continuing to use the trail. In one case a horse tripped, sending both horse and rider down a steep hillside. The woman was hurt and her horse had to be destroyed. This terrorist act was committed in the name of the environmental cause. It cannot be ignored, justified or excused. What if the woman had died? Her death would not have been an accident. What is the difference between this act of eco-terrorism and pre-meditated murder?

Monkeywrenchers go by the book. Dave Foreman founder of the well-known eco-terrorist group Earth First! co-authored *Eco-Defense, A Field Guide to Monkeywrenching*. The book details what to do and how to commit terrorist's acts. Of course since the disclaimer says the book is a joke, no legal action was taken. Remember, the communist method of communicating with comrades? They say what they mean, then dismiss what they said as a joke so the political significance is lost.

The book *Eco-Defense* promotes terrorism in the name of the environmental cause. Monkeywrenchers ambushed motorcycle riders by spreading nails on roads and placed spiked railroad ties inside tunnels so the riders would crash. Eco-terrorists also hammered spikes into trees so a logger's chainsaw or mill saw would hit it and cause serious damage. These acts of violence were promoted as a real 'high' for those who participated in sabotage activities. Earth First! publicly stated in April 1990, that they would stop spiking trees, but they lied. The March 1991 edition of *Earth First! Journal* revealed a different thought. The statement was; *"don't forget the (f-ing) spikes"*

The Nazi cause gave people this same sense of false glory. Committing violent acts against innocent people was justified in the name of protecting the sacred soil. The Nazis set out to cleanse the German soul and rid the earth of undesirable people. The Nazis were on a power trip and they went power crazy.

The environmental cause is being used to get people involved in the same kind of power trip. The Greens are encouraging a similar level of intolerance toward the American people. Eco-Terrorists commit acts of terrorism and harassment in the name of saving Mother Earth. The Nazis committed acts of terrorism and harassment in the name of saving the sacred soil of the Fatherland. The Green movement is cultivating hate against our own people in the name of Mother Earth. S.S.D.D. - Same Stuff, Different Decade.

Wrong is wrong, right is right. We cannot let this slide. When they came for the Jews, no one came to their aid. The rest is history. What is the difference between these violent attacks on American citizens and the initial Nazi attacks on the Jewish people? As a society, we cannot continue to ignore these actions in the name of the environmental cause. The Greens official political position is, they do not condemn Eco-terrorism. Creative sabotage is an individual decision. If the Greens were really non-violent they would condemn violence. Peaceful, tolerant, conflict resolution does not resemble Eco-terrorism.

Green intolerance is everywhere. Eco-terrorists throw blood on innocent people because they wear fur. Greens justify this action as punishment for a crime against nature. Wearing leather is now on the crime list and the message is: to protect the environment and animals, don't eat beef and don't wear leather.

These attacks are all part of the Green political strategy. The Animal Rights, Anti-Beef, Anti-leather message is intended to impact, then cripple businesses across America. The Greens want Americans to become so worn out with constant conflicts within our society that we become hostile toward our culture. This is when the Greens plan to present their ideas as our salvation. Lenin's instructions for revolution include staging conflicts to keep society in a constant uproar so citizens will welcome change. Hitler used the same tactic. The nonviolent Greens are using violence, verbally attacking innocent people, laying traps for others and disrupting our society with multiple mass protests to put Americans in a frustrated, submissive state of mind.

Animal Rights

Animal rights are another example of the difference between public perception vs. actual group philosophies and activities within the Green movement. No one condones cruelty to animals. American pets are part of the family. Caring for animals is not the issue. Our love of animals does not equal approval for Green politics and terrorism.

Barry Clausen, a private investigator hired to infiltrate Earth First!, obtained a copy of the Animal Liberation Front activist's handbook titled: *A DECLARATION OF WAR: Killing People To Save Animals And The Environment* By SCREAMING WOLF. Clausen states:

> *"They believe in a revolution to liberate animals and if necessary kill their oppressors – HUMANS. The contents of this handbook on murderous terrorism are distinctly characterized by its title and subtitle."*
>
> *Walking on the Edge*

The Greens goal to control our lives reaches far beyond Washington D.C. and environmental protection. The Greens, just like Hitler, stress citizen activism. The Greens justify abuse of their fellow Americans in the name of their cause. Activists are doing their 'Green-Duty' by braving confrontations to declare their politically correct positions with Nazi-style fury. Like the Nazis, these people are not stopping to think about what they are involved in. They are allowing themselves to become insensitive and mean. They are lowering their standards and sliding into uncivilized behavior.

Hitler's 'propaganda machine' convinced reasonable people to do unreasonable things. Excellent propaganda does not equal excellent political decisions or sound public policies. America's future, including our environmental future, is far too important to leave up to the Greens just because they can afford to broadcast hostile propaganda.

Animal Rights activists are a good example of how Greens are getting normal people to take aggressive action toward their fellow citizens. There is a difference between expressing a sincere concern for animal welfare and Nazi-style activism. The determining factor is in how people approach the situation. Nazi-style activists don't need facts. They assume they are right. Reasonable people take a different approach. They begin by talking to each other.

This author had a recent Green encounter. It began with a public announcement describing a car and asking the owner to report to the front of the store. Upon admitting ownership of said vehicle, a very angry woman began to share her opinion of how cruel it was to leave two small dogs in the car on a hot afternoon. Other customers did not have to strain to hear her remarks, which included 'others', were calling the authorities to take care of the situation.

This was embarrassing. Although briefly stunned, it was critical to respond to these accusations and stop the show. It was necessary to interrupt her to explain that although her concern was understandable, the dogs were fine and well cared for. The explanation included these details: the dogs had just been shaved to keep them cool, they had water and this stop involved enough time to run into the store and pick up a receipt. The scene ended on that note. Hindsight is always 20-20. What was left out is that the dogs ride along because one pet has epileptic seizures if she gets upset. If she's home alone, she barks at every noise because she's nearly blind. That upsets her. She is much calmer resting in her basket in the car. If she has a seizure, medication and care are immediately available. If anything, these pets are over cared for.

Perhaps those people thought the dog was barking because she was overheating but they could have asked instead of jumping to conclusions. There is nothing wrong with caring about animal welfare. The danger lies in the attitude and the way these situations are approached. People who have pets care about them. If a stranger is concerned about the feelings of animals, they ought to be just as concerned about the feelings of human beings. The Greens call for peaceful conflict resolution, but in reality, do not display common courtesy or kindness.

If we were operating by usual American good manners, the woman would have shared her concerns privately. She would have shown some respect for a fellow citizen. She could have asked how much longer the dogs would be in the car and she would have learned: the dogs were left in a cool car, the air conditioner had just been turned off, windows opened, they would only be there for a few moments and they were not being mistreated. What occurred in this situation was blind condemnation. The Nazis operated on blind condemnation.

There is a difference between concern and blame. Concern is something you share with someone. Blame is something you do to someone. The Greens increasingly confrontational approach to getting their way is a prime example of how Nazi-style political activism got out of hand. Animal rights activism is becoming more common and it includes the destruction of valuable research data, scientific equipment and research facilities.

We all share a love and concern for animals. We cannot allow ourselves to justify attacking innocent people in the name of animal rights or any other part of the Green movement. We need to remember there is a difference between assertive and aggressive behavior. To maintain a civilized society we must demand civilized behavior.

Industry must consider environmental concerns. Environmental groups must consider industry concerns. Industries can't be allowed to destroy the environment and the Greens can't be allowed to destroy America. We need honesty, communication and cooperation.

Basic Training Coming to a Mall Near You

So far, the Greens have played it safe. Eco-terrorists have been sneaking around at night disabling equipment, killing cows or stringing piano wire across trails when no one can see them. Now they mastered the easy stuff, it's time to get serious and more comfortable confronting American citizens.

The Greens intend to take terrorism shopping. Coming to a mall near you, Eco-terrorists plan to start harassing Americans about the wrongs of Capitalism and Christmas. In the name of the environmental cause, you or a family member may be singled out.

Many Americans agree, Christmas is commercialized but this is a different issue. American citizens ought to be safe in shopping malls. American citizens should not be exposed to terrorism in the name of anything. Is this military training for the Green troops?

This is another example of the contradiction between the Greens professed non-violence and their activities. There are varying degrees of violence. Mainstream Americans must understand intimidation and citizen harassment leads to increased levels of terrorism. These ideas are being cultivated by many groups associated with the Green movement. Earth First! took the lead on this one and told members to:

> "*go to the malls and: 'tear-it-up, shut-it-down and do-it-now'!*"
> *From the Trenches Newsletter*
> September, 1994

Beyond discussing money in terms of Christmas presents, how about eco-terrorism and it's effect on American families. How long could your family eat if you could no longer produce income and there was no money coming in? Monkeywrenchers intentionally break expensive equipment other Americans use to make their living. No equipment, no work. No work, no income.

How can the Greens espouse concern for the life of a tree and not the life of a family? If you are a loving and compassionate person, how can you not care if a horse and rider fall down a mountainside? What caring person could set traps for motorcycle riders or timber workers that could result in their violent death?

If the Greens were non-violent, they would not invent violent things to do. Professed non-violence contradicts the violent acts of many involved in the Green movement.

Contributing to the Delinquency of a Minor

According to a recent report featured in the newsletter *From the Trenches*, Earth First! is now recruiting students from high schools and colleges. Students are being targeted to join the cause and learn how to commit terrorist acts while they are minors and above the law. Students are also easier to recruit than adults because they operate on emotion and are very naive.

The Hitler Youth were also recruited at an early age to 'play political activist' so they would grow-up to be terrorists. Hitler involved children in a political movement and molded them into little Nazis dedicated to the cause.

The Greens are using the exact same approach. Greens are recruiting children and teaching them to take assertive actions in the name of the environmental cause. America's children are 'playing political activist'. They are learning to be dedicated to the environmental cause.

So many books are out now pushing children to be politically active. One of these books is: *The Kids Guide to Social Action* by Barbara Lewis. The book covers issues like; recycling, gun control, protesting, writing legislators, how to get a bill on the ballot and even includes forms for students to copy. The book is a resource guide for child activists.

It includes a list of organizations for children to contact for assistance. Environmental groups listed range from the Sierra Club to Greenpeace. Political contacts are also listed. They include youth groups we expect to see and one we might not expect to see, the surprise group is the 'Youth Section of the Democratic Socialists of America'.

Although calls for social change are not illegal, Socialism is not the American standard. Listing this organization suggests to students that socialism deserves equal consideration with traditional political groups. This is a subtle devaluing of our system of government and the economic standard this nation is based upon. We are not a socialist nation. We are a capitalist, free enterprise nation.

3

Eco Child Abuse

"It takes a whole village to raise a child"

African Proverb

The idea *"it takes a whole village to raise a child"* has been popularized in America. Why? The Greens plan to replace our tradition of private, independent child rearing with the Communist model, where society plays the major role. The village concept is a convenient message for the Greens to use to eliminate the family unit by eliminating our belief in and need for the family unit. The village concept is designed to condition Americans to accept the government must play an increasing role in family life. Since most Americans would not embrace this idea, the Greens are presenting it as a new way to help children. Greens are pushing community involvement and for non-family members (strangers) to become influential parts of a child's life. The purpose is to quietly undermine the family. Greens also support the 'Treaty on the Rights of a Child' which would give the world community the power to help decide how children, even ours, are raised.

We need to remember this is an African proverb. The American version would be 'it takes a whole family to raise a child'. Americans would not fall prey to these ideas if the entire list of Green goals for families was public knowledge.

Green Communists are using the environmental cause and village concept to conceal their goals. Murray Bookchin is a leading Green activist who is considered an authority in eco-philosophy. In September, 1990, Bookchin outlined these Green goals and family values:

> "*No longer is it enough to speak of new techniques for conserving and fostering the natural environment. We must deal with the earth communally, as a human collectively, without the trammels of self-interest, profit, competition and property that have distorted humanity's vision of life and nature since the break-up of tribal society. **We must eliminate not only the hierarchy produced by our market-oriented society, but hierarchy as such; not only the patriarchal family, but all modes of gender and parental domination; not only the classes produced by our corporate society but all the social classes and elites.**"*
>
> *Ecology, Anarchism & Green Politics Sept1990*
> Murray Bookchin
> Ecology and Revolutionary Thought
> Youth Greens - Left Green Network

This quote was featured in a youth Green publication. Youth Greens work with the Student Environmental Action Coalition, which is associated with the Democratic Socialists of America.

There is a difference between a community volunteer program that addresses a specific issue and being set-up to give the Greens a chance to promote Green values to America's children. The village idea is like a Green tightrope. We have to make sure to maintain the balance between steps to help children in need and steps to achieve the Green goal to eliminate the family unit. The Greens will attempt to gain control over American families by supporting efforts that give the government more authority in private family matters.

Americans ought to think twice before letting Green strangers interact with their children. Americans normally teach our children to stay away from strangers because of the potential danger. It would be wise to continue that practice.

Parents have been set-up to allow their children to join in Green community (village) activities such as a hike, a field trip or an environmental youth conference. A false sense of safety has been created because it is an environmental activity. Parents feel good their children want to help clean up the environment. Some parents may welcome a break while their children learn about nature and spend time in the fresh air. Most parents feel their children are learning how to be better people from these kinds of activities. Green activities seem harmless. Hitler made youth activities seem harmless.

> "*The mission of the Hitler Youth is neither religious nor radical, nor is it philosophical, political or economic. It is entirely natural:* **the young people should be led back to nature, they should recognize nature as the giver of life and energy.** *And they should strengthen and develop their bodies outdoors, making themselves well and keeping themselves well. For a healthy mind can develop only in a healthy body and it is* **only in the freedom of nature that a human being can also open himself to a higher morality and a higher ethic.**"
>
> Hitler, Memoirs of a Confidant
> Adolf Hitler
> (Bold Emphasis Added)

Hitler told parents their child's participation was not political or spiritual. He lied. German parents made an error in judgment. They trusted those involved in the Nazi movement with the hearts and minds of their children. German parents did not understand the personal and political ramifications that would follow. German parents allowed their children to participate in Hitler Youth activities because it sounded like a healthy activity. Most German parents did not worry about their child's involvement and others welcomed it.

America's children are being recruited into the ranks of the Green movement and indoctrinated with politically correct thoughts. Green youth activities are nearly identical to how the Hitler Youth were recruited. Greens, like Hitler, involve children in activities where the political values of the movement can be cemented in the child's mind. Nazi values were the core of all activities. Hitler organized youth camps and land service activities. According to Alfons Heck, German children did not rush to join the Nazis because of their dedication to saving the Fatherland. They joined to have fun, instead of working at home. Alfons blames adults for not stopping Hitler's Nazi movement.

> *"I developed a harsh resentment toward our elders, especially our educators from the Volksschule to university; not only had they allowed themselves to be deceived, they had delivered us, their children, into the cruel power of a new God."*
>
> A *Child of Hitler*
> Alfons Heck
> Hitler Youth Leader

Green and Nazi youth activities have these things in common:

- belong to special clubs
- have special badges and other propaganda items
- sing special songs
- say special new pledges
- get in touch with nature
- participate in parades
- meet national leaders in the movement
- are recognized, rewarded based on performance
- attend special youth conferences
- involve children at an early age

S.S.D.D. Same stuff different decade. The Green goal is the same as Hitler's. They need followers. They are abusing children for political gain in the name of saving Mother Earth.

The village concept conveys the Communist ideology that society rather than a family knows what's best for a child. The end result is group-think instead of the 'spice of life' and individuality produced by the traditional American family. Group-think is also the goal of environmental education, to cement the belief children must follow Green orders to save Mother Earth. This can lead to schools and society dictating children's values. America's communities have always played a role in the lives of our children. There is a difference between sponsoring a softball team and brainwashing a child.

Many programs currently operating such as Big Brother and Big Sister programs, mentor programs for students or speaker's programs are not the same as the village concept. These programs are well run. Participants are screened, the programs monitored and someone is accountable to parents.

Recruiting small children into a political cause seems to be the trademark of dictatorships. German children were recruited into the ranks of the Hitler Youth at age ten, some as early as age eight. Russian children joined the Little Octoberist while in kindergarten and then the Young Pioneers by age nine. The Greens are targeting pre-schoolers.

Earth Day, The New Children's Crusade!

> "If the millions of school kids who now raise Earth flags, plant trees and march in 'All Species parades' get their way, Earth Day will soon be bigger than Christmas."
>
> E magazine - April 199
> Mike Weilbacher

Telling the American people Earth Day is a children's crusade is like saying Germany's children trained themselves to be little Nazis. Children did not organize the Hitler Youth, adults did. Children are not organizing the Green Youth, adults are.'Greening' the schools is no accident. It is the

Greens way to your child's heart and soul. Earth Day is the inroad. Children are being indoctrinated with Green ideology in schools across the country. When people realized what Nazi really meant, it was too late. Germany's children were already brainwashed to pledge their allegiance to Hitler. Hitler youth believed the future was up to them so they became Nazi activists.

Greens understand the concept. Children have no political past. They operate on emotion so their political opinions can be easily molded. America's children have been led to believe, just like the Hitler Youth were led to believe, that they are the only ones who can change the world. The future is up to them.

Emotional Blackmail

> *"The execution of this great transformation must be left to youth."*
>
> *Hitler, Memoirs of a Confident*
> Adolf Hitler

> *"A lot of people think kids can't do very much work inthe world. But I think kids might be the only chance."*
> Anna Brown, age 11
> *Save the Earth-An Action Handbook for Kids*

Pretty heavy load for an 11-year-old child to carry. There is a big difference between children learning to be responsible and children being taught they are responsible. Getting a Green education is very different from learning facts about the environment. Green teachers encourage students to react to environmental horror stories. Children are encouraged to get angry and to get politically involved. The Greens are scaring America's children into political action.

What are some ten-year-old children doing instead of playing and having fun? Some are gathering under trees to figure out how to fix the hole in the ozone. Fear drives them to do this. Children believe if they don't come up with the answer, they will have to dig holes and live underground like gophers.

Eco-Child Abuse is a term that describes the Green method of using fear, peer pressure and lies to scare or force children into taking a political position or becoming Green activists. It happens when the Greens twist environmental issues to manipulate children. It happens when Greens create an unreasonable level of responsibility for children by telling children it is up to them to save the earth.

Where do children get these ideas? One example is found in a 1993 children's coloring book, *Helping Our Environment,* by Rudy Young. The author indicates this book represents a "new trend of teaching" and that it has "great support from leading educators and teachers worldwide". The book deals with political and environmental issues. One topic is zero population growth. Zero population growth occurs when the number of births is the same as the number of deaths. To make a point, the author asks readers:

> *"Why might zero population growth be a good idea for the future?"*

The author gives these reasons for zero population growth.

> *"There will one day be so many people on earth that they will begin falling over the sides"*

> *"There will be so many people on earth that there won't be enough skateboards to go around"*

> *"There will be so many people on earth that it will get too heavy and fall out of orbit"*

> *"There won't be enough food to feed everybody"*

How can this kind of science get the support of leading educators and teachers? This is not science. This is emotional blackmail. This form of political science mixes a political issue with fear to get a child to make an emotional decision. This is not an uncommon approach to environmental education. The alternative to zero population growth is either starving to death or falling off the earth. Which sounds more pleasant? These simplistic choices are intended to convince children the only way to live is to support zero population growth.

Most Americans think learning about the environment is a simple process and a healthy experience. In concept, yes, in practice, no. Environmental education is complex. We must make a distinction between children learning about the environment and children learning to go Green or die.

The Green Emergency Room

Would we allow anyone to take a class of 8 year olds into a hospital emergency room and tell them it was their job to save a bus load of bleeding accident victims? What would they do? How would they feel?

Feeling it is their responsibility to save the earth causes the same kind of emotional trauma. Children are feeling it's up to them to save the earth. Just like the bus load of injured people, the life and death threat is too much responsibility for little people. Children have no frame of reference to draw from. It is a crime to put them in this position.

We can't continue to let the Greens send our children into the Green emergency room. The responsibility for that level of political and environmental responsibility belongs with adults.

Who's In Charge?

Seven-year-old children don't drive cars. They don't know how to steer, let alone, the rules of the road. Eight year old children don't run for office because they don't have the necessary life experience.

Why are seven and eight year old children expected to write opinion letters to politicians on political issues as if they are adults? This is an unreasonable level of student involvement. This is part of the Green indoctrination process. Writing letters to politicians about environmental issues they cannot comprehend and signing petitions about issues they do not fully understand, is wrong. Participating in Green public protests against our country is not what America's children ought to be involved in.

The distinction must be made between an eight year old parroting facts and an eight year old comprehending a complicated issue from a mature standpoint. Evaluating facts and forming intelligent opinions is part of the growing-up process. An adult grasp of a national issue or the political process doesn't occur by age eight.

If you don't have an eight year old handy, ask to see a friend's. Look at this little person and ask yourself; can this child possibly understand these complex political issues? Should this child participate in national politics?

Like the Lion And the Cub

Like the lioness and her newborn cub, the lioness is unlikely to tell the cub, "Welcome to the world baby, now go catch dinner. Show me how it's done." It would not be natural. The natural process is for the lion to nurture, teach and protect the cub until it can manage on its own.

If the Greens truly believed or were concerned with nature's way, they would never use children. They would not put children in adult situations. They would not reverse the natural order of the role of parent and child. It is unnatural, unconscionable and unhealthy.

Children's hearts and minds are too precious to allow them to be used in this manner. The trend of parent-child role reversal is evident in Green theme television shows and motion pictures.

Who shall we thank for all this child activism?

> *"to what do we owe this recent surge of environmental responsibility among today's children?*
>
> *Many people believe that it begins with more activist-oriented ecology and conservation programs taught in schools.*
>
> *Kids are not only being trained to recognize potential environmental hazards in the home and their neighborhoods, but also are being taught to go out and do something about it.*
>
> *With this training comes a confident attitude that they can change old habits and long-standing public policy. "*

1993 Earth Journal
Buzzworm magazine –Editors

The Greens intention and political motivation for using children to advance their political goals is obvious. The Hitler Youth were also trained, in school, to be politically active and with that training, they learned to feel confident about their political opinions to change old habits and public policy.

The Hitler Youth developed very confident attitudes about many things, such as:

- what they were doing was right
- their role in politics was essential
- today, rule Germany and tomorrow the world
- allegiance to Hitler and the cause came first
- Jewish people were their sub-human arch enemy
- learned to feel good about having power over Jews

As the saying goes, 'children learn what they live and live what they learn'. It doesn't matter if *what* they learn is based on false information, if they believe it to be true. Hate and anger can still be learned. It was child abuse then and it is child abuse now.

Materials for activists-oriented learning are offered free to teachers by all the large environmental organizations. Targeting children for political gain ought to be considered a child abuse crime, punishable by law. There is a difference between parents taking their child to a Fourth of July celebration that is pro-American and the Greens sneaking into the schools to brainwash children to be anti-American. Going behind parents backs and sneaking into the schools to reach the children is exactly what Hitler did.

Hitler took advantage of children's innocent thoughts and emotions. The Green assault on America's children is unacceptable and unforgivable.

Many Americans are becoming increasingly concerned about Green assembly programs like the YES tour (Youth for Environmental Sanity) presented in schools. It's reported these programs are sending some children home in tears.

Our Money, Our Children, Is This What We Pay For?

Environmental education is not what it appears to be

> *"Members of Kids Against Pollution in Closter, New Jersey, have flown to many parts of the country to give talks about their work. They explain how they started their group in Mr. Byrnes's fifth grade class and how KAP has expanded to a network of 500 groups around the United States and in five foreign countries. The original KAP members are used to giving speeches by now, and they do it well. But some adults aren't too eager to listen to them - at first."*
> Save The Earth-An Action Handbook for Kids

How many school hours and tax dollars were used to pay for getting this children's activist group going? How many teachers are being paid with taxpayers money to start these groups across the country? Children have no experience to form, fund or run a functioning national organization. Ten-year-old children don't establish international contacts and fly around the country all by themselves. It just doesn't happen.

Following Hitler's example, the Greens are taking children out of the classroom, involving them in fun events and setting up special environmental conferences for them to attend. What child would not find this exciting? Hitler understood motivation. Exciting events without parent's supervision make children want to participate.

The Hitler Youth had to earn their way to Nazi political events. They were recognized by Hitler and held a special place in the event. The Greens have duplicated this approach. Children are earning their way to Green youth events through environmental activism. Children are publicly recognized by influential Green leaders like Vice President Al Gore as earth heroes. Green games, parades, songs, nature treks and personal 'adult-like' recognition are designed to become the preferred social life for a child so their political loyalties can be molded.

Recruiting The Little Green Army

Hitler built his youth groups using a psychological approach. He used teachers and organized special outdoor activities. He used a recognition and reward system. Children were convinced they were doing their duty and they were willing to give their lives to save the sacred soil of the Fatherland. Hitler lured thousands of children away from their families and instilled in them firm political beliefs and an unquestioning commitment to the Nazi cause.

> "I never once during the Hitler years thought of myself as anything but a decent, honorable young German, blessed with a glorious future...none of us who reached high rank in the Hitler Youth will ever totally shake the legacy of the Fuhrer. Despite our monstrous sacrifice and the appalling misuse of our idealism, there will always be the memory of unsurpassed power, the intoxication of fanfares and flags proclaiming our new age...Today Germany belongs to us and tomorrow the world."
>
> A Child of Hitler
> Alfons Heck
> Hitler Youth Leader

U.S. soldiers captured eight year old children, armed and fighting for the Nazi cause. Children were taught to act like adults and to have blind dedication to the Fuhrer.

There is nothing wrong with children learning to recycle. Everything is wrong with using children, like Hitler did, to grow a little army of political robots who did not question his ideas. The Greens would like us to believe small children are leading the charge to be environmental activists.

The reason for this facade is that it keeps the public's attention on the environmental issue and not on the Greens political motivation.

This strategy helps the Greens in several ways, they can:

- hide behind the environmental cause
- have access to America's children
- generate public concern and sympathy

The October 30, 1994 edition of *Parade* magazine featured the story, "Kids Voting". It is a new program to help young Americans learn the value of voting. This kind of program requires close attention. Following the election process is different than an in-school program promoted by an outside group. Pushing eight year old children to study a national issue to form a political opinion has questionable value. It may, as the article indicates, get more parents voting again, but the opportunity to influence the political opinions of young children poses a greater danger. If a child cannot understand a national issue, they should not be expected to form an opinion on one. The promoters of the program indicate it is strictly non-partisan. The Green movement is also said to be non-partisan.

Since the Greens have targeted children, any school activity involving students and political issues ought to be monitored by principals, teachers, parents, concerned citizens and elected officials to ensure the Greens cannot use our schools the same way Hitler used the schools. School programs like this one must be carefully evaluated on their educational value versus the potential danger of children being manipulated.

The Hitler Youth were indoctrinated by their teachers to believe, that their parents were wrong, if their parents did not agree with Hitler's ideas. Hitler preyed on children to create his little army of activists and began programming children as early as eight years old. We need to ask ourselves, is it wise and is it necessary to involve America's children in national politics? Is it in the best interest of young children to be involved in this subversive political movement?

The January 15, 1995 edition of, *Parade* magazine featured the article; "Mr. President, Here's Your Midterm Report Card". The article described a program sponsored by, *Weekly Reader* that surveys children and asks them to set goals for the President. A follow-up survey is taken so the children can grade the President on how he's doing to reach their goals. Students surveyed were fourth, fifth and sixth graders. The top issue of concern was the environment. *Weekly Reader* also prepared the, "Election '96 Program".

Education must encompass multiple subjects, politics included. It is disturbing that America's fourth and fifth graders are being encouraged to feel they are capable of passing political judgment on the President of the United States. Giving our President a report card complete with grades is arrogant and insulting.

Children are part of this nation's future. They may share the political concerns of their parents or teachers but concern is different than passing judgment or giving a political grade to adults, including the President. There is something wrong with this picture. The Hitler Youth were taught they knew better than their parents and other adults. They were a part of Nazi politics. Hitler made sure they knew, he personally depended on them. Children learned to be arrogant and insulting political activists.

Politics and children don't mix. It is dangerous territory. Children learning about our political system is not the same as children learning they have an adult voice in politics. These ideas are coming from environmental groups, radical teachers and Greens. America's children are not thinking of these ideas by themselves.

The tough questions on eco-child abuse are:

- Do students feel they have a choice?
- Was it a do or die message?
- Did the teacher use peer pressure to force action?
- Is it associated with grades?

Children are special little people. Their opinions and feelings are very important. Children need guidance as they learn how our country functions and how to be good citizens. We cannot allow children to become political pawns like the Hitler Youth. Children do not need to participate in national politics. Political interest groups should not be allowed to inflict their political views on children. Green education programs can have serious side affects. We need to protect our children by determining what is a reasonable dose of politics in education and at what grade level. We need to reestablish the ground rules. We need to make a distinction between teaching about a political issue and using carefully selected information to mold students political opinions.

> *"The environmental movement is one of the subversive element's last steps. They've gone after the military and the police and now they're going after our parks and playgrounds."*
> Mrs. Clarence Howard
> Daughters of the American Revolution

The Greens will continue to use children as political pawns unless we change the rules. The first step is to recognize the Greens are coaching our children. If the Communists were planning to brainwash America's young people, school would be the logical place to go. Children are there, all day long, by themselves. Children are so easily influenced by emotions. Being afraid of the dark is nothing compared to day and night end of the earth messages. Green movies, television shows, environmental studies, information provided to schools by environmental groups, Earth Day celebrations at school and other Green propaganda magnify the fear of environmental disaster in the eyes of children. The Greens intend to expand their opportunities to influence children.

> *"We support increased funding for education and a shift in decision making responsibility and funding control for education so that teachers are making most decisions about the curriculum, school goals and policies, specific students, school accreditation, and administrative and staff hiring, with significant involvement from parents, older children, and the local community."*
>
> Green Party Program

Why do teachers need this expanded level of authority? The Greens are pushing this so they can control the schools and ensure America's children get a Green education. Although the statement includes the line, 'significant involvement from parents' that is highly doubtful unless it's a Green parent. Make control possible by making control legal. The Greens have political support for their ideas.

> *"Grant expanded decision-making powers at the school level, empowering principals, teachers and parents with increased flexibility in educating our children."*
>
> *Putting People First*
> Governor Bill Clinton-Senator Al Gore

Perhaps President Clinton was not aware of the politics of the Green movement. Maybe the Greens copied his idea. Whatever the source, the ideas are the same. We can't protect our children from something we cannot see.

The Green objective is to get children politically committed before parents figure out there is a difference between environmental education and Green indoctrination.

Teaching Children Away From Their Parents

During an educational activist's conference, one teacher told the group:

> *"no one knows what I teach my kids when I close the door and you've got to be willing to risk it."*

Statements like these epitomize the attitude of Green educators. This conference was a Green recruiting event. Many teachers who attended did not share that opinion, others did. Teachers who share this Green teaching philosophy are the teachers in question. Radical teachers with radical ideas are influencing America's educational system. Dr. Pierce, a Harvard University Professor shared this idea on the teacher's role in promoting social change in the classroom. This statement was made at an educator's conference:

> *"Every child in America who enters school with an allegiance toward our elected officials, toward our founding fathers, toward our institutions, toward the preservation of this form of government ... all of this proves the children are sick...*
>
> *because the truly well individual is one who has rejected all those things and is what I would call the true international child of the future."*

> *Educating for the New World Order*
> Dr. Chester M. Pierce

Hitler used the educational system to teach children away from their parents and heritage by denouncing traditional values. S.S.D.D. Same stuff different decade.

Why Rewrite American History?

The majority of people first involved in the Nazi cause were teachers. The majority of the people first involved in the Green cause were also teachers. German children learned these ideas from their teachers:

- Don't tell your parents what you are learning
- German history is a lie
- Rewritten version of history is true
- German traditions are out-dated and old fashioned
- Your parents don't understand the Nazi party
- Children understand the Nazi party
- Jewish people are a blight on earth
- Germany's future depends on children

Radical Green teachers are giving America's children the same kind of permission and support to question authority as Hitler gave the Hitler Youth. The purpose of the rewriting history and attacking the idea Columbus was a hero is the Green way to get children to reject tradition. Children are learning:

- American history is a lie
- Not to believe official American stories
- American heroes are really liars and murders
- Children must raise a ruckus, protest
- Children understand Green ideas
- To be ashamed of being an American
- To condemn American way of life
- Parent's values and beliefs are old fashioned
- Children must make up for historical wrongs

Objective: influence children to embrace Green ideology by dissolving America's image in the eyes of our children.

*"When an opponent declares. 'I will not come over to your side,'
I calmly say, "Your child belongs to us already...What are you?
You will pass on. Your descendants, however, now stand in the
new camp. In a short time they will know nothing else but this
new community."*

The Rise and Fall of the Third Reich
Adolf Hitler

What's Wrong With Lies?

People believe them. Lies and revolutions are just like
kidnapping. Kidnappers don't usually notify the victim in
advance they are planning to kidnap them. If they were
completely honest, the person would have the chance to
avoid being kidnapped.

Nation-napping is no different. If revolutionaries were
completely honest about their objectives, it would give people
a chance to avoid that outcome. Beyond being deceitful, lies
cause serious problems. People base their opinions on what
they are told. They expect it to be true. They base their
decisions on it being true. Deliberate lies have countless
ripple affects.

Children believe what their teachers, parents and other adults
tell them. Children do not have an adult frame of reference to
understand what makes a society or government system work
or what makes a society or government system fail.

Children's books about the environment site capitalism and
the American way of life as the primary cause of our
environmental problems. Children are learning to dislike
America.

'Rethinking Columbus'

A radical teacher's publication entitled, *Rethinking Columbus* basically explains how teachers can reinvent America by rewriting American history. They begin by writing off our past as a historical myth.

America needs to worry about the rethinking Columbus effort. The reason children are being taught to rethink Columbus is because the story of Columbus introduces our children to the first history of this nation.

If American history is presented as myth or in a negative light, it will change children's values about America, our culture and our society.

There is a difference between exploring different aspects of history and deliberately focusing on one part of history and blowing it out of proportion for political purposes. Green teachers are using American history to shame children into accepting the Green political position and taking political action.

Active Duty

Green teachers are using the environmental cause and related subjects like the story of Columbus to teach children to rebel against their country.

For example, one fourth grade class wrote to their U.S. Senator asking why he voted to spend money on Columbus and the quincentennial. He sent them a copy of the story of Columbus from the, *World Book Encyclopedia*. The children wrote back to the Senator to inform him they believed:

- the story of Columbus was not true
- money should not be spent to honor Columbus

The Green subliminal messages twisted into this lesson are:

- Columbus didn't discover America, Indians were here first
- Columbus was a bad guy
- Columbus brought capitalism to America
- Capitalism is to blame for all environmental damage

The general idea is, if Columbus had stayed home, the world would be a better place and nothing bad would have ever happened to the Indians or the environment. Teaching this idea is wrong. No one knows what history would be if Columbus had not discovered America.

Changing the Definition of the Color Green

If you want to better understand Green politics, read a few children's books about environmental protection. Although the authors may not fully understand the political goals of the Greens, children's books teach Green political thought and stress political activism. The word Green is no longer defined for children as a color. Green is defined as:

> *"In recent years all over the world, green has come to symbolize sound environmental policies and practices."*
> *Hands Around the World*
> Susan Milord

This definition sets children and adults up to believe all actions or policies recommended by the Greens are automatically right. This message helps create blind followers. Some children's books portray children as violent, intolerant and aggressive activists leading the fight against capitalists polluters. Greens use the paint brush approach to depict all capitalists as one evil group. It's the Hitler technique. Some children's books contain outright lies. America's children are learning to see capitalism as opposite of environmental excellence. The Greens are creating the opinion socialism is better for the environment. Radical Green teachers are teaching Marxism.

> *"We are committed to the transformation of existing public school systems..."*
>
> Green Party Program

The Greens have modified their strategy to bring about a swift cultural transformation. To maximize their effectiveness the Greens are promoting alternatives like charter schools but have returned their focus to using our existing public education system because it allows them to reach more children faster.

Public education has been changed to the point is has become what one educator described as 'social' education. This means the focal point is not giving students a quality basic education. The focal point is teaching social ideas from alternative sexual preferences to alternative religions, alternative history and alternative environmental politics.

Freedom of Choice is Not the Issue

Most teachers are wonderful, caring individuals. There are obviously others who believe they have the right to impose their personal political beliefs on other people's children. That is not what the classroom is for

The intent of this book is not to insult the integrity of the entire teaching profession. The purpose is to alert all Americans; teachers, parents, bus drivers, counselors, principals, everyone, about Green politics in education. We all care about children and we cannot intelligently address the problem without alerting those involved at the source.

Curriculum content is not solely the teacher's choice. Teachers are responsible to the people who pay their salaries, the general public. Teaching personal or political philosophies to the public's children does not fit within the realm of their job description or public expectation.

Rewriting history vs. teaching American history, as written, is the issue we must address. Teachers are not hired to use their position of trust to take advantage of vulnerable young minds. That is not a job choice. People are expected to do what they are hired to do, as defined by the employer. Employers don't hire employees to do whatever they feel like doing.

The American people have not been asked if we want history rewritten. The American people, employ the educators. If the American people have not authorized educators to rewrite history, educators should not be teaching the rewritten version.

This is not a blanket indictment of educators. Educators may not be aware of the political objectives of the Green movement. This is as much a wake-up call for them as it is for all other Americans.

We need to work together to get the Greens out of our schools. It is also important to understand teachers have to work with school boards. Greens are encouraged to become involved in local politics to quietly influence areas like education.

America's children are getting 'Greened' from all sides, including Green cartoons.

'Captain Eco'

"Here's the picture, in a nutshell. Your planet's in serious trouble - from pollution, toxic waste and the loss of forest, farmland and fresh water....

Your parents and Grandparents have made a mess of looking after the earth. They may deny it, but they're little more than thieves. And they're stealing your future from under your noses."

Captain Eco-And the Fate of the Earth 1991
Jonathon Porritt - Ellis Nadler

This lovely thought comes from, *Captain Eco*, a children's book about saving the environment. The story is based around a cartoon character who comes from the soul of the earth to teach children how to save the planet. The story begins with a letter explaining to the reader that children took over in the 1990's and forced political leaders to support the Green Movement.

Other political leaders have blamed children's ancestors for political gain. From, *Hitler's Ideology*, by Richard Koenigsberg.

"Our ancestors contributed to the catastrophic splintering of our inner being"

Mein Kampf
Adolf Hitler

Jonathan Porritt's story promotes Green political ideas throughout and criticizes everything about life on earth. Eating beef, eating fast food, bankers, people who drive big cars and others are singled out as ignorant, selfish sub-humans. Humans are depicted as lazy, selfish, boneheads. The politics of emotion are used to make children feel guilty, fearful, angry enough to resort to violence and finally, committed to being Green political activists.

The story suggests many things to young readers; eat less meat, buy organic vegetables, fight for animal rights, use human waste for fertilizer and join environmental groups. The authors draw many conclusions for children, such as:

- parents don't know how to save the earth
- children are the only ones who can save the earth
- children must teach their parents what to do

'Captain Planet'

The *Captain Planet* cartoon series is based on a similar theme. Gaia is the spirit of the earth. Five children and a green-haired super hero fight to save the planet from the bad guys like, *Hoggish Greedly* and *Looten Plunder*. The Greens always win, defeating evil capitalists. They use clever names and spread the anti-capitalist Green message.

The cartoon is a slick combination of Green messages: it hints at eco-violence. Gaia is the earth's spirit. Children learn to see the earth as a living being. It is like the movie, *Pocahontas*, that promotes Green spirituality.

If your children watch, *Captain Planet*, start listening. What messages are your children receiving about the environment, our culture and Green politics?

The book, *Captain Eco*, was written by Jonathon Porritt. Porritt is also the author of, *Seeing Green* and *Save The Earth. Save the Earth*, was published by Turner Publishing, Inc, a subsidiary of Turner Broadcasting System, Inc. Turner Broadcasting also created, *Captain Planet and the Planeteers*.

Repetition Is The First Law Of Learning

Children's books about the environment encourage children to join environmental groups. Environmental groups encourage children to become members because it gives them multiple opportunities to encourage children to go Green. Memberships in Green organizations serve the following purposes:

- get Green ideas in the hands of children
- keep constant flow of Green ideas in front of children
- chance to instruct children on what to think and do
- memberships gives the Greens more money
- membership gives the Greens more political power

Remember, during a political show and tell, it's a numbers game. The more members the Greens can hold up, the more politicians will pay attention and vote green. Politicians ought to inquire if all Green group members are voting age?

At School, Are Halloween And Earth Day The Same?

Halloween is an event:

- one day
- children dress up in costumes
- community involvement, trick or treat

Earth Day is a celebration designed to promote cultural and social change. Earth Day is the vehicle to foster public acceptance for Green ideas.

Earth Day is a ceremony filled with Green ideology. Earth Day has been expanded to Earth week and Earth month.

The Earth Day Celebration:

What goes on:	What it means:
• is a day, week, month	• environmental programming
• all species parades	• reduce child to species
• multi-culturalism	• abandon melting-pot
• fly the earth flag	• replace American flag
• sing earth anthem	• replace America's anthem
• honor earth heroes	• replace American heroes
• public celebration	• recruit new Greens
• earth is a being	• Earth worship, Green spirituality
• Green fun-time	• get child in Green social circle
• Earth Pledge	• replace our Pledge of Allegiance

Why is it so important America's children accept the Green concepts of, 'All Species and One People'? Communists treat people like animals. The political motive behind 'All Species' is to raise children to see themselves as no more deserving than other species or animals. Children raised with this mentality will not expect to be treated any differently than animals.

The Earth Pledge of Allegiance:

> *"I pledge allegiance to the Earth, and to the flora, fauna and human life that it supports, one planet, indivisible, with safe air, water, and soil, economic justice, equal rights and peace for all."*

The Greens political purpose for 'One People, One Planet' is to condition our children to see themselves as global citizens instead of American citizens. Children raised with this mentality will lose their independent streak. Independence is the heart of America.

Creating group-thinking followers or drones is the objective. It would be easier for drones to obey Communists than it would be to try and force independent Americans to submit.

Earth Day is also the vehicle the Greens are using to introduce new symbols, values and traditions for children to identify with. The Greens need children to sever connections with our past and culture so they will accept a new one without question.

To accomplish this the Greens rely on Hitler tactics again. The Greens have manufactured Hitler's, *historic dishonor* by rewriting our history. Our children are learning America is something to be ashamed of. The Hitler Youth learned to be ashamed of Germany's past and proud to participate in the new order of the Nazis. Our children are learning to accept:

- new world order
- new Green symbols
- new Green heroes
- new Green pledge of allegiance
- new Green belief system
- new Green culture

There is a difference between teaching children values most Americans can agree with and teaching children new values most Americans don't know about.

The Earth Flag company helps clarify the purpose of the Earth Flag by advertising a message that suggests we should not burn the American flag, just replace it with the Earth Flag. Earth Flags come with a copy of the earth pledge of allegiance. Some schools fly the Earth flag all year, giving it the same status as the United States flag. The message is, both flags are equal, but they are not.

Everyday people want peace. Everyday people want a cleaner earth. If we do not fly a peace flag all year, why should we fly the Earth flag all year? The Earth flag is not our nation's symbol. It is not equal to the flag of the United States of America. Leaving the Earth Flag up all year is intended to give it equal status in the eyes of our children. It will be easier for the Greens to replace our flag if the Green flag is already accepted

If environmental protection was the goal, there would be no need to actively promote this gray area regarding the symbol of our nation.

Greening School Sports Programs

School sports programs are another target for the Greens. Competition needs to go. The Greens want our schools to shift from a focus on competitive team sports to programs that emphasize cooperative play.

The Greens believe competition divides people into winners and losers and that is not acceptable. The Green goal here is:

- nullify pride of achievement for those who excel in sports
- eliminate competitiveness, accept everyone is the same
- comfort children who have less or no athletic ability

Personal development and lessons learned from participation in competitive sports are invaluable. Physical skills, physical fitness, self-discipline and team work are lessons used repeatedly throughout the course of a lifetime. Why eliminate such a wonderful opportunity for those who are gifted athletes and others who just love to play? There is a difference between a personal choice not to participate in organized sports and not having the opportunity to compete in sports.

Is this the result of the Communists applying rule number one of the, *Communist Rules for Revolution?*

> *"Corrupt the young; get them away from religion. Get them interested in sex. Make them superficial;* **destroy their ruggedness."**

Is this attack on sports and competition designed to destroy our children's ruggedness? Competition is healthy. This is another effort to force us to be the same, eliminate individualism and turn us into Green drones with no ambition.

Would professional sports be impacted by the Greens emphasis on cooperative play vs. sports competition? Professional athletes are trained from childhood in their respective sport(s). Without this training-ground (for replacement talent), the quality and entertainment value of professional sports would diminish and eventually die-out. The multi-million dollar sports industry would not be exempt from the Greens goal to control the people and the economy of this nation.

Wild Animal Rights

The make-believe Indian white wolf myth and real life wild wolves are not the same. Children learning they can depend on wolves or safely swim with sharks is unhealthy. America's children are being led to believe wolves and sharks are their friends. Sell that to someone who has been attacked by a wolf or had a loved one attacked or killed by a man-eating shark.

As children, most of us were taught to stay away from things that could hurt us. We did not learn wolves were friendly creatures or that insects were just like us, bugs with feelings. The Green idea we are all the same creatures, who respond to each other in the same way, is insanity. If lions had human feelings, they would not attack and mutilate people. They would not attack defenseless children in campgrounds.

Animals do what animals do. Snakes and bees bite, even if we'd like them not to. The Greens are preying on children's emotions so children will write letters that parrot Green political messages on endangered species, animal rights and wolf reintroduction. Children are not toys. It is a crime, pure and simple, to diminish their natural sense of fear of wild animals. Self-preservation is a natural instinct. Taking this away from children is unnatural and is another Green contradiction to natural law.

Little Red Riding Hood

> "*At last some scientists began to wonder if wolves really were dangerous. They went deep into the forest to study how the wolves live. One scientist was walking in the forest when he met two wolves by accident. One wolf ran away. The other wolf walked right up to him. The scientist was scared. But the wolf just licked his face and trotted away! The scientists learned that healthy wolves do not attack people.*"
>
>

Wild Wild Wolves
Joyce Milton

Greens indicate healthy wolves are not a threat to people, but what if a person meets an unhealthy wolf? Can a child tell the difference? The message the child gets from this story is, do not fear, wild wolves will either run away or lick your face.

This is unconscionable disregard for a child's safety. Wild wolves are not the same as the family pet. There are multiple children's movies out which depict wolves as the mystic protectors of children. Children need to understand this is fantasy, not a fact.

Some may argue, this is a child's fiction story. What harm can one story do? It's not this one story that will do irreparable harm. It is the sum total of Green programming that creates the problem. Children receive Green messages about creatures and the environment from school, movies, cartoons, coloring books, television specials, environmental clubs and stories like this one. It would be easy for a child to believe the message is real, not fiction, and that is what is dangerous. It is not safe for children to think they can talk to wolves.

Wolves are now being reintroduced into populated areas. What happens if a child gets lost in one of those areas and disturbs a pack of wild wolves? What will the child do? What will the wolves do? The wolves may run away but what if they didn't. What if one was hurt or rabid? That innocent child would be in big trouble and may, because of Green programming, die a painful death. At least, if the child understood wild wolves were not the family pet, the child might not make its presence known and have a chance to climb a tree or sneak away. The child has no chance if it runs right up to the wolves. That action would invite attack.

Recently, a rabid mountain lion took on four adults and their dog. They managed to kill it with a kitchen knife and all survived the attack. They had a critical advantage. They were smart enough to be afraid of a mountain lion.

A woman was brutally attacked and killed by a mountain lion near Sacramento, California. She was jogging and the mountain lion was hungry. Sightings of mountain lions in populated areas, such as Sacramento, have increased since the ban on mountain lion hunting was passed by voters. Mountain lions are also showing up in southern California neighborhoods. A teacher was attacked and killed by a mountain lion while hiking.

Wild animals are unpredictable. No one can be 100% sure how a wild animal will respond to people. The animal's response depends on its circumstances at that particular moment.

The instant Green response to the mountain lions coming into cities is that too many people have invaded the mountain lion's habitat, forcing them to relocate. This sounds logical on the surface, but think about it. The lions are being forced out of their habitat because there are too many people living there. To get away from people, the lions decide to relocate to a metro area?

Some people believe the reason the lions are showing up in populated areas is easy food. Because of the hunting ban, the mountain lion population has grown and that would lower the populations of those animals they prey on. Supply and demand may be forcing the lions to look for other prey, like dogs, cats and people.

Oregon passed a law that bans hunting mountain lions and bears with dogs. According to seasoned hunters, it's almost impossible to find the illusive animals any other way. Since the ban, several incidents involving mountain lions have occurred in the state.

Early August brought two more sightings of lions in populated city areas. One involved a mountain lion that attacked and killed a cat in a back yard one evening. The other, involved a male mountain lion that was seen stalking a group of children as they played in a backyard pool. The lion was on the other side of a chain link fence until the family dog chased it away. What if the family had no dog? If mountain lions will change their illusive behavior and start looking for food in the city limits, so will wolves.

Too much competition in their natural habitat may be causing the lack of natural prey available to the lions. If some lions were relocated to less populated wilderness areas or their numbers thinned, nature would have time to recuperate and balance out.

It seems logical, if we can put a man on the moon, we can find reasonable and effective solutions to correct environmental problems, including these kinds of sensitive habitat issues. Child safety must be the first priority. The best way to combat Green propaganda is to make sure children understand that wolves and other wild creatures are not tame, safe playmates.

Wisdom of the 60's, Shall We Try Some More?

Do we have the maturity to admit that as individuals and as a society we've made a few errors in judgment? The counter culture of the 60's has produced some very harmful results. Our children are hurting. The early drug culture has led to our current drug crisis. Teen sex and teen pregnancies have sky rocketed. Why?

This quote is repeated because "corrupting the young" is also an objective of rule number one in the *Communist Rules for Revolution.*

> *"Corrupt the young; get them away from religion. Get them interested in sex. Make them superficial; destroy their ruggedness."*

We have been set-up to abandon traditional American values.

4

Facts or Fabrication?

The American people are not getting the straight facts on serious political issues. What we are getting is a lot of Green communist propaganda.

> *"The press is our chief ideological weapon."*
> Nikita Krushchev
> *Washington Post – 1957*

What is preventing us from getting good information? The Greens have systematically 'Greened' the media by convincing journalists it is their duty to go beyond reporting the news and use their influential position to:

- advocate the Green political position
- manage facts to control what Americans hear
- 'Green' public opinion
- help save the planet

The Greens have motivated journalists to accept this as their duty based on the idea time is running out and only they can help the ignorant masses understand what needs to be done. If journalists do not help sway public opinion, part of the blame for catastrophic environmental ruin will rest on their shoulders.

This is not a new tactic. Lenin and Hitler used it. Nazi propaganda and doctrine were spread by public information. Hitler controlled the airwaves. People heard what Hitler wanted them to hear.

The Greens operate on the end justifies the means. Slanted stories or out-and-out lies are acceptable. To intelligently move forward, we need to make a distinction between fact and fabrication. This distinction begins with our public information sources and extends to all the environmental information we have received to date. We need to understand the 'Greening' of our public information sources is a three-stage process. First, the Greens have successfully pushed the press to go beyond reporting facts to advocating the Green position. The second step was to get the media to go beyond advocacy and begin concocting news stories to increase public support for Green politics. The third step is Green control of mass communications. Then we will hear only what the Greens want us to hear. We are now in stage two and rapidly approaching stage three.

> "*The press should be not only a collective propagandist and a collective agitator, but also a collective organizer of the masses.*"
> Lenin
> *New York Times 1955*

This statement by Lenin explains why the Greens targeted the media and pushed them to go beyond reporting the facts on environmental issues and pressured them to help shape public opinion. Greens use fear and the emotional pull of a pending environmental crisis to manipulate the media to participate in what amounts to conning the American people.

According to James Tyson, author of the 1981 book *Target America*, there are thousands of communist propaganda agents working in the United States. Tyson explains the Soviets allocate over $240 million per year to fund these agents worldwide. Tyson backs up this estimate with information provided by an undercover agent for the FBI who was a member of the U.S. Communist Party. The communist agents operating in America are known as 'Pro-

Cells'. Pro-Cells are professionals such as journalists, advertisers, lawyers, doctors and other influential people.

On October 21, 1994, the *Associated Press* reported that Aldrich Ames, the CIA agent arrested as a spy, was paid more than $2.5 million by the Soviets. Mrs. Ames claimed she participated under duress. According to this AP story, after she was told where the money was coming from, she and Aldrich went to New York and spent $6,000 KGB dollars over the weekend.

Why are we spending millions of dollars to rescue the Soviet Union when it appears they have plenty of money to spend financing subversive communist efforts in the United States? Are we financing our own demise?

Creative Journalism

Creative journalism was evident in a 1993 *NBC* report on the condition of the Clearwater National Forest in Idaho. The story addressed accusations that heavy logging posed a threat to fish populations. *NBC* news showed photos of apparently dead fish lying in water and a scan of a large clear-cut mountain area. This was apparently to confirm to viewers that logging was killing fish. The clear-cut served as the background image for Anchorman Tom Brokaw.

Senator Larry Craig, (R-ID) publicly challenged *NBC* on the truth to the story and that resulted in an apology to viewers Brokaw explained that the fish *NBC* featured were not actually dead; they were only briefly stunned for testing. According to one report, *NBC* never responded to Senator Craig's charge that the clear-cut shown was also false information. Senator Craig indicated the clear-cut was really a burn area in a forest in Washington state and not located in Idaho's Clearwater Forest.

Tom Brokaw may have taken the heat for the creative journalism of an *NBC* staff writer. Mr. Brokaw may not personally research the stories he reads. Maybe he just reads a script. There is a difference between reading and writing the news. This story was contrived. False images were used to deceive the people and generate support for the Greens.

Tom Brokaw and other journalists could help put an end to 'creative journalism' by publicly advocating a renewed commitment to accuracy among his peers. *NBC* is not alone in creating biased news reports.

News programs ought to report the facts. Citizens ought to be allowed to form their own opinions. Manipulating the facts is a violation of the public trust. It ought to embarrass those who consider themselves professional journalists.

Americans who did not hear *NBC's* apologies may still believe the fish were dead because of timber harvest. We need to make a distinction between a news report and a news story.

- a news report is based on real facts
- a news story is based on make-believe

We cannot form intelligent opinions if what we are told is based on fabrication. In the past, there was a significant difference between the sleaze rags and the evening news. Now the tactics and integrity levels appear to be the same. Where do professional journalists draw the line? What do they want to be known for, truth or trash?

Journalists are expected to adhere to the same level of honesty they expect and need from their fellow Americans. Journalists must be able to trust what their surgeon or auto mechanic tell them. Their health and well-being depend on the integrity of other professionals.

If journalists depend on the words of others, then others ought to be able to depend on their words. We rely on journalists as our news source and our emergency broadcast system. We have every right to expect to be well informed, not misinformed.

Apologies after the fact don't fix the problem. Striking it from the record is useless if the jury already heard the remark. The media ought to better police themselves and penalize those who do not practice responsible public broadcasting. If a network or its representative is accused and found guilty of consistently and intentionally lying to the American people, it ought to result in regulations or penalties such as:

- repeat apology and correction several times
- warn, suspend or fire the person responsible
- fine the network a substantial amount
- warn viewers, material presented may not be factual

There is a difference between errors and lies. This could be a major step toward restoring the trust of the American people for the news and for this profession.

Green leaders also have an obligation to be honest with the people of this nation. It is not acceptable to further political goals by lying. The American people deserve more respect. Intentional lies and creative journalism add up to fraud. Public information, like news reports, impact people's lives and influence political opinions.

False information about the environment can lead to:

- a vote for a Green candidate
- a lower opinion of our fellow Americans
- generating financial support for a Green organization
- accepting or justifying Eco-Terrorism

Big Con Jobs Begin With Little Con Jobs

The speech by Chief Seattle, made famous by the Green movement, is not based on what the Chief said. The Chief's speech is a victim of creative journalism. The speech was improved by a film writer who thought the changes would create a stronger message for an environmental film.

The improved version of Chief Seattle's speech is repeated in environmental publications, children's books and many Earth Day events. The Greens know it is not true but continue to use it because it has more political value. Chief Seattle's speech is on the cover of a Green party brochure. Altering facts or not revealing all facts is how the Greens operate.

Green Rules of the Game, Manipulate the System

> *"...but there was a political decision that was made by those who introduced the Ancient Forest Protection Act, that by introducing a national bill at this time, you may have more enemies than friends...*
>
> *.. A lot of our strategy is to nationalize this issue, and if every Senator in the country could see that their state would be affected directly, they might not be willing to protect what we are saying is a very special and different, unique, ecosystem in the Pacific Northwest...*
>
> *...all native forests do deserve protection, they would all be protected, as well as native grasslands and native woodlands and native coastlines and so on under the endangered ecosystems act."*

Marc Liverman, Attorney
Conservation Director Audubon Society – Portland
LAW Conference 1991

This statement shows those involved have no problem intentionally deceiving our Senators, other political representatives or the American people. The language used by the Audubon attorney, '*protect what we are saying is special*' is interesting. The choice of words is significant. The language suggests other areas have already been targeted and the political plan is to over-emphasize the value of this particular ecosystem to establish a legal precedent to control ecosystems across the nation. Greens get political support by not sharing all the facts.

> "*Manipulation is persuading people to make up their minds while withholding some of the facts from them.*"
> Harold Evans
> British Journalist, 1971

Hitler lied whenever it suited him. The most important thing to remember is, this is the mentality of the Greens. This is not to suggest that every person involved with the National Audubon Society is a liar or a Green Communist. It is to confirm manipulating the truth in this manner fits 'the end justifies the means' mentality of the Greens.

This means the Greens:

- violate the public trust
- use support for environmental cause for political gain
- twist the issues to justify Green recommendations
- manipulate the public, politicians and political system
- work behind the scenes to achieve power and control

The Audubon Society was very involved in the Spotted Owl issue. From the beginning, one of the key reasons given to stop all logging was that Spotted Owls could only live and survive in old growth timber. The 1982 edition of the *Audubon Society Encyclopedia of North American Birds,* indicates something different. It indicates the spotted owl is flexible. It can live in tree cavities, on the floor of caves, on the ground near large rocks and even takes over nests other birds have abandoned. We were 'set up' to believe otherwise.

> *"... with the spotted owl, there was two years invested in doing nothing but press, public relations and media work before any litigation was filed, that's critically important.* The other important thing is that you never emphasize your legal theories to the press; you emphasize what you're saving. *The legal theory never appears as attractive to the public than the fact that you're saving big, old trees.*
>
> Andy Stahl
> Sierra Club Legal Defense Club
> Seattle Office: Resource Analyst
> Western Public Interest Law Conference-1988
> (Bold Emphasis Added)

The end justifies the means. The Green Movement continues to prey on emotions to achieve immediate political reactions and increase the size of their bank accounts as they continue to advance their political agenda.

> *"The Northern Spotted Owl is the wildlife species of choice to act as a surrogate for old-growth protection and I've often thought that thank goodness the spotted owl evolved in the Northwest, for if it hadn't, we'd have to genetically engineer it. It's the perfect species to use as a surrogate."*
>
> Andy Stahl
> Sierra Club Legal Defense Club
> Seattle Office: Resource Analyst
> Western Public Interest Law Conference-1988

The purpose for nationalizing Spotted Owl and timber harvest issues was to put control of the industry in the hands of the federal government. Slick public relations campaigns and media coverage across the nation created the impression the federal government had to step in or the owl would go extinct and timber harvest would cause severe environmental damage. Instead of a state issue to be settled by the state, it became a national issue that had to be settled by the federal government. That was the goal, to set the precedent for the federal government to intervene and control the situation.

We need to keep in mind; our government is not the problem. The Greens are using our system to bring down our system and they created this situation. Communist leader Gus Hall indicated in 1972 that one of their political goals was to nationalize American industries and demand those industries be controlled by federal laws (Public control).

Americans had no reason to doubt the facts presented on the Spotted Owl or any other environmental issue. If no one questions the Greens, they can simply move on to their next target and do the same thing. That is how the Greens operate. The Spotted Owl was never the issue. Taking control of one state economy at a time is the objective. The following statement made by Gus Hall in 1972 clearly defines this goal.

> *"Socialism corrects the basic flaw of capitalism. It sets human society on a new path. **The means of production, factories, mines and mills become the property of the people. They operate and produce only to fulfill human needs. They are not motivated by profits. This is the foundation for a new set of priorities, for new values...What is involved is a conflict of values."***
>
> *Ecology - 1972*
> Gus Hall
> (Bold Emphasis Added)

Off the Internet

Government control of production and distribution is how Communism functions. Green Communists are using the environmental cause to hide their efforts to gain control of industries and individuals across America.

"Tired of the same old system: Join the Communist Party, USA
Susan Wheeler wrote the following, excerpted from People's Weekly
World: Fledgling efforts to approach logging in the Northwest in a new
way that respects the requirements of whole ecosystems, already tentative
and frail, are in imminent danger of falling victim to timber corporations'
appetite for raw material to turn into profit.

Both houses of Congress have passed a measure that will open national
forest up to new assaults and essentially nullify the Clinton
administration's feeble Northwest forest plan and efforts to save salmon.
'Salvage' operations are touted as measures to remove untidy 'dead or
dying' timber, thus improving the health of forests, although
environmentalists have long pointed out that dead timber plays a crucial
role in the life cycle of forest ecosystems.

In particular, seven of the sales are within Oregon's Ten Mile Creek
watershed and neighboring watersheds. Ten Mile Creek is the site of a
unique research experiment designed to restore wild salmon runs by
recreating the conditions that foster successful spawning"

This article was featured in the "From the Internet" section of
the July/August, 1995 edition of *Ecologic* magazine. It is easy
to see from reading this statement that Wheeler has a more
than passing interest and working knowledge of timber
harvest and environmental issues. Wheeler promotes the
Green idea of managing entire ecosystems which includes not
removing any timber, dead or alive, from the forest. This
suggests the Communist Party is well informed and very
involved in this issue. Obviously the Communists have been
working many years to achieve their 1972 goal to gain control
of mill production.

The federal government is now directly involved in
environmental decisions regarding timber harvest. The
Communists have been successful.

Green Communists are using the environmental cause to
justify their calls for Americans to change our 'values' and to
accept their 'values'. Green values amount to Socialism and
"compulsory Green living". The Greens need to convince

Americans to surrender control of production and distribution to the federal government. Years of planning and propaganda were used to prepare the public to support the Greens taking legal control of the timber industry.

Government control of production and distribution is Communism. If we continue to accept Green control of business and industry in America, the Greens will continue to take control, one business at a time. Greens are also attacking individual rights. This is why environmental laws are the center of a growing debate across America. Environmental protection is not the issue. The issue is Green control of industries and individuals.

Wheeler's article uses the environmental cause to suggest:

- Capitalism is bad for the environment
- Ecosystem management is good for the environment
- Green values and communist values are the same
- Becoming a Communist will save the environment

If Americans allow the Greens to continue to twist and abuse environmental issues, the Greens will continue to transform our society step by step. If we allow the Greens to justify more and more government and social control over the rights and lives of the American people, from private property rights to free enterprise issues, they will successfully manipulate Americans into volunteering for Communism.

Since the Spotted Owl issue made the news, more owls have been found. The Greens avoid that topic. The Greens will advance Communism by keeping the public focus on fear of loss not facts. The Greens are not concerned with facts, only with accomplishing their political goals. We have been set-up to accept what the Greens say is true. We have been lulled to sleep. When an individual person or business is accused of an environmental crime, Americans need to say, prove it!

The Greens have spent hours and thousands of American's hard earned dollars convincing us to trust they are acting in our best interest. We need to realize we are seeing the goals of the Communist Party carried out. We need to stop trusting the Greens and start looking at environmental issues from a cautious, not emotional, political standpoint.

Create-A-Crisis

The ideas the Greens are promoting are based on a pre-set political agenda. Many of the environmental issues we are dealing with were outlined as political objectives years ago.

The *World Conservation Strategy* was put together in 1980 and it outlines how the Greens believe the world ought to be run. According to the conservation time line, the World Bank called for action on forest in 1989. That fits the time frame for the Spotted Owl crisis and setting the public up two years in advance of the alleged crisis.

Whittaker Chambers is a former Soviet agent who defected to the United States in the late 1940's. Chambers was a Senior Editor of *Time* magazine. During that period, he states in his book *Witness* that Henry Dexter White, Secretary of the Treasury helped create the World Bank and later ran the organization. Chambers states that he knew that Henry Dexter White was a Soviet agent. It is not hard to believe this is true considering career CIA officer Aldrich Ames was arrested and convicted as a Soviet Spy in 1994.

Greens want Congress to endorse the *World Conservation Strategy* and use it as a guide for environmental policies in the United States. The World Conservation Strategy includes this objective:

"set out a plan of action to bring about the required political decisions and allocations of financial and other resources."

In other words, the end justifies the means. Do whatever it takes. Set us up and manufacture support for the 'required political decisions'. The Pacific Northwest, according to the World Conservation Strategy, is a world heritage site and requires "careful allocation and management of timber concessions". To set us up to support the 'required political decisions', to gain control of the timber industry and the economy of the region, what happened?

- World Bank called for action on forest
- Manufactured a crisis to make it a national issue
- Spotted Owl became a federal issue
- Federal government involved in state economy
- Government involved in production and distribution

Government control of production and distribution is how business under Communism functions. The timber industry explained the Spotted Owl was a surrogate to conceal the political objective to control the industry and stop logging. Green attorneys openly admit the owl was used to help make logging illegal.

> *"The special role of disinformation is enhanced by the aggressive and ambitious character of communist external policy. This aims at **promoting and establishing communist regimes in noncommunist countries throughout the world by giving support to the extreme left-wing opposition, by gaining temporary political allies, by exploiting and deepening whatever internal crises may occur, and even by creating artificial crises.**"*
>
> *New Lies for Old*
> Anatoliy Golitsyn
> (Bold Emphasis Added)

Pick A Number, Any Number!

Speaking of disinformation, how many species are really going extinct? According to Green groups there is no exact number; one source sets the number at over 165,000 a year, another 500,000 by the year 2000. Another researcher indicates that the United States has recorded only 7 species, perhaps 13 total that might have gone extinct since 1973.

There appears to be a *slight* discrepancy. Are we losing 13 species in 21 years or 165,000 species per year? What estimate is true?

Where is the scientific data and list of species to support these claims? Science is based on actual data. If there are that many species dying, we ought to have a list of what they are, where they are and a record of how many there used to be. Without scientific documentation, it is impossible to form an intelligent opinion.

Where do the Greens get these numbers? The Green approach to science appears to be: pick a number, any number, and the bigger the number the better.

What Are the Facts?

There is no question we have some major environmental messes to clean up. These extinction numbers are just too far apart to be above board. Something is wrong. Losing 7 species over a 21-year period vs. losing 165,000 species per year makes a big difference in how we respond to the situation.

We either have a catastrophic problem or a manageable set of circumstances we can correct by making different and better choices. Wild claims don't cut it. Documentaries by Green groups don't reflect the overall picture. What America needs and deserves, is an in-depth look at the issues in question.

Before we can help determine what direction this country takes, we need accurate information. Our future depends on it. What television network is willing to help Americans uncover the truth? An on-going public debate would give us time to understand the environmental issues.

It is important to repeat, those involved in environmental careers, like any group of professionals, must be accountable for what they advocate. They must be able to back up what they are 'saying' with documented facts.

Huge discrepancies in claims, lack of unbiased public information and the subversive approach of the Greens continue to support the theory that environmental issues are being exaggerated to further the Greens political aims.

Americans are willing to do our share to correct environmental problems. We need accurate information to effectively address the tasks we face.

Incompetence or Dishonesty?

Environmental organizations have created the impression they are the most reliable sources for environmental information. Most Americans don't question their facts.

The 1995 book, *The True State Of The Planet*, edited by Ronald Bailey, challenges current reports concerning the environment. The book is the combined effort of some of America's leading environmental researchers. The authors present what they believe is an accurate interpretation of environmental science and make distinctions between environmental activism and environmental science. The book offers up to date information and disputes many of the claims made by the Green Movement. It is worth reading.

Americans who care about the environment recognize the reason environmental groups are presenting false information to the public. Roberta Parry of the U.S. Environmental Protection Agency wrote this letter to the Sierra Club. It appeared in the April 1995 edition of the magazine.

> *"In 'Conservation a la Carte',* **Paul Rauber incorrectly states that pesticide runoff into streams and rivers is the primary cause of water pollution in the United States** *....While pesticides have been detected in some drinking water supplies, nitrate, a nitrogen compound is by far the chemical contaminant most responsible for violations of drinking-water standards.* **Pesticides** *(which affect 27 percent of impaired stream miles)* **often seem to be used by environmental groups to gain the attention and dollars of the public,** *while the major causes of water pollution are ignored."*
>
> Roberta Parry
> Agriculture Policy Branch
> Office of Policy, Planning and Evaluation
> U.S. Environmental Protection Agency

This is not a mere violation of the public trust. It is blatant disregard for the truth. The article "Conservation a la Carte" was written by *Sierra* Senior Editor, Paul Rauber. Mr. Rauber may not do his own research, but when it's published, *Sierra* magazine and their staff are responsible for what is written.

With the resources available to the Sierra Club, the vast network of environmental facts and information that includes the EPA, there is no excuse to present inaccurate and misleading information.

We can only draw one of two conclusions. This error is due to incompetence or dishonesty. If environmental sources are incompetent, we can't rely on them. If environmental sources are dishonest we can't rely on them. How much more inaccurate information have we received on critical environmental issues? Correct information is essential if we are serious about taking care of the environment.

The environment is like a patient who needs help getting well. If we were the patient, we would want a diagnosis and treatment plan based on fact, not fabrication. False information could put our life at risk. Like an illness, the diagnosis and treatment plan for a healthy environment requires competent, honest information or we are putting the environment at risk.

What can we learn from this?

- Green groups are not always a reliable source for environmental information.

- Sensationalizing false information is acceptable if it increases membership and financial contributions.

- It is more important to increase public support for the Green political agenda than it is to tell the truth.

- Environmental protection is not the goal. If it were, the Greens would try to stop water pollution using the money to get the real contaminant out of the water.

Misrepresentation is counter-productive. If we accept this end justifies the means mentality, the Greens will continue to put political goals first. Do we want to stop pollution or fund a revolution? Like a wolf in sheep's clothing, many Americans don't see these groups as the political animals they are.

As the saying goes, necessity is the mother of invention. How much of what we are hearing is true? What has been manufactured to serve the Greens political agenda? Before setting public policies that will turn our society upside down and put an end to individual freedom in this country, we ought to get the facts. Gradual Green control will occur if Americans continue to trust what the Greens are 'saying' needs to be done. It's just a matter of time.

We have environmental problems and we have to decide how to handle them. We cannot allow the Greens *Chicken Little* messages to put us in a crisis level mentality. The Greens plan to create an unreasonable sense of urgency so Americans won't have time to consider the issues, facts or alternatives.

Panic Politics

America needs good laws, not more laws. There are too many bills presented for consideration each session. Over 260 pieces of Green legislation alone were introduced in the 101 and 102 Congresses. That is too many bills in one subject area. How can they receive adequate review?

This legislation overload is partly to blame for the problems we are experiencing within our government system. Third parties won't fix this. The two party system works, but it's gotten off track and needs our assistance to correct the problems.

Our political officials are overworked. They meet with constituents, serve on committees, vote on bills, make numerous personal appearances and campaign if they run for office again. What happens with that kind of schedule? The daily workload is divided among the staff. House and Senate staff review bills, listen to lobbyists and then report to the Congressman or Senator.

Solution

If we put a limit on the number of bills introduced each session we could slow down the process and regain control. The avalanche of legislation gets laws passed before they are adequately scrutinized. The crime bill, for instance, was about 2000 pages long. Just days before the vote, some political leaders had not even received a complete copy of the bill.

There was pressure to get it passed before the end of the session. The big push came from the Clinton administration. Lobbying groups started the routine. Trading favors and trading votes got it passed.

Where is the fire? Why do we need to be in such a hurry to pass precedent setting legislation? If politicians had more time to personally study proposed legislation and then discuss the ramifications with the people they represent, this kind of political insanity could be changed and avoided. Politicians ought to have time to focus on correcting and improving our nation, instead of stumbling through piles of proposed legislation.

Our political leaders ought to have plenty of time to study the issues and proposed legislation *before* voting. Then they could determine whether or not the law compliments our constitution, preserves our freedom, protects our culture and ensures our national security. Bills that don't meet these basic standards ought to be referred to the people or thrown out.

'We the people' share the responsibility for creating some of these problems. Running for political office has become a popularity contest rather than a race based on who will do the best job for the country and the people.

Many politicians end up being celebrities rather than concentrating on being effective legislators. The public expects politicians to make hundreds of public appearances while in office. Qualified people leave office due to the constant demand on their personal life.

After a day on the job, politicians are expected to give up their evenings and weekends to meet the demand for public appearances. Politicians, like the rest of us, ought to have time to re-group and relax. A number of public appearances are part of the job, but if legislators had time to ponder proposed legislation and go home at days end, they would probably do a better job.

Legislating Population Control

Population control and natural dying are also on the Green agenda. Natural dying and assisted suicide are meant to accomplish the same thing; lower the population. Like Hitler, the Greens are redefining life and death issues. The Greens are making death a political issue to diminish the value of life, from abortion to assisted suicide. The choice to use or not to use technology to save a life is a personal decision. Greens suggest using technology to save a life ought to include consideration of the value of the life in question.

Assisted suicide is considered an environmental issue because if the people who have been diagnosed as terminally ill or permanently disabled were to choose to die, it would reduce our population. In premise, the idea of choice is not completely unreasonable. Caution must to be exercised to ensure, if someone chooses to check-out, it is their decision, not legalized murder.

Hitler took control of life and death issues based on his values of the quality of the life to be saved. He began by ordering retarded children and the mentally ill put to death because they were considered 'useless eaters'. The same mentality was applied when the Jews entered the death camps. The Nazis divided them according to their labor value. The Jews were either sent to the left or the right. This was an instant sentence to live or to die based on someone else's judgment of a person's value to society.

German citizens allowed themselves to become immune to the pain of their neighbors. Hitler created a death culture using fear, terrorism and manufactured hate. He legalized murder.

The Greens are affecting our culture. They are making their ideas legal. We need to pay close attention to state ballot initiatives. The Greens, in 1991, specifically identified the strategy to use the ballot initiative process to:

- publicize their alternative ideas
- challenge the two party system
- advance Green politics

The Greens are using ballot initiatives to get pieces of their political agenda legalized. Voters don't know the initiatives are part of the overall Green agenda. This is another Green set up. The Green plan is to cause the transformation of our society one initiative at a time. The Greens camouflage their politics because they don't want Americans to vote or campaign against the initiatives. Every initiative they can slip by takes us one step closer to a Green future.

Jeremy Rifkin, author of the book *Entropy*, suggests we need to reduce our population to the level it was in the Solar Age to maintain the earth's carrying capacity. Rifkin estimates that population was about 1 billion people in 1800. After that time period, we changed from solar based to extraction based energy consumption.

Rifkin indicates the world's population should reach 8 billion by the year 2015. How many of us, worldwide need to go, to reach a Solar Age population? If we understand correctly, it seems we need to reduce the human population by 7 billion people over the next 20 years to reach 1 billion. Rifkin suggests these steps to reduce the population:

- License parents for no more than two children
- Penalty for more children is higher taxes
- Citizens volunteer to limit families to two children
- Sterilization programs, force could be necessary

David Brower, of Earth Island Institute and *'Free Willy'* fame seems to agree with Rifkin. Brower stated:

> *"childbearing should be a punishable crime against society, unless the parents hold a government license…all potential parents should be required to use contraceptive chemicals, for the government issuing antidotes to citizens chosen for childbearing."*
> *Dawning of the New Age of the New World Order*

Hitler shared the concept of superior people and population control. He eliminated the Jews, the retarded and others because they were, in his opinion, not fit to live. He considered them vermin and an enemy of the Fatherland, Motherland.

> *"We in the Green Movement aspire to a cultural model in which killing a forest will be considered more contemptible and more criminal than the sale of 6 year old children to Asian brothels."*
> Carl Amery
> Green Party

Earth First! founder Dave Foreman has an interesting point of view on population control. He seems to share Hitler's mentality of extermination.

During an interview with Jerry Mason, Foreman was asked what his three main goals were.

"my three main goals would be to reduce human population to about 100 million worldwide, destroy the industrial infrastructure and see wilderness with it's full complement of species returning throughout the world."

The population of the United States is about 261.6 million. If there were no one else in the world, the U.S. alone would have to reduce our population by 161.6 million to reach Foreman's goal for world population. Another population thought from Dave Foreman:

"Aids is not a malediction, but the welcome and natural remedy to reduce the population of the planet...should human beings disappear, I surely wouldn't mind."

Public information sources indicate that Dave Foreman came up with the idea for Earth First! while on a camping trip. According to the authors of *Trashing the Economy*, Ron Arnold and Alan Gottlieb, in 1979, Dave Foreman was actually propositioned by the Wilderness Society and the Sierra Club to form a radical environmental group that they would finance. The author's informants reported Foreman accepted that deal.

Mainstream environmental groups began publicly referring to Earth First! as 'the 'radical fringe'. Earth First! became the visible, radical arm for the Green movement. The terrorist activities of Earth First! make the politics of mainstream groups seem mild. Earth First! helped to:

- sensationalize environmental issues
- nationalize environmental issues
- make the political goals of mainstream environmental groups seem rational

This was another set-up. Trick the American people into supporting the political ideas of mainstream groups because they are less radical than those of Earth First!. This does not mean the political ideas of the mainstream groups are reasonable. It means, when politicians compare demands, the mainstream groups appear to be the lesser of two evils. This political hoax was also used to:

- increase public concern for the environment
- increase public support for Green politics
- increase public contributions

It worked, but picking the lesser of two evils is not a good way to set environmental policy.

What does this tell us about the integrity of these mainstream environmental groups? Betraying the trust of the American people is acceptable. The end justifies the means.

Taking Terrorism Mainstream

The Sierra Club has in the past publicly distanced themselves from groups like Earth First. A May 1995 article for *In These Times* magazine reveals Dave Foreman has been named to the elite 15 member Sierra Club board. Foreman is also on Sierra Club's five member executive committee for 1995-96. This ought to make it clear, radical politics and terrorism are part of the mainstream environmental movement. According to the article, Foreman will play a leading role. This also shows us the radical fringe was never really the radical fringe.

David Brower, founder of the Earth Island Institute, was also named to the Sierra Club board. He was once ousted by the Sierra Club for being too radical. Obviously, times changed.

We ought to be concerned that Dave Foreman is a part of the leadership of one of the largest mainstream environmental groups. It indicates that radical ideas are a part of the Green agenda.

The Nazi movement began as a tiny band of radicals. Those radicals gained recognition and then took their radical ideas to the mainstream. The masses began to accept those radical ideas and terrorism became a part of mainstream politics in Germany. The Greens seem to be following the same path.

The Greens are taking their radical ideas, including population reduction mainstream. Although the Greens have not yet publicly revealed plans to exterminate people to lower the population they have called for voluntary human extinction.

As a people and as a nation, we cannot ignore these facts. Reminiscent of the Nazis, some participants in the Green movement are lying to the masses and using terrorism to gain political power. Radical politics and acts of terrorism will not solve environmental problems.

Environmental efforts ought to focus on restoration and taking responsible steps toward preventing further problems. The current focus on spending millions of donated dollars on litigation or to finance terrorism is not the most effective way to solve environmental disputes.

These groups ought to focus on cooperation and spend those millions of dollars helping businesses and individuals correct the problems. They could be taking creative and cooperative steps to help boost our economy by paying unemployed citizens to replant burned areas or clean up riverbanks. Instead, Green groups focus on lobbying and lawsuits to change public land use policies to legally force their ideas on the American people.

The goal is not cooperation. It is control. The problem is three-fold. First, the Greens are not the only Americans capable of understanding an environmental issue. The Greens are not the only Americans who can think. Second, American citizens are loosing equal representation to a growing eco-dictatorship. Third, Americans do not realize the Greens have created this eco-monopoly to gain control of the land base in America.

The Green movement has become an eco-monopoly. An eco-monopoly is different than the number of people in America who support a healthy environment. An eco-monopoly is this author's term for Green control of public information regarding environmental issues. From 'spendy' Green documentaries to the daily news, the Greens have all but eliminated American's opportunity to hear both sides of an issue.

There is little difference how the Greens are controlling public information to sway public opinion and how the Nazis used public information to sway public opinion. One-sided propaganda convinced Germans that the Jews were materialistic scum who were no longer fit to live as they had been living.

One sided propaganda is convincing some Americans to believe others are materialistic scum who are no longer fit to live as they have been living.

The greatest problem with this eco-monopoly is that it dominates environmental decision making on the national level. The opinions of other American citizens aren't getting the attention they deserve because they cannot compete with the financial resources and the media prejudice the Greens have set up.

Almost everything we hear and see regarding environmental issues is based on information provided by environmental groups. Green groups are calling for radical change in America based on their ideas of environmental protection. Americans need to find a way to hear both sides of an issue before political decisions are made and ideas become law.

A few people resisted Hitler's lies. Those in the resistance movement made up their own minds. They resisted the Nazis and saved thousands of innocent people in the process. They approached that political mine field from the standpoint of 'what could be done' instead of 'what couldn't be done'

Every American wants to do what is necessary to protect the environment. Like most issues regarding the environmental cause, we do not know what is true. The only way we are going to find out is to get both sides in front of the people and figure out who knows what they are talking about.

Some population experts suggest we do not have a major population problem. Population issues affect us all and so will an oppressive government system. If the future of our nation and the world is at risk, isn't it time we found out what is going on?

Green Is Extreme

"The elimination of beef and other meat from the human diet is now required if we are to have any hope of saving the planet and ensuring our children's future."

> Biosphere Politics
> Jeremy Rifkin

Rifkin is a political leader in the Green movement and is aggressively pushing this part of the Green agenda in Washington D.C. The Greens want control of production and distribution. This includes controlling our natural resources, economic base and food supply.

What would it take to get control of, or put an end to beef production? Find a way to prevent ranchers from raising and supplying beef to the American people.

Can the Greens actually eliminate beef and other meats as a food choice in the United States? Consider the 'Big Guns' involved in this Green coalition, all targeting the individual rancher.

The beef business is a prime example of Green politics in action.

>*"What everyone likes is the Big victory you load them cattle trucks for the last time and they go driving off into the sunset and they never come back. "*

>*"But you can win a lot more victories than that ultimate one, you can win a lot more victories by making him (the rancher) pay for what he does out there and by making it so expensive in his operation and making so many changes for him to continue to run his cattle on the public lands that he goes broke, he can't do it, he has to come up with other ways to be a rancher. "*

>*"When you get right down to it, the boots and the hat, boy for them guys, its a way of life."*

>*"The ultimate picture is of course, the last cattle truck driving off into the sunset, but that's not how you win."*

>*"How you win is one at a time, one at a time, he goes out of business, he dies, you wait him out, but you win."*

Roy Elicker
National Wildlife Federation Counsel

Does this sound like a sincere plea to protect the environment or a plan to put a ranching family out of business? To end production you have to destroy the producer. Make control possible by making control legal.

It sounds like the Nazis secretly discussing the fate of Jewish businesses, but this is the type of heartless dialogue common among Green activists.

Elicker also pointed out how activists can use endangered species to put cattlemen out of business. These mean-spirited attitudes are carefully concealed from the general public.

This does not mean all representatives of the National Wildlife Federation are Communists. It does mean, this is how the Greens are using concern for the environment to destroy the beef industry.

Put A Little Green In Your Life

Would you burn down your own home? That's the idea the Greens are selling to the American public to justify the end of beef production.

Why would a rancher destroy the land that feeds them? If cattle can't eat, they die. If what the Greens say is completely true, the rancher would have put themselves out of business a long time ago. To produce beef for this nation, generation after generation, they had to take care of the land.

Put yourself in the same situation. Put a little green in your life. Boy, for you guys it's the football, your computer, your music, your clothes, your career, *'boy for you guys, it's a way of life'*. Yes, it is. It's a matter of freedom and personal choice.

According to this Green political logic, your choice of clothes (and other personal preferences) makes you automatically guilty of being an anti-environmentalist. It doesn't make sense, but what if people believed it? By the same token, ranchers should not be labeled or judged automatically guilty because of their chosen profession and dress code.

Ridiculing personal preference to imply guilt, as opposed to addressing the issue in question, is asinine. You might hear that approach on a playground. Kids use the saying, 'you're ugly, and your mama dresses you funny', but when was the last time, in a political discussion, an adult accused you of having cooties?

Why are the Greens attacking cowboy clothes? It is an effective manipulative tool for the Greens. The purpose is to cloud the public's judgment. There is a method to the madness. A few, well-placed remarks dehumanize the issues.

Greens have mastered the communist art of diverting the public's attention. The tactic is called character assassination. It prevents people from discussing the issue in question. The Greens do not give people the facts or explain the consequences. Instead, the Greens keep the jokes flying and people laughing. The result is, the audience forgets the issue, likes the Green comedian and leaves with a strong dose of the Green political perspective. It is a very effective method to avoid the factual and the human side of an issue.

America needs to take a step back and re-evaluate these issues: Health care, animal rights, anti-hunting, gun control, population control, natural dying, privatization of our educational system and political correctness.

The objective is to get Green political ideas legalized before we understand there is a difference between concern for the environment and being coerced into submitting to the Green political agenda. If allowed to go unchecked, America's response to environmental sensationalism will give Green Communists time to accomplish their mission.

It doesn't matter what is true. It matters what people think is true. It's all a matter of perception. The Greens are good at creating false perceptions.

Most big businesses are made up of small, individual businesses. Beef production is the result of individual ranching operations. If the Greens put one rancher out of business, the industry will not be destroyed. If the Greens are successful putting many ranchers out of business, one at a time, it adds up to the end of an industry. That is a big deal. We have lost a food choice. Families have lost their independence and their income. America has lost economic strength.

The National Wildlife Federation representative spelled out the Green strategy. The end justifies the means. The objective is to put Americans out of business one at a time. The big victory comes from each little victory. That's how the Greens are winning.

This has nothing to do with the environment or the Greens would focus on the environment, not issue blanket (dehumanizing) orders to put people out of business.

What's to win?

Is this a game or a war? It's a war against America being waged on one citizen and one group at a time. If we accept government control of other people's lives, we begin to sacrifice our freedom. Gaining control of one person, one group, one step at a time, is the political strategy.

"We're in a war, the war of industrial civilization against the natural world"

Dave Foreman, 1991

Reports indicate the 'Unabomber' revealed he was part of a group that wanted to break down society and divide it into smaller units. The Greens have a similar goal. They want to create bioregions and establish small communities.

The Unabomber stated in a story by the *Associated Press* on April 26,1995 that the goal of his group was:

"the destruction of the world wide industrial system. Through our bombings we hope to promote social instability in industrial society and give encouragement to those who hate the industrial system."

(Bold Emphasis Added)

The goal to completely transform our society is also a Green goal. The communist strategy is to cause chaos within our society to destroy American's desire to fight for our country.

"Visualize Industrial Collapse"

Earth First!

*"my three main goals would be to reduce human population to about 100 million worldwide, **destroy the industrial infrastructure** and see wilderness with it's full complement of species returning throughout the world."*

Dave Foreman
Earth First! Co-Founder
(Bold Emphasis Added)

The political messages of the Unabomber, Earth First! and Dave Foremen seem to be the same.

Success does leave clues. Hitler realized before the people of a nation would accept a new set of cultural values, the old set of traditional images and patriotic symbols had to be systematically devalued. This is what the Greens are doing.

Our collective American 'way of life' and culture is under attack. The goal is to convince us our past isn't worth preserving so we will accept new Green symbols, new Green ideas and abandon American values and traditions. We've been lead to believe these are uncontrolled, spontaneous Green ideas about how to save the earth. In reality what we are seeing is the controlled execution of the Green's long-term plan.

The Greens are working to transform our society by destroying what makes our society work. Animal rights, condemning meat consumption, insulting cowboys and ridiculing American history are all part of the plan. Cowboys represent a key part of our history. They are a symbol of our courage, heritage and pioneering spirit. The Greens are using 'character assassination' to dissolve the cowboy image and contaminate our sense of pride.

The Greens are twisting environmental issues to put ranchers out of business and gain control over the land base and what we eat. We are to live happily ever after eating roots and rice. Whatever the issue, endangered species to animal rights, we need to recognize when we are being set-up for Green Communism or the Greens will continue to manipulate us.

Using Your Imagination

Writers, producers, directors and actors are being asked to further the environmental cause by using entertainment to sway public opinion. Many of these Americans do not understand the environmental cause has been hijacked and they are helping advance the Green's political goals. Some do. Greening Hollywood is a big deal. Entertainment is a powerful tool that can be used to *condition* the American people and our children to embrace Green ideas.

The fall 1989 issue of *InCONTEXT* magazine featured an article on "Redefining Entertainment". The article focused on how entertainment could be used to transform values and promote social change. Entertainment was a miracle tool to:

- popularize the transformation of society
- attract masses to concept of change
- unite audience and create a following
- create anger toward enemies presented on screen
- send subliminal messages to sway political opinion
- change the world

Norman Fleishman was interviewed for this article. Fleishman is known as the conscience of Hollywood and indicates he was influenced by Joe McCarthy. He states:

> *"I was around the progressive movement as a child, so I agreed with McCarthy only about one thing: that the storytellers were the most powerful people in the world. He went after the storytellers, had many of them blacklisted in Hollywood, because he felt their power. In a sense I followed in his footsteps, only I've taken the opposite tack. I do what I can to assist and support them and inspire them, if I can, by way of these meetings I've held over the years."*
>
> (Bold emphasis added)

Excuse me? Joe McCarthy's mission was to stop communist storytellers from using entertainment to spread propaganda and subliminally influence the American people. Fleishman indicates he has 'taken the opposite tack'.

The opposite of stopping communist storytellers from using entertainment to spread propaganda is to help communist storytellers use entertainment to spread propaganda and subliminally influence the American people.

Later in the article, Mr. Fleishman states:

"So we need to popularize these things that we believe in, add the element of entertainment- the gripping, the holding, the entrancing....I'm not saying this is an iron-clad plan to change the world, but I do believe in the possibility of transformation."

Is Mr. Fleishman saying he helps communist storytellers spread their political beliefs or is he saying he uses the power of entertainment to impose his political beliefs for social transformation on unsuspecting Americans?

America, we must stay mentally alert for subversive messages woven into entertainment. What Fleishman is advocating is not honest. It is based on deception. It is more like a con job or a sting operation. Entertainment is supposed to be entertaining; a performance, a party, something people do for amusement. Americans do not expect entertainment to be used as a political tool to change their values and political beliefs.

It is significant to mention that issue of *InCONTEXT'* was sent to Governor Bill Clinton. The Winter, 1990 edition of that magazine included this letter to the editor:

"Thank you for sending me a copy of your recent issue of InCONTEXT. **I enjoyed the article featuring Norman Fleishman on 'Redefining Entertainment'. His behind the** *scene's work has educated many Hollywood writers about the important social and environmental issues that are increasingly the concern of the 'middle'. I wish you continued success in your goal to make the major cultural shifts our world is now experiencing to be as graceful and as positive as possible."*

Bill Clinton
Governor of Arkansas
(Bold Emphasis Added)

What major cultural shifts was Governor Clinton speaking of? Mr. Clinton indicates he supports using 'behind the scenes' tactics to manipulate the American people and using entertainment to spread biased political messages.

Most Americans do not expect entertainment to be used to brainwash them into accepting new political ideas for social transformation. Political ideas are like any other product. Quality products and ideas are sold on their merit and value to the buyer (honesty). Shoddy products or questionable ideas can't be sold on merit. Shoddy ideas or products require conning the buyer into accepting a product or idea by using misleading information (deception). It's like beach front property in Arizona. After you buy it, it's too late.

Many writers, stars and producers are unaware the Greens have long courted Hollywood to promote their political ideas using news and entertainment sources. This is why news includes make-believe facts and make-believe entertainment is used for Green political brainwashing. This is completely unreasonable.

The environmental cause and Hollywood stars are not to blame. The 'Greening' of Hollywood is the problem. 'Behind the scenes' politics take unfair advantage of trusting Americans. Using entertainment to indoctrinate unsuspecting consumers, including children, is underhanded.

> *"A red cancer is gnawing at the vitals of this nation and the world. The Communists are working at being Communists 24 hours a day. Let us work at being Americans 24 hours a day."*
>
> Cecil B. deMille
> Movie Director – 1948

Case In Point

In one episode, the television program *SeaQuest* focused on a crew member, who craved a mouth-watering hamburger. The crew member had to get the meat illegally. He had to smuggle it on-board and secretly prepare the hamburger.

Just as he was ready to take that first bite, the captain walked in and ordered the crew member to surrender the hamburger. The captain justified this action by reminding the guy meat consumption was illegal and it was his duty to enforce the law.

Earlier in the show the audience learned that meat had been outlawed by the government. It was determined meat was bad for public health so meat had been banned and was no longer a food choice.

As soon as the captain was outside the door, he decided the hamburger looked good, so he took a couple of big bites, then tossed the remainder in the trash. He deprived another, but indulged himself and wasted the rest.

Case in point: Do as I say, not as I do. In a communist country, the privileged few get what the masses are denied.

Where Do We Draw the Line?

There is a difference between life in a free society and life in a communist society.

Support for environmental protection does not equal American's support for a political revolution and a switch to Communism. When Green political objectives become public knowledge, the people who continue to publicly support the Green agenda, ought to be the first to walk their talk. They ought to stop their lives, give up their wealth, their property and live by the Green rules they are trying to force on others.

Communism is based on the double standard do as I say, not as I do. Russian leaders preached equality to the masses and went home to live in private luxury. Do as I say, not as I do is the communist double standard.

Examples of the do as I say and not as I do, double standard can be found frequently within the environmental cause. Here are just two examples.

The Sierra Club played a key role in nationalizing the Spotted Owl issue to stop logging in the Pacific Northwest. According to a 1994 story by the *Associated Press*, William Arthur, the regional director for the Sierra Club, made this comment during panel discussions with President Clinton criticizing the timber industry:

> *"We cut like there's no tomorrow and tomorrow caught up with us yesterday."*

This statement would suggest to most people that Arthur believes too many trees have been cut and that no more should be cut down. Think again. Soon after he successfully helped close down small mills and put hundreds of loggers out of business, specifically because cutting down trees was harmful to the environment, Arthur cut down 70% of the remaining trees on his property. The money Arthur made was designated for home improvements. According to the report, twelve years ago Arthur cut down enough trees to put himself through graduate school. Arthur justified his reverse political position, stating:

> *"the Sierra Club doesn't have trouble, with logging when it's appropriate."*

According to the report, Ken Kholi, a spokesperson for the timber industry indicated that Arthur, representing the Sierra Club was among eight other environmental groups suing the Colville National Forest. These groups were suing them for not protecting old growth trees. Kholi indicates Arthur cut down some of the same kind of old growth trees he was suing to protect.

According to an article in *Ecologic* magazine, May 1995, Jon Roush, President of the Wilderness Society harvested 80 acres of old growth trees on his property. The Wilderness Society President sued the U.S. Forest Service in 1983 and prevented them from logging in the Bitterroot Forest due to the harm it would cause to the environment. Roush owns a ranch in the Bitterroot area. It borders the land he prevented the Forest Service from harvesting. According to the article, the Roush ranch is worth $2.5 million.

There's nothing wrong with cutting trees on private property. There is something wrong with making sure other Americans don't have the same right. That is, the do as I say, not as I do, Green difference. There is no excuse, no clever justification, for this misuse of power. These self-proclaimed environmental protectors are hypocrites. They accept donations to prevent others from logging and then log themselves.

Some things just aren't right. Judge Helen Frye awarded the Sierra Club Legal Defense Fund of Seattle, Washington and the Western Environmental Law Center of Eugene, Oregon $1,005,512 in November 1994. This money was paid to reimburse these groups for the dollars they spent on the Spotted Owl case. This is all perfectly legal under the Endangered Species Act. This allows all Americans to help fund Green groups. First, the Sierra Club Legal Defense Fund uses the money donated to them. Then, they reach into every taxpayers pocket to pay them back for the money they spent to stop timber harvest in the Pacific Northwest.

"You can't save a forest and cut it down too."
William Arthur
Sierra Club - February 1994

The Sierra Club guy can harvest his trees and make a profit. The Wilderness Society guy can harvest his trees and make a profit, but other Americans should not harvest trees for profit according to the Greens. Again, it's do as I say, not as I do.

Things Can't Get Any Worse

That's exactly what the Jewish people thought. The Jews kept trying to be reasonable, to work with the situation, to comply, until things got back to normal. That didn't happen.

Hindsight is always 20-20. What the people did not realize is that Hitler and his Nazis were lying, unreasonable people. Reasonable people dealt with Hitler like he was a reasonable person. That was a critical mistake.

People don't treat known enemies in a trusting manner. They keep their guard up. America's guard is down because of our genuine concern for the environment. The Greens refer to the environmental cause as a war.

Americans have tried to reason with the Greens. It is a waste of time. We need to take Green politics and ideology seriously. We must realize we are dealing with a fanatical, unreasonable minority. We need to recognize it is a war.

People tried to reason with Hitler. It was a waste of time. Hitler played for power while others played fair. Hitler was serious about his Nazi ideas. The Greens are serious about their ideas. Hitler didn't play fair. The Greens don't play fair. The Greens want it their way or none.

A Dangerous Message

The film, *The Last Supper* with Jason Alexander, (co-star on Seinfeld) was reviewed. The movie is about college students who kill people they determine are not politically correct or are anti-earth. The movie is supposed to be a comedy about getting rid of the people who bug you.

Another comedy film with a Green twist is *Serial Mom* starring Kathleen Turner. This movie is also about how a seemingly ideal suburban Mom gets carried away with killing people who bother her. This movie includes a scene where Mom and garbage men are discussing the neighbor who doesn't recycle. The conversation concludes that someone ought to kill that neighbor to help save the environment.

These movies are intended to be funny and entertaining. The underlying social message is not humorous. It promotes extreme intolerance toward other people.

The distinction we must make is between free speech and accountability. The message the public hears is the responsibility of the writers and others in this area of movie making. Fostering hate towards our fellow Americans and suggesting those people ought to be killed because they are not politically correct is where Hitler began.

It takes just as many strokes on the keyboard for a writer to express ideas in a positive rather than a negative manner. If the script was not about a serial killer, the writers might take this approach. The Mom states she will never give up trying to teach her neighbor the value of recycling. Mom could enlist the support of the garbage guys to help the neighbor learn to recycle, even if the three of them had to do it for her.

Justifying killing people to protect the sacred soil is what Hitler did. According to the book, *The World Must Know*, Hitler and his propaganda minister Dr. Joseph Goebbels understood he needed the masses to, '*unite them behind his rule*'. They began by lying and manipulating the masses to:

- believe they had an evil enemy
- believe it was a question of life or death

They accomplished this by:

- using Hitler's speeches and personal drama
- managing public information press, radio and film
- presenting all information with a Nazi slant
- playing on sympathy and fear
- adding a spiritual, tribal, ceremonial quality to events
- repeating Jews were savage, greedy, vile creatures

Hitler made the Nazi cause the center of public life. Hitler played on emotions to get the public to agree with his solution to a manufactured political dilemma. He used propaganda to get support for Nazi ideas from economics to saving the sacred soil of the Fatherland. This decade, public information and entertainment are being used to Green public opinion and make the Green cause of saving Mother Earth the center of public life.

An episode of *Seinfeld* featured the character Elaine dating a Communist. Several times during the show, her lines expressed how 'cool' it was to date a Communist. Is it just a joke or a subliminal political message that Communists are cool?

Actors and actresses are not Communist because they deliver a line. Entertainers are not responsible for the content of a script unless they write it. Actors and actresses perform. The question isn't about performance, it involves using performances to create a specific public perception.

The entertainment industry has to take a serious look at its responsibility factor in American politics. The industry must address what is fair use of their product and what is misuse. Integrating political messages and using emotional appeals to get consumers to take a political position is not fair use. It is a conflict of interest and a violation of professional ethics.

This is not about censorship. It is about ethics, responsibility and recognizing this art is being abused for political gain. There is a difference between entertainment and indoctrination.

Powerful Allies

The environmental movement enjoys the support of some very powerful allies who may have no idea what they are really lending their names to.

Robert Redford is a good example. He's been involved in the environmental cause for years. A 1989 article on the Greens indicated Mr. Redford might even be the Green white house hopeful. He indicated he was not.

The official Green Party program came out a few years later. Mr. Redford may be one of many Americans who doesn't fully understand what he is supporting. It appears he may not.

Every American needs to understand the Green's political plans. What happens in this country affects each and every one of us. We won't be able to protect the environment if we lose our freedom to take action. We don't have to stop caring for the environment to stop a Green revolution.

When Robert Redford discovers he would lose control of Sundance under the Green system, he may want to publicly withdraw his support for the Greens. Greens want to end private property ownership, land speculation and development in general. Redford built a beautiful resort in an undeveloped area. He even cut down trees. He proved Capitalism, concern for the environment, development and free enterprise can work hand-in-hand.

Our American Culture

A culture is what is created when groups of people develop a certain way of living or 'way of life'. A way of life includes traditions and those are then passed on from one generation to another, creating a lasting culture.

Where we live and how we live is part of who we are. Freedom is the ability to make personal choices about our lives. Some people love life in the big city. Surfers live for the beach. Other Americans thrive on life in the suburbs. Some prefer the country. Each life choice carries with it the joy, challenges and responsibilities connected to living in that particular place.

Hitler proved you can destroy a culture right in front of people's eyes. Nazi domination occurred gradually. Hitler made control possible by making control legal, one Nazi law at a time. The Greens are concealing steps to eliminate our freedoms and our culture one Green law at a time.

It's important to understand how the Green agenda mirrors Communism and the connection between Green leaders and communist activities in the United States.

Earth Island Institute is directly associated with the Green Party and promotes their agenda. Staff members teach seminars on Deep Ecology (earth worship). These training sessions are offered to teachers, Green activists and community organizers. Americans were urged to donate to Earth Island in the promo before the movie *Free Willy*. Earth Island founder David Brower was an active leader in the Green movement.

Brower also founded The League of Conservation Voters and Friends of the Earth. Friends of the Earth was linked to the communist front organization, NLG.

James Tyson, author of *Target America* identifies Friends of the Earth as an affiliate of the National Lawyers Guild or NLG. Tyson indicates NLG affiliate organizations promote communist ideas and help form other groups to do the same. Tyson summarizes the political purpose of the National Lawyers Guild with this statement from an NLG leader:

> *"I am a double agent, I want to use the System to bring down the System."*
>
> William Kunstler
> NLG Convention - 1971

Jonathon Porritt was an Executive Director for Friends of the Earth. It appears the environmental cause is the vehicle the Greens are using to bring down our system.

The editors of the *Earth Island Journal* surveyed various environmental groups to gather ideas for 50 more things Americans could do to save the earth. The list was published in the Winter, 1990 edition of *Trilogy* magazine.

Nine ideas from that survey are listed below. Before reading the list imagine if membership in any of the environmental groups surveyed may be associating you, or lending your financial support to further one or all of these goals.

Does your support for the environmental protection equal support for these political goals?

- Be a total vegetarian
- Disconnect your power lines
- Don't have children
- Live on $140 a month
- Set a maximum wage
- Don't own pets
- Let domestic cattle go extinct
- Don't use batteries
- Use washable cloth instead of toilet paper

Are the individuals who developed this list using washable cloth instead of toilet paper? Are they living on $140.00 a month? Have they disconnected the power lines? If not, it's do as I say, not as I do politics. We ought to take these goals seriously because the Greens take them seriously. The Greens plan to attain these goals by using different excuses to justify specific legislation. They don't have to propose it themselves. They get others to do it for them.

For example, setting a maximum wage is a socialist step to Communism. Congressman Ron Dellums bill; "A Living Wage, Jobs-for-All Act" supports the Green goal. Americans are not expected to notice Dellums bill is a step toward Socialism or that the political goals of the Greens and the Democratic Socialist and Eco-Socialists match.

Americans who are involved in environmental efforts for personal rather than political reasons may not understand the Green agenda. It's hard for Americans to see what's going on politically if their attention is diverted to other issues.

A key to Hitler's success was he operated like a magician. He kept people paying attention to the wrong things so no one noticed what was actually happening. Hitler kept his message simple and repeated it often. The bigger the lie and the sensationalism, the better.

The Greens have imitated this technique. The Greens keep their message simple and repeat it often: Save this, Save that, but Save it! The Greens also play on fear and hype to motivate the public and politicians to support their ideas. Like Hitler, the Greens are keeping the public focused on the wrong issues to generate fear and unrest. The focus is on Green doom-and-gloom:

- threat of global warming
- threat of animal extinction
- threat of human extinction

The focus is on the topic, the emotional hook and the urgent need to take drastic steps to save the earth by surrendering control of the environment and our lives to the Greens.

The focus ought to be on:

- public awareness, public debate
- alternatives to the drastic steps the Greens propose
- diverse scientific opinions on the subject
- political and personal ramifications of a Green future

We can and must learn from history.

"It is possible to lead astray an entire generation, to strike it blind, to drive it insane, to direct it towards a false goal. Napoleon proved that."

Alexander Herzen
Russian Journalist - Political Thinker

5

Shades of Green

The Green strategy is to bring about a massive shift in our values by using different issues and avenues to either create conflict or send subliminal Green messages to the American masses. The goal is to get support for Green ideas without being obvious. Green ideas come in many 'shades of Green'. Each plays a part in eroding American traditions and values. Green politics are based on the following Ten Key Values:

1. Ecological Wisdom
2. Grassroots Democracy
3. Non-violence
4. Social Justice
5. Decentralization
6. Community-Based Economics
7. Feminism and Post-Patriarchal Values
8. Respect for Diversity
9. Personal and Global Responsibility
10. Future Focus/Sustainability

These 10 key values are simple and extremely vague. The reason for simplicity is, to draw the masses to simple, nice-sounding ideas. The reason for being vague is, to allow the Greens to use the vagueness of these terms to change our values. These intellectual, progressive sounding terms like 'personal and global responsibility' are designed to be 'all encompassing'. This way they can be 'adjusted' to mean anything and mask the steps to transform our society and modify our behavior. The plan is to 'adjust' the meaning until they create a 'revolution'. Revolution means overthrowing our government and destroying our freedoms by justifying

Socialism then Communism. We must make very careful distinctions. We are dealing with a well-financed, well executed, calculated political effort. We must face, expose, and publicly debate the political goals of the Greens or they can succeed.

The Greens have been planting and cultivating alternative ideas to challenge our standards and public policies for years. The Greens use various issues to camouflage their political agenda including:

- Third Party Politics
- Ballot Initiatives
- Rewriting American History
- American Indian Rights
- Green Spirituality

From public health to labor issues, children's rights to religion, the Greens color the issues from an environmental angle to drag another segment of the population into the overall movement. The next steps in the 'Greening' process are to slip-in Green political ideas and start implementing those ideas under the banner of environmental protection.

Dealing with the Greens is like playing a game of cards with a stacked deck. The players think they are playing by the rules with the same odds of winning, but that is not the case. The deal looks fair but the dealer knows what cards he gets and how he's going to play them.

That leaves the rest of the players at a definite disadvantage. This is how the Greens are advancing their program. They have stacked the deck so the American people don't realize they are being deceived and cheated. Here are some of the ways we've been set-up to lose.

Third Party Politics

Many of us are ready to do almost anything to help stop the decline of America. We are tired of watching others devalue the standards and ideals on which this country is based. We have even considered supporting a third political party.

Part of the communist assault on our country includes weakening our system of government. Green Communists are promoting third party politics to change our two party system, divide the vote and put Communists in power. The Communist Party plan to deceive voters and run Communists as independent candidates is outlined in a January, 1989 *Political Affairs* article the "Impact of the 'Independent Plus' in the Election of '88" by Joelle Fishman.

> *"To break the two party lock on the system, the* **Communist Party joined in coalition with a number of independent parties to support the Uniform Federal Voting Act** *sponsored by Rep. Jon Conyers Jr.* **This bill would liberalize ballot access laws for independents and new parties.** *It demands full support of the 101st Congress along with the* **Universal Voter Registration Act introduced by Sen. Alan Cranston.**"

> *"The Communist Party...decided not to field a presidential ticket in 1988...Instead the National Committee urged all state organizations to reach out to other independent forces and strive to run Communist candidates, where possible, on independent or coalition tickets..."*

> *"the idea of electing left and Communists independent candidates to public office is now on the agenda. The groundbreaking campaigns of 1988 opened the way"*

Political Affairs-Marxist Journal
January 1989
(Bold Emphasis Added)

Fishman was, at that time, the chairwoman of the Communist Party of Connecticut. Senator Cranston was identified as a Green legislator in the Rifkin's book, *Voting Green*. Senator Cranston has since retired and is now involved with Mikhail Gorbachev's environmental organization, which is directly linked to Green Communist activities in the United States. Former Senator Cranston may not know about the Greens political agenda, then again, he is working with Gorbavchev who is pushing Green ideas that smack of world Communism.

Hiding behind the environmental cause and lying about their politics allows Green Communists to sneak in the back door and trick the public into voting for a Communist camouflaged as a Democrat, Independent, Labor or Green candidate.

> *"Just as Communist, left and progressive independent campaigns found common ground with the 'progressive wing' in the Democratic Party in the effort to defeat Bush, so the common ground widens to shape the course of the country under the incoming administration. Many of the independent campaigns related to, or found their beginnings in the Jackson movement. The Rainbow Coalition and labor-based coalitions...provide the arena for ongoing grassroots organizing toward the 101st Congress, future elections and political empowerment."*
>
> Political Affairs-Marxist Journal
January 1989
(Bold Emphasis Added)

July 1995, the *McAlvany Intelligence Advisor* reported:

> *"Former Communist Party Vice Presidential candidate, Angela Davis has been named as the new executive director for Jesse Jackson's Rainbow Coalition. Davis has also served on the Central Committee of the Communist Party U.S.A."*

Independent candidates are part of the communist plan to divide the vote and disrupt our electoral system. The Greens are setting-us-up to support Proportional Representation and 'use our system to bring down our system' to make control possible by making control legal.

> *"it's very difficult for Greens and kindred spirits to overcome the virtual two-party monopoly of the political process. What we need in the United States is the proportional representation that Europe has (i.e. if 18% of the people vote for Green Senate candidates, then 18 percent of the Senate would be Greens). Greens around the country are beginning to talk this up and may well make proportional representation a battle cry for the 90's."*
>
> John Rensenbrink
> National Spokesman, Green Party

Third parties and ideas like Proportional Representation are easier to resist when we understand the goal is to destroy our system of government and put the Greens in power. Hitler capitalized on Germany's multi-party chaos to seize power.

If we cannot get our political leaders to carry out the will of the people then a third party may be necessary. Before we commit to that solution, we ought to remember our government is based on a two party system for good reason. Multiple parties create division, confusion and upset the checks and balances of our government system. Imagine what life and taxes would be like if we experimented with different political philosophies every four years? Third parties sound enticing but they could create more problems.

Mr. Perot said some things Americans wanted to hear in 1992 but he dropped the ball at critical points in the campaign. Many people, discouraged with the leadership offered by the Democrats and Republicans, voted for Perot. There could not have been a more effective way to put the current administration in the White House. This is not to suggest Mr. Perot is a Communist. It is to point out how third parties can influence an election by splitting the vote.

The two party system may not be perfect but it gives us a choice of two distinctly different concepts of how America ought to be governed. The communist strategy involves encouraging multiple parties because it disrupts and breaks-down our electoral process. Multiple parties put America on shaky ground. America cannot risk sending a Watermelon, Green on the outside, Red on the inside, to the White House.

John Drakeford, author of *Red Blueprint for the World,* noted:

> *"In a democracy Communism's objective is to destroy everything that gives stability to the highly developed capitalist state. The legislative, judicial and executive branches of the government must all be destroyed to prepare for the next form of government. William Z. Foster, the former chairman of the Communists Party in America, stated it very clearly when he said:"*

> *"No Communist, no matter how many votes he should secure in a national election, could, even if he would, become President of the present government.* **When a Communist heads government in the United States - and that day will come just as surely as the sun rises - that government will not be a capitalistic government but a Soviet government, and behind this government will stand the Red Army to enforce the Dictatorship** *of the Proletariat"* [1]
>
> (Bold Emphasis Added)

Wishful thinking, or is this part of the calculated political effort by the Soviets to take over our country? We must be very careful whom we elect and the laws we support. The founding fathers gave their lives to give us a legacy. It was their love of liberty and extraordinary wisdom that produced the Constitution, the Declaration of Independence and our system of free government. It is visionary now, over 200 years later. Our system of government is not the problem. The problem is that some people in it are abusing their positions of power. We ought to stick to the two party system unless we are convinced beyond a shadow of a doubt that it is our political system, not people, that is causing problems.

We don't need to reinvent government. We need to clean up the one we have. It is like a priceless antique. With a little elbow grease it will be as good as new. Throwing it out would be a tragic mistake. America is the envy of people around the globe. Our culture, freedom and system of government are the reasons. The Green goal to devalue our system of government is no different than their reason for devaluing our past. If we dislike what we have, we will be more likely to try the Green alternative.

Rewriting American History

> "*The German people have in the year 1936, in the fourth year of the National Socialist regime, ended the period of their historic dishonor*
>
> My New Order
> Adolf Hitler

The Greens use Hitler's tactic of dwelling on injustices of the past to sensationalize calls for change in the present. Hitler ignited the Nazi movement by:

- ridiculing Germany's past to produce historic dishonor
- rewriting history to a politically correct Nazi version
- using nature, save the sacred soil of the Fatherland
- calling for social change, new traditions for a new age

At the same time Hitler was devaluing Germany's past he was offering Nazi ideas and values for a new and brighter future. The German people accepted their past was dishonorable and anxiously left it behind to support Hitler's new age ideas and new world order. They did not stand up and protect their traditions and culture.

The Greens have ignited the Green movement by:

- ridiculing America's past to produce historic dishonor
- rewriting history to a politically correct Green version
- using nature, save the sacred soil of Mother Earth
- calling for social change, new traditions for a new age

The Greens want us to accept our past is dishonorable so we will fall for their mix of new age, new order and new world government. They hope we will not 'catch-on' and stand-up to protect our traditions and culture. The Greens are effectively eroding our feelings about our past by 'Greening' American history; rewriting history to be Green and politically correct. One example is the Disney hit, *Pocahontas*. The movie presents a historical figure in a Green light. *Pocahontas* is portrayed as a mythical, eco-feminist champion of nature who talks to trees. June 19, 1995, *Time* magazine featured a review of *Pocahontas* by Richard Corliss. Corliss said:

> *"GREEN POWER: As teacher of the land's bounty with John Smith as her student, Pocahontas becomes the first eco-feminist."*

There is no question. Pocahontas was a heroine. The question involves using the power of entertainment to spread Green ideas and values about eco-feminism and Green spirituality. This is the link to Green politics. The movie is an example of Green subliminal, psychological programming. Americans think they are enjoying a simple boy meets girl story. In reality, the mix of fantasy and fact promotes:

- Green version of American history
- Green spiritual values
- Green eco-feminism

Cartoon characters are a clever way for the Greens to introduce alternative spiritual values to children and adults without being obvious.

American history was modified to promote a Green politically correct version of a historical event. Good entertainment has a lasting effect. When children study the true story of Pocahontas in school, will they identify with the 11-year-old Indian girl who did not have a romance with Captain Smith or will they identify with the Disney version of the 20-something Indian maiden who became romantically involved with Captain Smith? Will they see Pocahontas as an eco-heroine? Will they embrace her spiritual values? Will they believe they ought to talk to trees?

> "I developed a harsh resentment toward our elders, especially our educators from the Volksschule to university; not only had they allowed themselves to be deceived, they had delivered us, their children, into the cruel power of a new God."
> A Child of Hitler
> Alfons Heck

This decade, the 'God' is Green. Children operate on emotion. They do not understand the difference between fantasy and fact unless it is explained. Entertainment, like anything children are exposed to, can have a lifelong affect. The distinction must be made for children; that fantasy is based on imaginary things, like daydreams. Facts verify actual events and depict the truth. *Pocahontas* may be billed as a fantasy but because it tells a story about an actual historical event, it will be accepted by many children as real. When facts are distorted and mixed with fantasy it can create confusion and incorrect assumptions.

Richard Corliss mentioned another message conveyed in the movie *Pocahontas* was:

> "the standoff with the white man is one of eco-heroes vs. strip miners, defenders of an idyllic homeland against greedy invaders."

The idea of 'defending an idyllic homeland against greedy invaders' mirrors the environmental message Hitler used to justify taking action against those he labeled the 'greedy invaders' of the Fatherland. Hitler also made up lies about those 'greedy' people so children would believe those people were bad and the Nazis were heroes so children would want to grow-up to be Nazis. Hitler understood children could be indoctrinated with new values. The 'greedy invader' message also contributes to creating shame for our past by depicting invaders or explorers (i.e. Columbus) as bad guys. Mixing seemingly harmless fantasy with revolutionary politics is a dangerous trend. It is the Green way to change our attitudes about our past, our present and our future.

Hollywood has a free hand. It's still a free country. Actors, writers and other Hollywood leaders need to understand the Green agenda or they will continue to be used by the Greens as a 'mouth-piece'. To turn this around, every American needs to recognize Green propaganda and the reason for the constant negative interpretation of America's past. Greens emphasize the negative to manufacture historic dishonor. 'Greening' Hollywood means promoting Green values while simultaneously sending strong messages to destroy our traditional values and national pride.

Disney Studios may or may not be aware the Greens are using the magic style of Walt Disney to transform our society and change our values. If the public objected, Disney might stop integrating Green messages into future films.

Discovery Happened

The Greens would like us to believe we can turn back the hands of time, make-up for the mistakes of others, (instead of learning from them) and create a perfect world to save the planet. All we have to do is turn our society upside down and accept the Greens vision of eco-topia. These are simply emotional hooks to guilt and scare us into eco-Socialism. The Greens used passage into the 21st century as another hook to inspire us to take leave of our senses, abandon our past and follow the Greens into a new age like the Germans followed the Nazis.

The Greens are romanticizing Indian lore and magnifying any unfortunate actions taken against the Indians for one reason, to devalue our past from Columbus forward.

Christopher Columbus was not a bad guy because he sailed over and discovered America. Going out and discovering things was what people did back then. It was not an easy job. It took courage, dedication and amazing fortitude.

Put yourself in place of Columbus. Can you imagine waiting years to get on a ship, manned by a bunch of convicts (because no one else would go) and setting sail across uncharted waters to prove the world was round? It was a major risk and a major accomplishment. Columbus is a hero.

We can't pretend to have the ability to put things back as they were before Columbus discovered America. We can work with what we have. The best we can do is to look at the environmental situation, see what we can do, then do what we can to prevent harm and correct damage. The Greens are condemning our past for these reasons:

- to manufacture historic dishonor
- use past mistakes to gain emotional political support
- blame Americans for all environmental ruin
- blame Capitalism for worldwide environmental ruin
- infer a return to a primitive lifestyle will save the earth

Our Cup Is Half Full, Not Half Empty

What if another empire stopped by first? What if aliens landed and beamed the Indians to Mars? What if cannibals landed and ate all the people? Things could have been worse. This land mass, known as America, was to be discovered by people at some point in time. Those people might have chosen other ways to deal with the Indians. They might have completely eliminated the tribes instead of placing them on reservations. Although the reservation was not a perfect solution, it was better than annihilation.

History is not perfect. No one can assume to know what they would have done under the same circumstances. Like our own lives, we can focus on what makes our cup half empty or what makes our cup half full. What about all the wonderful things that have happened since Columbus discovered America?

Erasing our Culture

The attack on Columbus is part of the Green objective to erase our frontier culture. Greens are also courting the Indian culture to get us to abandon our historical relationship with cowboy legends and western culture.

The number one rule in the 'Communist Rules for Revolution' is to destroy our ruggedness. American culture is based on rugged individualism. Cowboys are rugged individuals. The Greens are steering us away from cowboys because they are our heroes, symbols of strength, bravery and honor. Cowboys also symbolize modern day ranching and beef production. Greens aim to get two birds with one stone. Disrespecting our past paves the way to disregard these values as key parts of our present and future culture.

Hitler was the #1 Nazi. What role did culture play in the Nazi movement? How did the man known as the #2 Nazi feel about destroying the existing culture?

> *"Every time I hear the word culture, I release the safety catch on my revolver."*
>
> Psychopathic God
> Hermann Goring

The Green attack on western culture presents a revealing contradiction between what the Greens say they support and what the Greens practice. If the Greens truly respected multi-cultures, they would respect our culture. America is the melting pot. People came to America to become Americans and blend into this unique culture. America is the culture of one based on the contributions of many. The Greens are pushing multi-culturalism to establish marked divisions and promote individual cultures instead of a united culture. If the Greens truly respected different cultures, they would not be working to systematically destroy ours. The Green plan to erase our culture involves erasing different pieces of it. Here are a few tactics the Greens are using to diminish the value of our frontier heritage:

- present cowboy life, from clothes to ranching as outdated
- devalue all frontier traditions, horse racing to rodeos
- attack John Wayne for his stand against Communism
- replace cowboy and other heroes with new Eco-heroes
- condemn cattle grazing on public lands
- push vegetarianism, make meat consumption unpopular

The Indians are also victims in the Green assault on our past. As a minority group, they were targeted by the Communists years ago. The Greens aligned with the Indian nations to advance Green goals. Greens are using injustices of the past to sway public opinion in their favor. The Greens focus on bad so we'll believe bad is all there was.

We Don't Have A Time Machine

The cowboy and Indian wars were an unfortunate consequence of westward expansion. People can pretend they would have handled the situation differently but they were not there. We ought to remember, it's a two way street. Both the Cowboys and the Indians did things to be ashamed of.

According to one documentary, Indians tacked living children to trees and left them to die. Certainly scalping wasn't a pleasant experience for the cowboys but it is what the Indians did back then. Cowboys destroyed villages and killed men, women and children. Indians burned down homesteads and killed men, women and children. It was war. People on both sides were hurt and many lost their lives. Nothing we feel will ever change the situation for those who got scalped or burned at the stake. We cannot alter the events that shaped that time in history.

History is a part of our everyday lives. Everyone can look back over their lives and say, *'gosh, wish I'd handled that differently'*. We don't have a time machine so we can't go back and do it over. We can't teach people hundreds of years ago how to behave, not Columbus, the cowboys or the Indians. We ought to pay attention to what went right instead of allowing the Greens to judge the evils of every historical action. The Green assault on our past goes way beyond the Indian wars.

The Greens are attempting to create shame for every part of American history from the cowboys to the bombing of Hiroshima. Rewriting history is the way Greens hope to destroy our national pride. It is a political tactic we can't ignore. Playing up the Indian culture is intended to make a mockery of our past. Hitler created a new Germany by diminishing the value of the old Germany. He rewrote history as if it began with the Nazi movement. The Greens are rewriting history to create a new America. Pitching our past is not necessary if the goal is cleaning up the environment.

White Man's Law

The Greens have also used the American Indian to disrupt the way our society functions. Two Indian boys were found guilty of nearly beating a deliveryman to death. This case received national attention due to a question about how the boys ought to be punished. A tribal leader pleaded with the Judge to allow the punishment to be based on tribal law and tribal traditions instead of 'white man's law'. The tribal leader was granted this request. Instead of going to jail, the tribal punishment was for the boys to be banished to a remote island where they were to survive off the land for 18 months.

Dateline - NBC featured an in-depth follow-up report on this incident. The report revealed the following:

- banishment was never part of that tribes traditions
- restitution promised to the victim has not been paid
- boys put on an island 15 minutes from their homes
- boys were not living off the land
- boy's parents provided them with food and supplies
- tribal leader was not keeping track of boys as promised
- one boy applied for a driver's license during banishment

Most Americans honor keeping their word, some don't. The tribal leader combined the emotional plea of tribal tradition with a guilt-trip about 'white mans law' to con the Judge into agreeing to banishment as an alternative to prison-time. The tribal elder did not honor his word. He lied to the Judge about banishment being a tribal tradition and the boys did not receive the punishment that was agreed to.

No matter how our emotions are twisted, America can't afford to start playing favorites when it comes to enforcing the law. We cannot use a different set of laws and punishments for every sub-culture in America. It would create massive turmoil and increased frustration.

Chief Seattle

The Greens have added to their political power by aligning with many small special interest groups such as the Indians. The political goals of these groups are carefully intertwined into the politics of the environmental cause to create a stronger political force. Many little groups supporting each other equals one large lobby pushing the political goals of the minority groups. For instance, the Greens are using Indian beliefs to promote alternative land use values.

A prime example is a speech by Chief Seattle. Greens recite it on Earth Day, put it on posters and generally praise it as the guiding light of the environmental movement. The words the Greens are praising were created by scriptwriter Ted Perry in 1971. In 1992, the words attributed to Chief Seattle were exposed as forgery. Why do the Greens use it?

> *"How can you buy or sell the sky, the warmth of the land? The idea is strange to us. If we do not own the freshness of the air and the sparkle of the water, how can you buy them? Every part of the earth is sacred to my people."*
> Bold Emphasis Added)

The spoken words are beautiful and anyone who loves and respects nature understands these sentiments. If we put our feelings aside, what is the political motivation? The Chief's message is used by the Greens because it promotes the idea people cannot or should not own the earth. It is important all Americans realize this is a key part of the Greens subversive plan.

The Greens use the Chief's speech to:

- repeat private property ownership is wrong
- suggest private property ownership harms the earth
- infer shared ownership is better for the earth
- send subliminal message: Socialism is better for earth

If we accept 'no one can own the earth', we accept the end of private property ownership. The Chief's speech camouflages promoting socialist land use and a communal lifestyle. The root word of communism is commune. Karl Marx summed up Communism in a single sentence, *"the abolition of private propery"*. Communism is the goal.

Here's where the 'bait and switch' comes in for the Indian tribes. The Greens state they support treaty rights and tribe's rights to own their lands. The Greens operate on 'the end justifies the means' rule.

If Socialism is legalized and Communism follows, the sacred places of the Indian nations will be lost right along with the property rights of every other American.

How can the Greens break their promises? Read the 'Green fine print'. It allows the Greens to change the rules. The Greens reserve the right to change their program at any time so they can change their political position any time.

> *"**The Green Program** spells out in considerable detail the values, policies, and forms of governance that compose a Green alternative to the current order. **It is a living document that remains open to further democratic development and change.**"*
> Green Party Program

Tribal Ways

The Greens are using the Indian lifestyle to create the impression 'living off the land' was good for the earth, the creatures and that it was an easy, romantic journey. The purpose is to get Americans to equate the tribal lifestyle with environmental excellence. The flip side involves using environmental doom to justify our return to a simpler lifestyle. There's nothing wrong with a simpler lifestyle. The question is, who decides how simple we ought to live? It is important to note that recent reports indicate the Indian lifestyle was actually quite hard on the environment.

Animal myths are also part of creating a fantasy feeling. The mythical white wolf is portrayed in movies as the spirit guide that rescues humans lost in the wilderness. The political purpose is to gain public support for:

- the government to create more wilderness areas
- reintroducing wolves into populated rural areas
- building the spiritual belief we are one with animals

The Greens are creating the tribal mentality and using the village concept to advance their agenda in several key areas:

- make the communal lifestyle appear more appealing than our desire for individuality and self-reliance

- prepare Americans to accept responsibility for international environmental ruin so we'll finance Green goals like electricity for the Third World

This brings up a very important distinction between what the Greens say they want to accomplish and what the end result would be if we lose sight of the obvious. The Greens are talking out of both sides of their mouth.

To save the earth, Greens say Americans must:

- drastically reduce our quality of life
- share our wealth with Third World countries
- disconnect our power lines

Wait just a second. To save the earth, Greens say we ought to disconnect our electricity. On the other hand, to save the earth, Greens say we must provide electricity to others. We must provide electricity to the Third World so the people will stop using wood for heating and cooking.

Part of this makes sense. Helping Third World countries stop depleting their wood resources by introducing electricity makes sense. What does not make sense is the Green idea to disconnect our power lines.

If we disconnect our electricity we would create the same situation in America the Greens say we need to correct in the Third World. A keen sense of the obvious suggests this is not a good idea.

Greens hope to dupe us into accepting a major reduction in our quality of life as the only way to save the environment. We aren't expected to notice the Green proposal is a lose-lose situation for America. We share our wealth and lose our electricity.

It's a Green shell-game. The strategy is to keep our focus on 'the crisis-of-the minute' and off the end result. The end result is 'compulsory Green living', rationed lentils and lights out by 10:00 PM.

Mr. Gore's idea of a Global Marshall plan goes way beyond sharing our wealth and technologies with other nations.

"Indeed one of the biggest obstacles to the Global Marshall plan is the requirement that **the advanced economies must undergo a profound transformation themselves.** *....The new plan will require the wealthy nations to allocate money for transferring environmentally helpful technologies to the Third World...however,* **any such effort will also require wealthy nations to make a transition themselves that will be in some ways more wrenching than that of the Third World,** *simply because powerful established patterns will be disrupted."*

Earth in the Balance
Senator Al Gore
(Bold Emphasis Added)

A transition *"more wrenching than that of the Third World"* is expected for advanced economies like ours. If the Third World will face a difficult transition 'up-to' advanced technology, what is a *"more wrenching"* transition for advanced economies? A transition 'down-to' scarcity where *"established patterns will be disrupted"*. Clinton predicted in 1990 that we would be experiencing 'major cultural shifts'.

Anatoliy Golitsyn, an ex-KGB officer who defected to the United States, warned Americans in his 1984 book *New Lies for Old*, that world Communism was still the goal of the Soviets. The epilogue of *New Lies for Old* by Larry Abraham states the communist plan is to merge the United States with the Soviet Union so our resources can continue to support them. Abraham states:

"There is only one way: Increase their standard of living, while drastically reducing ours."

If we continue to allow the Greens to use the environment as the excuse to give the government control of our property, our paycheck, our weapons, our lives and our country, it will be too late to debate the issues. Americans will be in the same position the Jews were in Nazi Germany. We will be at the mercy of those in power.

Like Hitler, the Greens are selling sacrifice, personally going from abundance to scarcity to preserve the species.

> *"The sacrifice of personal existence is necessary to secure the preservation of the species."*
>
> Mein Kampf
> Adolf Hitler

Another note on the tribal lifestyle. People in Third World countries hunt wildlife for food and for pagan rituals. This could reduce wildlife numbers or endanger species.

Americans hunt wildlife but have developed sophisticated alternative food sources so we do not have to rely on hunting wildlife to feed our families. This is one reason our wildlife is abundant. If wildlife protection was the goal, ranchers and hunters ought to be receiving praise instead of condemnation by the Greens. It was the hunters and ranchers who initiated many of the efforts to protect and enhance wildlife habitats.

Think It All the Way Through

Another Green idea to improve our lives and the health of the environment includes the opportunity for city-dwelling Americans to volunteer to be relocated to rural areas to do socially useful work. Although this idea sounds nice, it requires some additional consideration. Remember, the Greens have duplicated Hitler's tactics because they worked.

Hitler called for the relocation of thousands of people out of the cities to work on farms. The Jewish people didn't think relocation to work on farms in the country sounded too bad. The Greens, like Hitler, are also calling for a major reduction in the human population. It would be wise to be wary of relocation programs to move people out of densely populated areas to rural America. When the Nazis needed the Jewish people to cooperate they promised them better conditions at the other end of the trip. The Nazis also used starvation as a way to control large numbers of people and curb resistance.

Control of food production and distribution is also part of the Green agenda. The idea of buying only 'locally grown foods' is the Green way to 'set the wheels in motion'. This may sound like a good idea and it would help local businesses but before accepting it is a good idea, take a trip into the Green future.

How many products do you buy that are not produced locally? The Greens political objectives include:

- limit services to local area
- limit production and distribution to local area
- terminate trucking
- eliminate private automobiles
- shut down most airports
- mandate non-consumptive use of wildlife

What if the Greens achieve these goals? What if the locally grown products were not enough to feed all the people? What if the crops fail? What if there was a natural disaster? People could not fish or hunt for food because consuming wildlife would be illegal. Supplies would quickly run out at the local market and people could not easily hop in the car and drive elsewhere to obtain food. This would leave people at the mercy of those in power.

America's food producers have organized methods of production and distribution that ensure a constant food supply. If floods destroy the California crops, other states can balance out the loss by selling their crops. Endangered species and wetlands issues are just two of the excuses the Greens are using to justify political action and more government controls.

The Greens are working hard to cripple the following food producers.

- Farming
- Beef
- Sheep
- Poultry
- Hunting
- Fishing

From a local perspective it may appear to be insignificant. From a nationwide perspective the result would be a complete departure from the way American food is supplied. How many people in this country depend on the grocery store for the products we put on the dinner table? We take for granted they will always be there, thinking to ourselves:

"This is America, there's no way this could happen."

Never happen? It is happening. The Greens are effectively working toward achieving their goals using environmental issues as the club to sabotage individual producers. Fishermen can't fish, ranchers are losing their grazing permits and farmers are besieged by animal rights activists. Reintroduction of species from wolves to grizzly bears creates more disruption. Biodiversity preservation and Ecosystem management are the key tools the Greens will try and use to disrupt operations and seize control of our land base.

This will continue unless we start asking questions and evaluating each issue. How long will it take for the Greens to get the job done if they continue to go unchallenged?

This is not about protecting the environment and working together to improve the situation. This is about gradual steps to take away individual rights and replace them with government regulations. Make control possible by making control legal. America's ranchers, farmers, fisherman and others involved in food production and distribution feed this nation. We all depend on them doing their part to produce and distribute our food supply. They also produce enough food to share with other nations in time of crisis.

If the Greens are successful in their campaign, what will we eat and where will we get it? The time to ask those questions is now, before the Greens achieve their goals. We ought to protect these businesses as if our life depended on it. Another option is to take the Green's advice that 'becoming a vegetarian is the single most important thing we can do to save the earth'. It would be easier for the Greens to legalize 'compulsory Green living' complete with rationed lentils. Greens know it's cheaper to feed the masses roots and rice.

Hitler destroyed a way of life, a culture right in front of people's eyes, one person, one group, one step at a time. He made control possible by making control legal. We can't let that happen to America. If we continue to accept government control of these people's lives we are beginning to accept control of our lives. Those businesses and industries that have not yet been impacted by the Greens will not be exempt. They are just lower on the priority list. The Greens want it all. They want legal control of this nation and your life.

Political VooDoo

Hitler knew that before people would accept a new set of cultural values the old set of traditional values and patriotic symbols had to be systematically de-valued in their eyes.

This is why religion is a key target for the Greens. The spiritual dimension of the environmental movement can be summed-up in a single word, atheism. Communists are atheist. It's political voodoo. The Greens are weaving myth, magic, goddess, deep ecology and more into environmental themes to grow the movement. The goal is to attract people who believe in these things and entice others to try these things so they feel part of the movement and vote Green.

How are the Greens using religion to advance their goal to create atheists? The Greens are two-faced. At the same time they are promoting atheism they are publicly quoting bible verses to get religious leaders to vote Green. The Greens are de-valuing organized religion because it is the moral foundation of this nation. The Green plan to transform American's spiritual values involves a series of seemingly insignificant steps. Each small step is designed to further dilute our values and beliefs. The following progression shows how the shift toward atheism is to occur:

- Get religious leaders to focus on environmental issues
- Get Americans to accept nature as part of worship
- Increase religious focus on creation instead of creator
- Use fear of extinction to shift emphasis to
- Use political issues to cement belief nature comes first
- Establish acceptance of Creation First, Creator Second
- Focus changed, door has been opened to atheism

Communists are atheists. Communism is a form of faith to Communists.

"We say the name of God, but that is only habit. We are atheists."

Nikita Krushchev

Religion is the Green's enemy. Communists believe religion is the opiate of the people and must be destroyed. The Greens are infiltrating religious ranks to use religious leaders, reach their networks and sway voters.

Hitler invented an earth-based, spiritual-political movement and used those elements to change the values of a nation. The Greens are using these same ideas to convert the values of this nation. The Greens have almost changed our decision-making process from logical and traditional value-based to a pseudo-religious, emotional, earth-based process. Spiritual environmentalism is designed to blur the lines until we can't see straight.

The environmental cause is being used as a recruiting tool to entice Americans away from traditional moral principles and into believing in Green spiritual principles to:

- weaken America's moral fiber
- increase acceptance for Green politics
- promote socialist policies
- lessen resistance to Communism

The Greens are accusing Americans of not caring about the environment to challenge us to prove how much we care. We can prove we care by blindly accepting Green values and political recommendations. The more Americans that fall for the spiritual side of Green politics the easier it will be to sell Socialism as the other half of the environmental solution.

Green religion incorporates various belief systems all rolled into a form of new values and environmentally-correct ideas. Spiritual Ecology and Eco-Psychology are good examples of how Americans are again being set-up to accept 'compulsory Green living'. The January 1, 1995 edition of *Parade* magazine featured a plug for Eco-psychology with this quote from *Self* magazine:

> *"Feeling depressed about the planet? Perhaps you need a couch session with an eco-therapist. Eco-psychology, a new trend in psychotherapy, helps people deal with their anxieties about problems like endangered species and deforestation. What's the best therapy? According to one eco-shrink, daily walks in the woods and establishing a relationship with a tree."*

Hugging a tree will not help solve environmental problems or reduce anxiety about deforestation or endangered species. Doing something positive for the environment would be better therapy than suggesting people do something useless like finding a tree to hug.

Suggesting a person help clean-up a beach or riverbank would help a person feel there was hope and they had some measure of control. They could see a positive result from their efforts and learn to think of positive ways to help the environment. That would be a feel-good and healthy prescription. They would learn to feel helpful instead of helpless.

Advising someone who is worried about deforestation to go find a tree to be friends with only magnifies their problem. Being friends with a tree suggests trees have human qualities, like the tree in *Pocahontas*. The person who was once worried about deforestation, now has the added problem of thinking the way to deal with it, is to have a meaningful relationship with a tree. This advice would increase a person's anxiety about deforestation because it increases the focus on trees and puts trees on a personal, human level.

This eco-advice could lead to complications. It could lead to an eco-obsession. What happens if the tree dies or is struck by lighting? The patient would feel like a close friend had died. This would cause more emotional unrest.

Professional therapists would see this pitfall. They would find productive ways to address environmental concerns and avoid recommendations that could backfire. Giving depressed people the impression, hugging trees will help them feel better or lessen their concern about deforestation is not healthy.

Vulnerable People Are Easy Prey

There is a substantial difference between having a healthy respect for the magnificence of trees and unhealthy, borderline insanity. Vulnerable people are easy prey. The Greens have multiple reasons to introduce eco-therapy. One reason is it encourages Americans to equate tree hugging with environmental health.

This is not to suggest that all psychologists or eco-therapists are Green. This advice was given by one eco-therapist. This is to show the Greens political motivation behind eco-therapy. It is a catalyst to spur emotional, earth-based decision-making. This is like the story of *The Emperor's New Clothes*. The king ran around half-naked because he did not trust his instincts and believed the lie he was told. The Greens would like us to run around like idiots but most Americans will see through the hoax. Remember, mandatory tree hugging on Sunday is part of 'compulsory Green living'. Again we are set-up to try Green Communism. Eco-therapy helps the Greens:

- promote nature as our mother, a human being
- condone fanatical behavior as a normal part of life
- infer nature worship can save the earth
- convince normal people to do abnormal things
- create and recruit fanatics

The Greens are using Hitler's approach to mental health. Hitler got the masses to abandon traditional values by:

- reconnecting to the sacred soil of the Motherland
- feeling a religious dedication to the Nazi cause
- equating being a Nazi with saving the Fatherland

Greens infer we don't care about nature so we'll feel bad and try their suggestions about how to remedy the situation.

The Greens are programming Americans to think we must:

- reconnect with nature, our lives are 'interconnected'
- have a religious devotion to Green politics
- equate being Green with saving Mother Earth

Hitler also used trees to cement a commitment to the Nazi cause. He sent children out to pick the bugs off of trees. The Greens send adults and children out to hug trees. Same stuff, different decade. Hitler also convinced normal people to do abnormal things. We can avoid repeating the German's mistakes by not falling for the same emotional traps.

Spiritual Ecology and the 'Council of All Beings'

The 'council of all beings' ritual is an emotional trap. This ritual is discussed in Carolyn Merchant's book *Radical Ecology*. Following is this writer's interpretation of Merchant's explanation.

According to Merchant, Spiritual Ecology was invented by Joanna Macy and John Seed. It is not something that has been passed down for generations. It involves a spiritual ritual where the beings of the 'Three Times' are summoned by participants. These are beings that, it is believed, have helped the earth, are helping and will help the earth in the future.

This ritual is referred to as the 'council of all beings'. The basic idea is that all beings are given a voice and an opportunity to share their concerns about environmental issues and how it is affecting them. Humans form a circle and wear masks to represent nature or specific beings. They can be a fox, a river, a tree or any other element of nature. Next participants take turns role-playing beings and listening as humans.

The 'council of all beings' ends with humans requesting help from all beings. Each being responds, removes their mask and becomes human again by entering the circle where all the humans bond together and then disperse for merry-making. This ritual is to raise our consciousness about other beings feelings on environmental issues. Accepting toads and trees as equal beings is part of the message.

Earth Day parades give the Greens the opportunity to spread this concept by using little children to wear the mask of one creature or another and convey the message they are equal to animals. Big Green people also dance around dressed as trees, animals or fish to display the 'all beings' idea. Special emphasis is placed on certain species depending on the political value. More fish people appear if the Greens are pushing the salmon issue. If we put this in perspective, it's not hard to see it is a political tool. The Greens are working to change how our children see themselves and their place on this earth.

Religious Leaders See Green

June 16, 1991, The *San Francisco Examiner* featured a report by Richard Powelson titled "Religious leaders see green, Agree to take up environmentalism." Powelson reports:

> *"Sens. Albert Gore D-Tenn., and Tim Wirth, D-Colo., active environmentalists in Congress, helped organize meetings with religious leaders June 2-3. Paul Gorman, executive director of The Joint Appeal in Religion and Science in New York, the name of the coalition of religious leaders, said the leaders now will get more involved in Congressional action, such as seeking to testify at hearings on environmental action. "They won't be talking about fuel efficiency standards or how much global warming there is," Gorman said."*

If religious leaders are involved in Congressional action on the environment they must discuss issues like global warming. Religious leaders are being used by the Greens to lend their good will, influence and support to Green politics. Church leaders and others ought to start making distinctions between religion, Green politics and environmental protection. They are different issues.

Greens are using religion to destroy religion because America's religious values are the fundamental link to America's strength. The Greens have merged Hitler's ideas into their campaign to bring about a complete social transformation. These ideas include:

- new age, new order
- occult, myth, goddess
- sexual deviance
- land reform
- earth-based values
- earth is seen as living being

We need to recognize the combination of politics, earthly spirituality and visions of a new age are the same psychological traps Hitler utilized. Hitler was insane but people fell for his ideas. They thought transforming society would equal a better life. Curiosity killed that cat.

Many Germans rushed to become Nazis without thinking. Many Americans are rushing to be Green. Some have jumped off the deep end into Nazi-like environmental fanaticism. Just because they've gone Green, doesn't mean they have to stay Green. The Greens have promoted the environmental cause as the politically correct thing to do. It was politically correct to become a Nazi. Think it through.

Hitler grounded the Nazi movement in a quasi-religion. He convinced people to abandon their moral and religious beliefs and to put their faith in the Nazi cause. The Hitler Youth denounced their faith in God when they pledged allegiance to Hitler. Hitler lured people from all levels of society to join the Nazi movement. The Greens are on the same wavelength.

Many involved in the environmental movement are promoting the idea that a 'religious transformation' and not science is the best way to save the earth.

> *"To look for a technological solution to the ecological crisis would be a lethal mistake. Scientific analysis points, curiously, toward the need for a quasi-religious transformation of contemporary cultures."*
>
> *1993 Earth Journal*
> Paul Ehrlich

Paul Ehrlich has been very involved in the environmental cause for years. He is best known for his predictions on the population crisis. Many of his predictions are reported to be wrong.

The Greens are working to eliminate religious values and transform our culture from many angles. Look at what has been popularized in America: psychic readings, numerology, goddess mythology, occult, deep ecology, witches, tree hugging, reincarnation and a tremendous focus on Indian myths. These are to tempt Americans to change our values. How does this relate to communist values?

The August 7, 1995 edition of *U.S. News & World Report* featured an article titled "Yeltsin's Eyes and Ears". According to the article Russia's top officials receive *"horoscopes and advice on the occult"* and a psychic *"corrects his karma"*.

'Greening Religion' also helps the Greens establish trust on the home front so parents will allow their children to participate in environmental events without asking questions. For instance, children are learning drumming in school. This is intended to be a spiritual experience to introduce children to an alternate belief system.

The Greens are quoting from the bible to convince church leaders to include environmental messages in their sermons. Protecting the environment does not need to include social transformation, earthly spirituality or any other form of Green political voodoo. America's religious leaders need to understand the Greens are advocating:

- organized religion is an out dated addiction
- adherence to dogmatic beliefs is religious escapism
- blame Judeo-Christian religion for environmental ruin
- ideas about God must be shattered and erased
- a new religious paradigm and a new faith is needed

> *"Once the ruling power is in our grasp, we must seize the evil in Germany by the root and tear it out, **to make way for the new faith, for the new religion."***
>
> Memoirs of a Confidant
> Adolf Hitler
> (Bold Emphasis Added)

The Greens are also calling for a new faith and a new religion. Deep Ecology is a key part of the Green spirituality and political ideas. Many Green groups, including Earth First! support Deep Ecology ideas.

The March 1991 issue of the *Earth First! Journal* featured a chart called the "Eco Depth Gauge". Readers were instructed to read through each definition until they reached the one they did not agree with. The definition just above that one revealed their level of commitment to environmental protection. Deep ecology means different things to different people. Here is the Earth First! "Eco-Depth Gauge". Where do you fit?

Superficial	We should take good care of our planet, as we would any valuable tool.
Shallow	We have a responsibility to protect the Earth's resources for our future generations.
Deep	Wilderness has a right to exist for its own sake.
Deeper	Wildlife has more right to live on Earth than humans do.
Profoundly Deep	Humans are too great a threat to life on Earth.
Radically Deep	Human extinction now or there won't be any later for this planet. A painless extermination is needed.
Abysmally Deep	A quick annihilation is too good for humans. A horrible, fatal illness from outer space is only fair.

It is important to understand the Deep and Deeper levels are evident in Green politics and spiritual ideas. Deep ecologists believe the only reason to use any part of nature is to meet a basic need and a major reduction in human population is required if human life and non-human life are to continue to co-exist.

> *"If I were reincarnated I would wish to be returned to Earth as a killer virus to lower human population levels."*
> Prince Philip of Great Britain
> Leader, World Wildlife Fund
> *From the Trenches, 1994*

Earth Day is a Holy Day for the Greens

Earth Day is the day Greens honor their spiritual connection to Mother Earth. Earth First! publishes its journal on pagan nature holidays. Another group that organizes Earth Day events year round calls itself Sun Day. Since many Americans associate Sunday as the day of worshipping the creator, the name Sun Day connects these earth activities to a religious day but shifts the emphasis to creation. In September 1989, the Unitarian Church placed an ad with the heading "Eco Spirituality, A Class of Readings, Discussions and Rituals". The church offered these topics for discussion and rituals:

- Creation Spirituality
- Deep Ecology
- Gaia, a Living Being
- The Greens and Bioregionalism
- Native Religions
- Animal Rights
- Ritual and Action

The Greens are using this religious variety to glamorize Creation Spirituality, atheism and to gain political support.

> *"Spiritual ecology, in contrast to utilitarian ecology, pays homage to the awe of nature and the wonder of creation."*
> *Biosphere Politics*
> Jeremy Rifkin

Synonyms for utilitarian are: practical, functional and workable. In other words, practical and functional utilitarian environmental policies are different than spiritual ecology. The principle focus of spiritual ecology is to pay tribute, honor and even worship creation. Rifkin's distinction between utilitarian and spiritual ecology fits with the Greens *goal* to base environmental policies on spiritual values not on what is practical or workable. This gives the Greens more ways to justify policies and laws that do not have to make sense. It makes control possible by making control legal.

> *"The task of saving the earth's environment must and will become the central organizing principle of the post-Cold War world."*
>
> Putting People First
> Senator Al Gore

Other political leaders have demanded for society to be transformed and organized around a new set of ideas.

> *"Our ideology is intolerant ... and peremptorily demands the complete transformation of public life to its ideas"*
>
> Psychopathic God
> Adolf Hitler

The Vice President demands saving the environment must become our 'central organizing principle'. There is no question we must protect the environment. The question is, on what principles will our environmental policy decisions be based? Will the decisions be based on functional, workable utilitarian principles or based on the Green principles?

> *"Indeed, it may now be necessary to foster a new environmentalism of the spirit."*
>
> Earth in the Balance
> Senator Al Gore

Freedom of Religion is not the issue. The issue is, Green spiritual principles are influencing our political leaders ability to render fair judgment about environmental policies. Consider our land use policies (public and private), our economy and our population policies. Biodiversity and ecosystem management play major roles in these issue areas. The Biodiversity Treaty signed by President Clinton in 1993 has the support of many of our political leaders. What is biodiversity? Biodiversity means valuing all organisms on every part of the earth except for humans. Human activity is blamed for the loss of biodiversity. One solution to preventing the loss of ecosystems and biodiversity is to create large wilderness areas where human activity is limited or forbidden. Our government is expected to dramatically increase the number of protected areas to preserve biodiversity. Why does this affect every American? Biodiversity and ecosystem management are terms designed to be 'all encompassing' and vague. Just like the Green's 10 key values, these two terms can be twisted to justify taking nearly any action in the name of environmental protection.

EnviroScan is published by Public Relations Management Ltd. of Ontario, Canada and reports on business and environmental issues. The September, 1994 issue used this quote to explain the meaning of biodiversity to readers:

> *"...the point of radical environmentalists protests and actions is the preservation of biological diversity. A term from the science of ecology,* **the biological diversity of a place is, in a nutshell, its resemblance to what it looked like before people interfered with it...** *Biodiversity might be more properly called ecological diversity, because, as radical environmentalists use the term,* **it refers to not only plants and animals but to mountains, rivers, oceans as well - the non living and living aspects of an ecosystem...Human interference tends to lessen this biodiversity."**
>
> Rik Scarce
> Eco-Warriors
> (Bold Emphasis Added)

EnviroScan emphasized the meaning of biodiversity, stating:

> *"Clearly,* **the preservation, maintenance and enhancement of biodiversity** *(biological diversity) - as encouraged by radical environmentalists -* **means returning the environment to its condition before any human involvement or impact. Biodiversity demands the elimination of human participation in the environment."**

What are our political leaders doing about biodiversity and population issues? Who supports these Green political ideas?

> *"Ultimately there isn't a chance of persuading people, civilizations and countries to take biodiversity seriously **unless they first understand, from the depths of the human spirit, the need to relate to Creation, to be sensitive to the realities of suffering and mistreatment, and to have a larger holistic spiritual view of what Creation is about.**"*
>
> Bruce Babbitt
> Secretary of the Interior
> *From the Trenches - 1994*
> (Bold Emphasis Added)

Our immediate problem is Green spiritual ideas are affecting America's public policy because they are affecting America's policy makers. We have a major problem.

> *"To some, **the global environmental crisis is primarily a crisis of values.** In this view, the basic cause of the problem is that we as a civilization base our decisions about how to relate to the environment on premises that are fundamentally unethical."*
>
> *Earth in the Balance*
> Senator Al Gore
> (Bold Emphasis Added)

Before moving forward, we need to decide what values we are basing our decisions on. Are they Green Communist principles or the principles in our Constitution?

> *"Socialism corrects the basic flaw of Capitalism. It sets human society on a new path. The means of production, factories, mines and mills become the property of the people. They operate and produce only to fulfill human needs. They are not motivated by profits. **This is the foundation for a new set of priorities, for new values...What is involved is a conflict of values.**"*
>
> *Ecology - 1972*
> Gus Hall
> (Bold Emphasis Added)

As If By Magic

Magical Blend magazine appears to be based on the conviction our society is going to experience a major social transformation. The purpose of the magazine is to prepare people to deal with this transformation by helping them reach a higher level of spiritual awareness.

The April 1994 edition of *Magical Blend* featured an article by Vice President Gore regarding the relationship between the people and the planet. The Vice President shares his ideas that we are global citizens, that we must reconnect with nature and that we need *new* leadership.

The Clinton-Gore ticket gave America new leadership. What new leadership is the Vice President talking about? The Vice President also indicates in his article that readers ought to help force political change by lobbying representatives. He suggests America needs:

- new attitudes
- a new model
- new stories to pass on to our children.

Vice President Gore points out our political leaders can't do this alone and suggests to readers that they begin pushing for change. Gore indicates the push ought to come from the bottom-up, from the grassroots. He advises readers that politicians can help but support shouldn't be coming from the top-down. Support for new leadership is not coming from the bottom-up if the Vice President is generating it from the top-down.

Magical Blend magazine comes complete with ads for celtic pentagrams, witchcraft, voodoo, soul retrieval, pagan rituals and other adventures in magic. *Magical Blend* is a curious place to find an article by the Vice President of the United

States. It is a unique audience from which to seek political support for change, a new faith and new leadership.

> *"Regardless of how high the cultural importance of a people maybe, the struggle for daily bread stands at the forefront of all vital necessities...**To be sure, brilliant leaders can hold great goals before a people's eyes, so that it can be further diverted from material things in order to serve higher spiritual goals...**The more primitive the spiritual life of man, the more animal-like he becomes until finally he regards food intake as the one and only aim of life."*
>
> *Hitler's Secret Book*
> Adolf Hitler
> Bold Emphasis Added)

Deep Ecology mirrors Hitler's ideas of spiritual manipulation. The Green value to take nothing more than you need is the invitation to divert people's attention from material things, encourage a survival mentality and scarce existence in the name of serving higher spiritual goals.

> *"We want you to join this common effort to unite our country behind a higher calling."*
>
> *Putting People First*
> Senator Al Gore

When political leaders ask us to change our values and answer a higher calling, we ought to think twice.

The Green Bible

A quotation from Vice President Gore appears in the *Green Bible,* right along with religious leaders, deep ecologists and Green activists. This is a free country. It is not a crime to be included in the Green Bible. It only indicates, those who compiled the series of quotations believe the Vice President's thoughts compliment Green spirituality.

The Vice President has written forewords to books that discuss and seem to support ideas like Deep Ecology. One book titled, *Climate in Crisis* includes this statement by then Senator Gore.

> *"The solutions we seek will be found in a new faith in the future of life on Earth after our own, a faith in the future that justifies sacrifices in the present, a new moral courage to chose higher values in the conduct of human affairs, and a new reverence for absolute principles that can serve as stars by which to map the future course of our species and our place within creation."*
>
> (Bold Emphasis Added)

What are these higher values and absolute principles? Are they rules, laws or religious values? Are these the central organizing principles? These are some of the questions Americans must answer before changing our values, answering a higher calling or trying a new faith.

The author of *Climate in Crisis,* Albert Bates suggests solutions to environmental problems require a worldwide reorganization of the way we live and relate to nature. Bates indicates saving the earth will require Americans to reconsider these values:

- individual rights
- creation of wealth
- private property rights
- reproductive rights
- patriotism

Bates declares a new paradigm is needed to solve our environmental problems. Don't forget Senator Al Gore wrote the forward to this book that does suggest he generally agrees with the message.

Bates ideas for the new paradigm include:

- elimination of individuality
- eliminate acquiring wealth (Capitalism)
- receiving uniform income
- sharing wealth equally
- equalizing worldwide standard of living
- adopting an ecological world view

The reason for this massive social transformation is to protect the environment. What Bates calls for seems to be the end of Capitalism and the establishment of world Communism. Believing we all share this earth and must lend a helping hand to those in need has long been an American tradition. Americans volunteer to share their wealth and talents with others. The key to our success and generosity is freedom.

There is no question that we can always improve the way we operate. We can consume less and alter behaviors to correct environmental problems. What Bates describes sounds like 'compulsory Green living'. Why will world Communism solve the ecological challenges we face?

Then Vice President Gore recommended a new publication called: *Macrocosm USA, An Environmental Political and Social Solutions Handbook with Directories.* Before the Vice President would recommend a book, certain steps would usually occur. The office of the Vice President would first review the publication to determine if it was something Mr. Gore would want his name associated with. After initial scrutiny, it would be passed on to Mr. Gore for his approval or disapproval.

We would expect the Vice President to review the contents before providing a personal endorsement. At the very least, prior to printing, approval of the page on which the Vice President's quotation was to appear would surely require checking spelling and placement.

"There are many crucial challenges that await us in the next few years...I need your help now as we work to build a better future for all Americans. I appreciate your expression of support and generosity. Thank You for Macrocosm USA."

Vice President Al Gore

Praise for this publication indicates the Vice President agrees with the book purpose to promote social change and other progressive ideas. We can always use innovative ideas. The question of endorsement concerns where the Vice President's quote is located and what is also featured on the insert highlighting the contents of the book. An article by the radical, environmental, terrorist group, Earth First! and the Green Party is listed on the insert. Other controversial groups such as Eco-Socialist, Democratic Socialist, and the Communist Party of the United States are listed in the book. The book offers a mixed bag of controversial and mainstream groups.

It is not a crime to promote change in a free country. It is not illegal for the Vice President to lend his name to a book. What we need to ask ourselves is, if it's appropriate for the Vice President to endorse a book that identifies Earth First! as a selling point? The administration indicates it condemns terrorism. So why is the Vice President endorsing a book that promotes a famous terrorist group? This endorsement communicates to readers that the politics and actions of Earth First! are acceptable to the Vice President. It's hard to imagine anyone involved in environment issues would not know about the sabotage and terrorist activities encouraged by Earth First!

The book is an alternative resource guide for progressive political opinions. The authors want to revolutionize politics and cultivate social change by promoting ideas for the social transformation of America. Listed on the insert along with the Vice President's quotation are Green ideas such as Bioregionalism, co-housing, economic conversion, vegetarianism and land trust. The Green Party is only briefly discussed in the book. One article indicates this is because it's still too soon to bring up Green politics in America.

Synonyms for *Macrocosm* are universe, cosmos, earth, world and creation. One article on religion indicates:

- that existing religions are old fashioned
- that due to global changes, existing religions will die out
- this will occur for a new vision of God to reign

What every American needs to realize is that Green spirituality is not really about an earthly religion. The Green faith is Communism. Greens are doing everything they can, in any way they can, to destroy our way of life, our economy and our strength as a nation. America is under siege. It's time our political leaders do what they were elected to do, protect and serve the American people based on our constitution and our principles.

> *"If we are to give the leadership the world requires of us, we must rededicate ourselves to the great principles of our Constitution...our nation needs the services of organizations who will remain vigilant in the defense of our principles."*
>
> President John F. Kennedy
> (Bold Emphasis Added)

6

Sold Out

Are Americans being mentally prepared to accept drone status? Recently PBS aired a program called *Human Quest*. The message seemed to be since people in different cultures smile when they're happy and shed tears when they're sad, that means people around the world are the same. The idea is that if we re-educate ourselves to think differently, we can all live as one people because we all fit the same mold. One speaker suggested we could go to *'re-training camps'* and learn to think properly.

The Green slogan 'One people, One planet' defines the message of this program. The other idea that 'we can learn to think differently' has been fine-tuned by the Communists. It's called brainwashing. People who did not agree with Lenin or Stalin were sent to slave labor camps to complete a *'re-education'* process. If they were lucky, they came back from Siberia, politically correct.

This is not to suggest the *Human Quest* program or its speakers are Communist. It is to understand the reason for the message 'we are all the same'. That level of thinking diminishes the value of individuality. Independent thinking is not part of the communist program. If we accept there is nothing special about being an American we've been re-trained to think properly. The purpose is to promote group-think.

Another step toward group-think involves a distinct sector of our society, gardeners and farmers. The Greens singled them out because they can manipulate their love of the soil into Green votes. Hitler took advantage of the same sector.

> *"Hitler found the farmers some of his strongest supporters. He singled them out as guardians of the holy soil."*
> A Child of Hitler
> Alfons Heck

The guardians lost sight of reality. Greens are using the 'sacred soil' part of Hitler's message to create a 'whatever it takes' mentality to save Mother Earth. This is the same mentality the 'guardians of the holy soil' took on. There is real potential for a repeat performance. The Greens have put soil on a 'holy' level again. Green terms like biodiversity and ecosystem are so vague they can be twisted to justify taking nearly any action in the name of saving the earth.

> *"Biodiversity... as radical environmentalists use the term, refers to plants, animals, mountains, rivers, oceans, non-living and living aspects of an ecosystem... Human interference tends to lessen this biodiversity."*
> Eco-Warriors
> Rik Scarce

Guilty Man Flees When No One Pursues

When people have something to hide, many times, they accidentally draw attention to it. Criminals often volunteer information they could not know unless they participated in the crime. This is the general idea of the 'guilty man flees when no one pursues' theory. Guilty people often give themselves away by accidentally pointing out what they didn't want anyone to know.

Recently, Earth Works Press published, *It's a Conspiracy, The National Insecurity Council*. It's a subject way outside the realm of their usual environmental publications. The book looks at different conspiracy theories. Considering their focus is the environment, it is extremely unusual they would spend time and money worrying about conspiracy theories. There is a logical explanation. The book suggests conspiracy theories are silly and Americans are just insecure. Conspiracy theories have nothing to do with the environment, so why are the Greens drawing attention to the subject? The Greens are trying to counter 'being exposed for conspiring to use environmental issues to overthrow our government' by setting us to dismiss the possibility. Guilty man flees when no one pursues?

Apply the 'guilty man flees' theory to the following statements made by a well known environmental activist. Gaylord Nelson, the founder of Earth Day recently gave a talk about Earth Day and the environmental movement. He brought up an odd point, then discussed it at length. It was the idea, some Americans had twenty years ago, that April 22nd was chosen for Earth Day because it was Lenin's birthday. Nelson got the audience laughing and joked away any connection. After twenty years, why is this an issue? Earth Day has the national spotlight on April 22nd. Most Americans don't know it's also Lenin's birthday. If Lenin's birthday is not an issue, why bring it up? Guilty man flees when no one pursues? Nelson's advice to the audience included this thought.

> *"Think Green, and then you will do what's right."*
> Gaylord Nelson
> March 1995

There is another interesting point about Communism and Lenin's birthday. To rekindle the Russian spirit and commitment to Communism, Krushchev, in 1955 ordered April 22nd to become the day to remember Lenin. This act changed the focus from the day Lenin died to the day he was born. This gave Leninists the chance to celebrate Communism instead of mourning the death of Lenin. April 22nd is the day Communists celebrate Communism. Now, it's the day the Greens celebrate Earth Day!

Do guilty women flee when no one pursues?

> *"Now that the Cold War is over it appears that some Americans are searching for a new scapegoat to blame for the current chaos in the country. Environmentalists have quickly become the new target for the right. Although it is dispiriting to be assailed as the destroyer of the American way of life, the backlash is not necessarily a reason to despair."*
>
> > *Voting Green – 1992*
> > Carol Grunewald Rifkin

The American people have shown overwhelming support for the environmental cause. What does the Cold War and chaos in our country have to do with environmentalists destroying the American way of life? Guilty woman flees when no one pursues?

Senator Al Gore points out in his book, *Earth in the Balance*, Americans are:

> *"hostile to the messengers who warn us that we have to change, suspecting them of subversive intent and accusing them of harboring some hidden agenda, Marxism, or statism, or anarchism. ("Killing the messenger," in fact, is a well-established form of denial.)*

Subversive intent? Marxism? A hidden agenda? Killing the messenger? What does Marxism or statism have to do with the goal to clean up the environment? Guilty man flees when no one pursues?

Having different opinions is what a free society is all about. A republic/democracy is not intended to be a one way or none operation. The Greens are setting Americans up to feel sorry for them to keep our attention off critical political issues. The Greens are planting the idea they are being treated unfairly to discredit in advance, those Americans who question Green political ideas. Why do questions about Green solutions to environmental issues pose such a threat to those whose professed goal is environmental protection? If Americans are asking questions about environmental issues and suggesting options, it ought to be considered positive. Asking questions means people care and want to help make good decisions.

Democratic problem solving involves a 'give and take' attitude toward finding solutions to complex problems. That is how win-win agreements are reached. Give and take does not mean consensus. Consensus is a Green Communist word created to re-train us to accept group-think by eliminating our majority rule process. Consensus means manipulating people to do it the Green way or none. If environmental excellence were the goal, discussion would be welcome. There is a difference between welcoming different opinions and pretending to welcome different opinions.

The Greens also use the anti-environmentalist label to eliminate discussion. *Greenpeace* even put out a book called, *The Greenpeace Guide to Anti-environmental Organizations*. The Green thought-police are trying to make it a crime to question the Greens. This suggests the Greens believe they alone have all the right answers. This fits Porritt's vision of Green dictators. The Greens have one solution for all environmental problems, the complete social transformation of America. Shouldn't we get a second opinion? The environmental community, like any other group of professionals must be accountable for what they advocate. There is a huge discrepancy between the Green practice of demanding accountability of others and the Green practice of not being accountable to others.

The Greens have an intolerant approach toward problem solving. The Green position of 'No Compromise' clearly illustrates their position. Communists operate on the, my way or none, approach to politics and power. The Greens manipulate themselves out of accountability using poor-me tactics and shifting the burden of proof to those who question them. Are the Greens infallible? Professionals, from surgeons to insurance adjusters, recommend second opinions. There is a vast resource of intelligence and ingenuity in America. Why should we trust our lives and our future to the opinion of an intolerant minority? That is a dictatorship. It's Green Communism.

> *"John Wayne. One of two great symbols of American machismo and proponents of a belligerent national posture, especially toward communist states, was actor John Wayne; the other is Ronald Reagan."*
>
> *Earth – 1987*
> Anne H. Ehrlich, Paul R. Ehrlich

Why are environmental activists pointing out John Wayne and Ronald Reagan were belligerent towards communist nations? Communist leaders have a history of committing unconscionable acts of abuse and have murdered thousands of innocent people. Communism is a threat to our nation. This kind of Green statement stands-out as 'guilty man flees when no one pursues'. Perhaps those who do not think we ought to resist Communism think we ought to submit to Communism.

Criticizing John Wayne and Ronald Reagan is also another attempt to discredit our past.

Destroying America's Heroes

John Wayne is an American legend, a hero and a patriot who loved his country. On screen he often played a cowboy who fought the Indians to help tame the west. Mr. Wayne drew the line between right and wrong. He could be pushed just so far, and then he stood up to the liars, manipulators and the rest of the bad guys. His characters reflected what being an American meant, an independent, honest person who had the courage to stand up for what was right.

> *"He gave the whole world the image of what an American should be."*
>
> Elizabeth Taylor
> *Duke, We're Glad We Knew You*
> *Reader's Digest, October 1979*

These attitudes and national pride are heartfelt and characteristic of the American people. These values are an intricate part of our nature and our culture.

> *"There's right and there's wrong. You gotta do one or the other. You do the one and you're living. You do the other, you may be walking around but in reality you're dead."*
>
> John Wayne - The Alamo
> *Duke, We're Glad We Knew You*

The Greens intend to destroy our character by making us weak and clouding our judgment of right and wrong and re-train us to forget who we are. We need to remember what we stand for.

Bad Guys Do What Bad Guys Do

Despite the Green idea that Americans are lame to be concerned about Communism, the emergence of Russia's Vladimir Zhirinovsky ought to have thinking people thinking. He is radical, mean and politically dangerous.

"I say quite plainly, when I come to power, there will be a dictatorship. I may have to shoot 100,000 people, but the other 300 million will live peacefully"

Vladimir Zhirinovsky
July, 1994

There is a difference between cultures. Many people around the world have kind hearts, others do not. The Olympics prove people from different cultures can get along with each other. Believing Mr. Zhirinovsky thinks like we do is a mistake. Zhirinovsky probably isn't kidding about slaughtering 100,000 people.

The Greens profess we are all one people. It's a nice idea, but it's simply not true. Every culture is unique. Different cultures grow different attitudes. Every nation has good guys and bad guys. Bad guys do what bad guys do.

The explorers who discovered the cannibals and the headhunters can serve as a reminder to the rest of us. The explorers may not have anticipated the particular habits of those tribes when they first met. After initial encounters, they understood. Those people had a different set of values.

International Cooperation or International Domination?

The Green movement is not about cooperation. It's not about science. It's not about the environment. It is about Communist control of America and the world. Look at the environmental conditions in other parts of the world. Their resources are in bad shape because they have not been cared for. In contrast, Americans have developed our resources. If we had not used our intelligence to do so, who would help the less fortunate? Who would bail out the starving Russians?

We need to make some changes and correct environmental errors but that does not require the complete transformation of our society.

For years, volunteers have joined the Peace Corps and helped developing countries learn how to manage their resources so they can help themselves. Citizens of the United States already share our wealth, information, food, people and financial resources. Many American volunteers have been repaid for their kindness with hostile acts of brutality, like beatings, rape and murder.

There is a difference between international cooperation, which we already do, and international domination. Maybe we can do more to work with other nations but we can't help the world if we can't help ourselves. Choice is the determining factor. Freedom and independence are the only reasons America is not in the same environmental condition as other countries, including Russia.

We have been free to use our brains and our backbones to stand up for, care for and build our resource base. Capitalism and the desire to make the world a better place is the reason. During the process of developing our resources, mistakes have been made. Americans want a healthy environment. The goal of creating a healthy environment should not require submitting to a communist world government.

Self-fulfilling prophecy is when people believe what they are told, even if it is not true. If good students are treated as if they are stupid, grades usually go down. The opposite is also true. If poor students are told they are intelligent, grades usually improve. We don't have to fulfill the Greens prophecy and accept world government because they say we must. We can make up our own minds. Some futurists suggest Americans will accept subordination to Japan, Europe or the Greens gracefully. This forecast is due to both our foreign policies and internal conflicts that are weakening our nation. The same futurists suggest America can avoid domination if we change our focus from external affairs to internal affairs.

That sounds like awfully good advice. We need to make the future of our country our first priority. We ought to be able to focus on America and correct our internal affairs without hurting the rest of the world. This would not mean America would ignore world affairs. It means we would cooperate with other nations without being controlled by other nations.

A healthy nation is like a healthy family. If the family is the last priority, it will break down. A family can't base their future on what is best for the neighbors. They don't have to ignore or fight with the neighbors to make sure their family is healthy. A nation is no different. We must focus our attention on internal affairs if we intend to get America healthy and keep America healthy.

Our Greatest Enemy

We do not have to continue to be pushed down this Green path to hell. We can work together and support each other like we have in the past. We can regain control of our lives and help get this nation back on track. Our greatest enemy is ourselves. Americans are famous for practicing a live-and-let-live attitude.

We need to realize we are dealing with a radical and intolerant political ideology that is pushing tolerant people to the limit. We cannot continue to allow the politics of special interest groups to shape America's destiny. We've got to take a stand and take responsibility for our future and the future of our country.

Basic Ingredients Of A Revolution

Revolutions stem from a conflict of values. Principles and values are what guide the people and the governments of nations. If a group decides to change the values of a nation, it is because their values conflict with the existing principles, ethics and morals that guide that nation. If this group is allowed to impose their values on that nation, revolution has occurred. Then new values and principles will guide that nation. The wisdom of John F. Kennedy is worth repeating to illustrate how important our principles are to this nation.

> *"We must rededicate ourselves to the great principles of our Constitution...our nation needs the services of organizations who will remain vigilant in the defense of our principles."*
> President John F. Kennedy

When one group decides to impose their principles and values on a nation, the group:

- devises plans to overthrow government
- develops ways to build public support for new ideas
- uses that support as political clout to seize power

'Subvert the Dominant Paradigm' is the Greens revolutionary call to overthrow our governing model. Greens intend to impose their political ideas on this nation. If the American people do not stop them, Green principles and values will become our guide as to how our government and society function.

You Decide

The following represents a summary of the strategic aims of the CPUSA, set at their national convention in 1969, in contrast are the political aims of the Green movement.

U.S. Communist Party Objectives and Strategies.

Mission: Seize permanent power over the American economy and government system. The communist plan of attack included these ideas.

- Build alternate political party, rival two party system
- Build or infiltrate a cause the American masses support
- Reform Capitalism and society, use minority issues
- Build alliances with radical, anti-establishment groups

1995 Green Movement, Green Party Political Profile

- Greens are a radical alternative third party
- Green environmental cause has America's support
- Greens reflect communist goal to destroy Capitalism
- Green movement represents multiple minority causes

The Communists had to find a compelling reason for Americans to accept society must be reorganized so businesses operated only to meet the basic needs of the people and not to make a profit.

To achieve this the Communists would have to change our values. They would have to find a way to forbid free enterprise and generate support for economic conversion.

To convince Americans that Capitalism is a flawed system, in need of change, Communists focus in on these points:

- Capitalist system creates 'have' and 'have-nots'
- Capitalism is only 'good for a few'; it 'hurts most people'
- Present Socialism as a better alternative

How are the Greens using environmental issues to promote anti-Capitalism?

- The earth cannot afford capitalist system
- Environmental problems can't be solved under Capitalism
- Capitalism is cause of environmental ruin around the world
- The only solution is a new society based on Green values
- Utopian Socialism is best plan for people and environment
- Change is necessary to save mankind

Communists had to find a way to convince Americans that:

- Public control of production and distribution is better
- Produce only what is needed and stop consumerism
- End Capitalism, put people before greed or personal profit

What do the Greens insist we must do to save the environment?

- Public (government) control of economy and business
- Public (government) control of all natural resources
- Public (government) control of production, based on need
- Public (government) control of distribution: goods, services

Lenin: "People not Profit". Greens: "People Before Profit".

To convince Americans to change our way of life, the Communists outlined these ideas to persuade us to try Socialism because our society was no longer adequate.

- Riot against society, create chaos, justify in name of cause
- Create strife between classes, promote a classless society
- Program the masses, plant communist ideas everywhere
- Challenge Americans to try new ideas and higher values
- Goal is revolution but only talk about it until ready to act

Green political activities match those Communist goals.

- Eco-terrorism excused in name of environmental cause
- Greens promoting a classless, genderless society
- Greens push Socialism as an environmental imperative
- Ecological future depends on changing all our values
- Greens talk about Revolution, because they plan one

Subvert the Dominant Paradigm or Overthrow the Governing Model.

Green politics and ideology fit the communist plan to seize control by imposing their values and principles on our society. The environmental cause is their path to power.

United States Communist Party Goals Set in 1930.

- Eliminate American Pride
- Eliminate patriotism
- Patriotism out of schools
- Diminish individualism
- Teach Marxism

Have those Communist's goals been achieved?

- American history is being rewritten to degrade our hero's
- Where is American patriotism
- Pledge of Allegiance and other events out of schools
- Global citizen focus over U.S. citizen and individuality
- Green teachers are teaching Marxism

Coincidence, or the result of a calculated political effort? TV is filled with classless, genderless, weakling images. It's a good set-up for the Greens. Where are America's rugged heroes? Thank goodness there are still a few who understand courage is the harder choice and freedom is worth the effort. The message of the movies *Braveheart* and *The Patriot* are exceptional.

Review the *Communist Rules for Revolution. How* many more symptoms can we identify? Who started these trends?

1. Corrupt the young; get them away from religion. Get them interested in sex. Make them superficial; destroy their ruggedness.

    - recreational sex, free contraception
    - males speaking in feminine tones
    - males wearing earrings & hair barrettes
    - drugs, alcohol and gangs

2. Get control of all means of publicity. Get peoples' minds off their government by focusing their attention on athletics, sexy books, plays and other trivialities.

    - Green journalism
    - Green entertainment
    - Televised trials

3. Divide people into hostile groups by constantly harping on controversial matters of no importance.

    - Multi-culturalism
    - Labeling: Hyphens before American
    - Anti-environmentalists vs. environmentalists
    - Politically correct speech

4. Destroy the peoples' faith in their natural leaders by holding the latter up to contempt, ridicule and obloquy.

    - Ridicule of America's historical leaders and legends
    - Columbus
    - John Wayne
    - Cowboys bad, Indians good

5. Always preach true democracy but seize power as fast and as ruthlessly as possible.

- Clinton and Gore's Way to Govern:
    - Executive Orders
    - Proclamations
    - International Environmental Treaties
    - More federal control using environment as excuse
    - Sweeping calls for major legislation and change:
    - Healthcare
    - NAFTA/GATT
    - Crime Bill
    - National Biological Survey
    - Terrorism Bill
    - Biodiversity Treaty

6. By encouraging government extravagance, destroy its credit; produce fear of inflation, rising prices and general discontent.

    - United States Government Budget 1.61 Trillion
    - EPA budget 6.6 billion
    - Deficit
    - Foreign aid: 1995 goal, over $7 Billion

7. Foment strikes in vital industries; encourage civil disorders and foster a lenient and soft attitude on the part of government toward these disorders.

    - UPS
    - Eco-terrorism
    - Animal Rights terrorism
    - Baseball, Airlines

8. By special argument cause a breakdown of the old moral virtues; honesty, sobriety, continence, faith in the pledged word, ruggedness.

   - Special Argument Number 1: Environmental cause
   - Pre-Nuptial Agreements
   - Law Suit Mania
   - Opening Adoption Records
   - Sexual Revolution

9. Cause the registration of all firearms on some pretext with a view of confiscation of them and leaving the population helpless.

   - Crime bill
   - Gun control
   - L.A. riots
   - Koresh, Weaver, Lamplugh
   - Anti-Hunting
   - Wildlife protection
   - Public health or security
   - Oklahoma Bombing

We cannot attribute all these events to communist activities in America, though many events are probably connected. We need to focus on protecting the principles and values that are America's foundation. The 'Communist Rules for Revolution help us see the kind of traps Communists use. Communists are committed to achieving the Party's goals.

> "The policy of the Leninist Party, it's wisdom and conscience, correctly express what is realized by the people, it's thoughts, aspirations and hopes. And we are convinced that the great cause of communism, to which the Party has devoted itself, is invincible."
>
> Mikhail Gorbachev
> 1985 – Speech

Advance Means Retreat, Retreat Means Advance

Another tactic used by Communists is that retreat really means advance. They fake being weak when they are strong and act strong when they are weak. This strategy keeps their enemies misinformed so they can be caught off-guard. After 20 years of service, a veteran officer in Russia's KGB Anatoliy Golitsyn defected to the United States and wrote the book, *New Lies for Old* in 1984. He warned the Communists were using disinformation, meaning putting out false information, to mislead us. Disinformation is used to divert attention from what is really going on in the Soviet Union. According to recent press reports, Russia's military is disorganized and weak. Other researchers contend the Russians are building their strength while we continue to downsize our military.

> *"Idealism did not stop Hitler; it did not stop Stalin. Our best hope as sovereign nations is to maintain strong defenses. Indeed, that has been one of the most important moral as well as geopolitical lessons of the 20th century. Dictators are encouraged by weakness; they are stopped by strength. By strength...I do not merely mean military might but the resolve to use that might against evil."*
>
> Margaret Thatcher - March 1995
> *IMPRIMIS*, journal of Hillsdale College

During a 1994 interview with *Audubon* magazine, Gorbachev referred to Communism as *'ideological garbage'* and indicated Communists had made a mistake trying to impose their values and government model on others. Advance through retreat?

Many Americans feel Communism appeared to die a very sudden death and have been slow to trust the Communists. Some Communists must have foreseen or planned the event.

> *"the August '91 coup was totally staged for Western consumption is evidenced by the fact that the **papers for the Gorbachev Foundation were filed with the California Secretary of State in April '91, four months before the pseudo-coup.**"*
>
> McAlvany Intelligence Advisor - March 1995
> (Bold Emphasis Added)

Anyone who has been involved with the legal process of creating a foundation or business understands it takes months of advance planning and documentation prior to filing papers with the State. Who knew Gorbachev was coming? Another consideration is these things cost money. Who financed Gorbachev?

The environmental movement is funded largely by the Environmental Grantmakers Association (EGA), which is supported by 138 foundations and groups, including:

- Ford Foundation
- Pew Charitable Trusts
- Rockefeller Brothers Fund
- Rockefeller Family Fund

The Gorbachev Foundation has received long term financial commitments from the following foundations:

- Ford Foundation
- Pew Charitable Trusts
- Rockefeller Brothers Fund
- Rockefeller Family Fund

The prologue for, *New Lies for the Old*, was written by Larry Abraham. He states, in 1953, the Director of Research for the House Special Committee on Tax Exempt Foundations was Norman Dodd. Dodd learned during a meeting with H. Rowan Gaither, Jr., then President of the Ford Foundation, that the Ford Foundation was *"following a covert plan"* and working directly with the White House to achieve this goal:

> *"we shall use our grant-making power to so alter our life in the United States that we can be comfortably merged with the Soviet Union."*
>
> H. Rowan Gaither, Jr.
> President - Ford Foundation-1953
> (Bold Emphasis Added)

According to Abraham, Dodd asked Gaither if the American people would be informed of this. Gaither told Dodd:

> **"We wouldn't think of doing that, Mr. Dodd."**

This is a significant point. It appears there are some very wealthy people who believe in the 'Do as I say, Not as I do' communist philosophy. They also believe, they alone know what is best for the American people, world Communism. Seemingly unrelated issues reveal disturbing facts and direct links to what we are experiencing in America today and the political objectives laid out by:

- Russia's Communist Leaders
- Leaders of the Communist Party U.S.A
- Ex-KGB Agents that Defected to the United States
- American Grant Makers, Foundations
- Prominent American Citizens, Pushing Social Change
- Mikhail Gorbachev
- Environmental - Green Movement Leaders
- Green Party
- United Nations

It is the opinion of this author that those Americans involved in this effort are either working with the Soviet Union because they are Communists, because their beliefs parallel Communism or because they have been duped into accepting the philosophy of Communism under a different name. This is possible. The new name given to communist values back in the early 70's was 'humanistic values'.

When comparing the concepts of 'humanistic' political ideas from John D. Rockefeller's 1973 book *The Second American Revolution*, to Gorbachev's vision for Green Cross International, to the goals of the Green movement and to the Green Party Program, the political objectives are unmistakably the same. Rockefeller's book looks like the outline of the Green Party Program and most of the goals set by the CPUSA. Some of the ideas Rockefeller promoted to bring about the second American revolution are also evident in Green politics and Communism. Some of those ideas are:

- Planned Society
- Guaranteed Annual Income
- Public ownership of business
- Physical needs provided to citizens as basic human right
- Redistribution of the wealth
- Economic conversion
- Reconsideration of social classes
- True democracy
- Degrading American history
- People before profit
- Diversity, community
- Socially useful work
- Atheist instead of traditional religion

Rockefeller uses the terms, basic human rights and financial insecurity to justify the call for a guaranteed income and other basic needs. Those are the terms Congressman Dellums uses in his promotional information for: H.R. 1050, "A Living Wage, Jobs-for-All". It is also the language of Communism.

John D. Rockefeller made this statement:

> *"there are many who have doubts about a guaranteed annual income, fearing it would create an enormous class of drones... but I am confident that there will be far fewer drones than many of us think..."*

Citizens living under Communism have often been referred to as drones. The confidence of his statement: *there will be far fewer drones than many of us think,* suggests that Rockefeller and others planned to impose these ideas. He states in the affirmative: *there will be far fewer drones,* as if it's only a matter of time.

The environment is severely degraded in Russia. Why? Communism is the reason. Russian citizens may have been concerned about environmental issues but they did not have the freedom or desire to take steps to correct the problem.

When the government has control of people's lives, people lose hope. People stop caring and operate like drones, completing their daily tasks. They know they don't have the power to change anything so they exist in a form of slavery. They depend on the government to provide the basics. They work and the government decides what they earn and how they live.

> *"They pretend to pay us and we pretend to work"*
> Soviet Workers Joke

It may be a joke in Russia, but it isn't very funny when it appears this way of life is planned for the American people. Rockefeller's ideas for promoting this kind of humanistic revolution in America include many of the same ideas the Greens are calling for today such as:

- need new leadership to head America in this direction
- acceptance of utopian or humanistic Socialism
- calls for social change
- calls for citizens to develop a higher consciousness
- need for decentralized government

The values Rockefeller outlines match the Socialist to Communist transition and Green ideas to revolutionize our society. Like the Communists, Rockefeller infers the problems we face can't be solved with our traditional values of:

- family ties
- patriotism
- conventional view of success
- traditional religion

To fully understand the extent to which Americans have been set-up, take a closer look at Rockefeller's idea family ties and traditional religion won't help to solve our problems.

The communist agenda includes destroying the traditional American family by replacing our values of privacy, independence and belief in God with their values. This is why Green Communists are promoting the village concept, co-housing, communes, community not individuality and atheism. It's interesting to look at the alternatives Rockefeller outlined over 20 years ago and compare them to what Hitler promoted, what Vice President Gore promoted and what has been successfully popularized in America. Rockefeller suggested these alternatives to traditional religion:

- eastern religions
- a higher level of consciousness
- extra sensory perception
- transcendental philosophies
- a metaphysical religious consciousness

- mysticism
- paganism, occult
- survival and nature
- sensitive to the mystery of life

Rockefeller suggests this will curb Americans '*overemphasis on science and behavioralism*'. If you're planning to use spiritual politics to shape America's public policies, especially environmental policies, it's a good plan to set-us-up to dismiss scientific facts and rely on Green ideology.

The *Second American Revolution* calls for radical changes to America's basic principles, ethics and values. Rockefeller explains that is the only solution to the problems we face. Rockefeller also quotes, *The Greening of America*, by Charles Reich regarding the revolution Reich predicts will take place in America in the 20th century. Reich said it would:

> *"change the political structure only as its final act."*

This sounds like John Drakeford's explanation of how Communists use scientific Socialism as a transition stage that is followed almost immediately by the violent overthrow of the political structure to establish the dictatorship. Drakeford sites this from the *Communist Manifesto*:

> *"We openly declare that our ends can only be attained by the forcible overthrow of all existing social conditions."*

Is this part of the communist agenda for the United States?

> *"Yes, we advocate a peaceful, electoral path to socialism. However, we have to be honest and say that we cannot predict, at this stage, whether a peaceful transition will be possible."*
> Gus Hall
> National Chairman - CPUSA
> *Political Affairs, January 1989*
> (Bold Emphasis Added)

According to information related by Larry Abraham in Golitysn's book, *New Lies for Old*, Mikhail Gorbachev, in a 1989 speech to the United Nations suggested that the United States and the Soviet Union would work together as world police to protect the environment and stop international terrorism.

Golitsyn a policy planner for the KGB before he defected to the West over 20 years ago warned the West part of the political strategy of the Soviets was to fake the fall of Communism and the liberation of Eastern Europe. Golitsyn warned us over 15 years ago this was the Communist's plan. That was well before Gorbachev entered the picture.

If Americans accept world government and an international police to enforce anti-terrorism and environmental laws on American soil, we would need some strong motivation to justify that level of submission. Beyond Green predictions of environmental doom, what might convince us we need help to control terrorism? Experiencing major acts of terrorism in America could do the trick. If Communists planned 15 years in advance to fake the fall of Communism, it stands to reason they could also plan to bomb the World Trade Center and the Oklahoma Federal Building to make terrorism an issue here.

According to retired United States Air Force Brigadier General, Benton K. Partin, the collapse of the federal building in Oklahoma could not have been caused by a single car bomb. General Partin's opinion is based on 25 years of military experience in all phases of weapons development, from initial research to design and system testing.

> *"When I first saw the pictures of the truck bombs asymmetrical damage to the Federal Building in Oklahoma City, my immediate reaction was that the pattern of damage would have been technically impossible without supplementing demolition charges at some of the reinforced concrete column bases (a standard demolition technique)."*
> Benton K. Partin
> *McAlvany Intelligence Advisor-May-June 1995*

General Partin suggests when Communists carried out terrorist activities in the past; the wrong group of people had been conveniently set-up to take the blame. Partin also questioned why the federal building was destroyed before all the evidence could be carefully evaluated to see what other clues might be found. General Partin also indicated according to his research on the communist's plan to force the United States into Socialism, the Oklahoma bombing is right in line with the strategy to foster violence and escalate terrorist activities. General Partin suggested the Communist's objective is to push the American people to support disarming citizens.

What political issue is likely to be brought up as a companion issue to government steps to control terrorism after the Oklahoma City bombing? Gun control is a likely candidate.

The number nine rule for Communist revolution is:

> *"Cause the registration of all firearms on some pretext with a view of confiscation of them and leaving the population helpless."*

Every American wants terrorism stopped and prevented. The Communist Rules for Revolution include preaching true democracy but seizing power as fast as possible. If the goal is to create a police state, enact gun control and render citizens helpless, then the call for high-tech surveillance equipment for wire taps of all militia groups and other citizen groups serves the Communist's plan. Giving the President of the United States the power to declare any group or individual a terrorist threat is an extreme and dangerous step.

Creating an unreasonable level of national hysteria about isolated incidents provides the excuse for some in positions of power to justify authorizing the government to take extreme action against American citizens. The incident at the Branch Dividian compound is a prime example of how things can get out of hand and turn from investigation to brutality. Most Americans are law-abiding citizens and cannot be blamed for the actions of a few. One bad apple doesn't spoil the barrel. The blanket indictment by the press and some politicians of all militia groups is completely irresponsible. It's like declaring all Americans who belong to X-Y-Z auto club must be investigated because another member is accused of causing a traffic accident that killed hundreds of people. What if this reactionary mentality was applied to other heart breaking tragedies? What about the incident involving Susan Smith and those two little boys that were drown? That was a gut-wrenching situation, but should it result in a government investigation of every divorced white female with two sons? The situation regarding the militias is no different. Acts of violence are acts of violence. The alleged actions of some militia members should not result in the condemnation of all members based on the assumption these Americans are guilty of a crime. What happened to, 'innocent until proven guilty'?

It is critical to keep our heads and work toward eliminating terrorism without sacrificing the basic rights of innocent Americans. We do not know if these terrorist activities are coincidences or calculated political moves by the Communists. Caution is the watchword. As a nation we do not need to react, we need to respond to this situation intelligently. We also need to understand the Communists are actively pursuing their goals in the United States. Gus Hall pointed out in his 1994 address to the Young Communist League, that he and his comrades have been:

> *"initiating, leading and participating in all great labor, political and progressive movements for reform and change...committed to socialism as the only viable...inevitable solution the inherent flaws, problems and crises that the capitalist system cannot solve. "*

> Gus Hall
> National Chairman - CPUSA
> *Political Affairs - June 1994*

Whittaker Chambers, the former Soviet agent who defected in the late 1940's indicates in his book *Witness*, that the greatest mistake Americans make is assuming that Communists think like we do. Chambers warns us, we have nothing in common with Communists. He stresses Communists have irreconcilable viewpoints on:

- morality issues
- standards and judgments
- the fate and future of mankind

Chambers suggests that Communists will engage in espionage *"to the degree they are Communists"*. The deeper their faith in Communism, the more they are willing to risk. It seems what Chambers wants us to understand is Communists think differently than we do. They have different moral and ethical values and will do 'whatever it takes' to accomplish their objectives.

This is how Hitler's mind worked. Reasonable people spent countless hours trying to understand, reason-with and make lasting agreements with Hitler. Hitler had his own agenda. He promised people anything to get them to cooperate then he would do as he pleased. He did not worry about right or wrong. Hitler's purpose was to advance the Nazi cause. If making a phony agreement helped, he made a phony agreement. Efforts to form lasting alliances were useless. It kept his enemies off guard.

Chambers indicates Communists operate by the same morals and do not see lies or espionage as betraying anyone. They believe the salvation of mankind depends on world Communism and that means the destruction of the capitalist system, *"which they believe to be historically bankrupt"*.

We should not blindly accept the Soviets no longer run a dictatorship, that the plan of world Communism is dead or that the Cold War is over.

A recent article featured in the August 7, 1995 issue of *U.S. News & World Report* suggests Chambers is correct and our values don't match communist's values. According to the article, *Yeltsin's Eyes and Ears,* the former KGB secret police who rained fear are back in business with all their former power to abuse innocent people. These powers include reestablishing their own prisons and wire tap privileges. The KGB has been split into two different organs; the Presidential Security Service and the Federal Security Service.

The Communists have not really changed their operations. It is a masquerade. They are pretending to change their values.

When We Least Expect It, Expect It

"the new Green vision places the environment at the center of public life, making it the context for both the formulation of economic policies and political decisions"

Voting Green – 1992
Jeremy Rifkin
Carol Grunewald Rifkin

"the task of saving the earth's environment must and will become the central organizing principle of the post-Cold War world"

Putting People First- 1992
Senator Al Gore

"The only ultimate solution, of course, is the creation of a planned society in which the quest for profits has been abolished...."

Ecology 1972
Gus Hall
National Chairman, CPUSA

What we're talking about is creating new forms of life on the basis of new values"

From Red to Green – 1994
Mikhail Gorbachev

Rifkin: transform public life, earth-based planned society
Gore: transform public life, earth-based planned society
Hall: transform public life, new values, planned society
Gorbachev: transform USA, earth-based planned society

"Our ideology is intolerant...and peremptorily demands ...the complete transformation of public life to its ideas"
Psychopathic God
Adolf Hitler

Like Hitler, these calls for the complete transformation of public life are based on personal, political and philosophical ideas. Hitler also used the same idea. The earth was his 'central organizing principle'. When political leaders call for this kind of radical departure from the way a society functions, it's time to pay close attention. History can repeat itself, but only if we let it.

Gorbachev's Propaganda Machine

Greens are recruiting celebrities to lend their support to environmental issues. This helps the Greens in several ways:

- draw media attention, good chance to nationalize issue
- opportunity to persuade the celebrity to go Green
- if not, celebrity will still 'appear' Green in public eye
- emotional hook to encourage fans to go Green

Many Americans don't understand the Greens political goals or tactics but every American needs to. Only then can we avoid becoming victims of communist propaganda. Gorbachev's Green Cross International or GCI appears to be just another environmental organization. It is not. Gorbachev and GCI have specific plans to implement a Green world government. Gorbachev is hiding behind the environmental cause to impose his values on America. Gorbachev was asked to be the keynote speaker for the 1994 Environmental Media Association Awards. Some questioned Gorbachev as an appropriate choice. This comment by Joseph Farah appeared in the *Los Angeles Times*:

> "*this is the same lifelong Leninist who presided over perhaps the most environmentally irresponsible nation in history.*"

Gus Hall lead people to believe Communists had better environmental ethics than Americans. Hall stated in 1972:

> "*One can judge a social system by its history.*"
> *Ecology-1972*
> Gus Hall

This is true. According to reports, the environment is in bad shape in Russia. Our environment is in better shape. Without our American way of life, citizens would not be free to care for the land or make enough profit to fund the 'bail-out' of the failed Russian economy.

Mikhail Gorbachev helped organize GCI and is the President of that organization. GCI Board of Trustees includes some of the same people involved in Green politics in America: Ted Turner, Robert Redford, Carl Sagan and Yoko Ono. The priorities of Green Cross International include:

- creating a new paradigm for a global civilization
- shifting basic values of how we view nature
- creating international environmental laws
- a world court to settle ecological conflicts
- local chapters to control international ecological threats

Gorbachev's goal is for GCI to serve as the global umbrella organization to handle global environmental issues. Gorbachev's vision includes using his celebrity status to promote these ideas and stimulate public concern for the environmental crisis. Global Green is the United States chapter of GCI. Gorbachev personally helped to select Diane Meyer Simon to serve as President of Global Green. Gorbachev and Meyer Simon met with leaders of major environmental organizations in November 1993 in Washington D.C. The purpose of the meeting was to get support for Green Cross International and Global Green. It was also to test the waters to see if the major environmental groups would accept GCI as the global environmental umbrella group and Gorbachev as their spokesperson. The 1995 edition of the new international environmental magazine, *Grassroots* featured an interview with Meyer Simon. She announced the results of that meeting with the major environmental groups. Meyer Simon stated:

"We expected some degree of resistance but instead heard a great willingness to join arms...they expressed a common need for someone to talk about values, whose words resonate with people in the streets as well as those in leadership."

Gorbachev met with the major Green groups in 1993 and was selected to be the keynote speaker at the Environmental Media Association Awards in 1994. Is this a coincidence, or the result of a calculated political effort to move Gorbachev into America's environmental spotlight? Gorbachev's vision is to create a 'new environmental consciousness' that includes changing all our values. Gorbachev made the following statement in the article, *From Red to Green, Audubon* magazine, Nov-Dec. 1994.

*"We must change all our values ...What we are talking about is creating new forms of life on the **basis of new values.**"*
Mikhail Gorbachev
(Bold Emphasis Added)

This may sound like a new idea but it's not a 'Gorbachev original'.

*"Socialism corrects the basic flaw of capitalism. It sets human society on a new path. The means of production, factories, mines and mills become the property of the people. They operate and produce only to fulfill human needs. They are not motivated by profits. **This is the foundation for a new set of priorities, for new values...What is involved is a 'conflict of values.'**"*
Ecology-1972-Socialism and the Environment
Gus Hall
(Bold Emphasis Added)

Times haven't changed. The communist's strategy to take over our country in 1930, 1969 and 1972 all include the goal to gradually change American's values. It is the exact same message Gorbachev is using in 1995. Gus Hall, in a 1988 article for the *World Marxist Review*, indicated the Communists understood they needed to come up with some creative ways to get Americans to go along with their ideas. Hall also indicated the Communists knew magnifying environmental doom would create the fear of human extinction and that fear could be used to persuade Americans to fight Capitalism.

> "*The fact is that* **the bigger the stake the people have in the struggle for a more livable world, the better fighters they are in the fight to save humanity from extinction. The challenge is to formulate the tactics of unity in struggle that can be molded into an unbeatable fighting force** *for human progress and human preservation*".
>
> Gus Hall
> National Chairman - CPUSA
> (Bold Emphasis Added)

Avoiding extinction was the emotional hook selected by the Communists. Have environmental issues been twisted and exaggerated to intensify fear of a global environmental crisis to scare Americans into anti-Capitalism? Part of Hall's plan included 'formulating tactics' to mold us into fighting for Socialism. Now, just 10 years later, Gorbachev's Global Green is creating a new television program called *Sacred Places*. This program will focus on the environment and feature prominent individuals who have experienced a Green 'spiritual awakening'. Green values for global environmental protection will be woven into the program. Meyer Simon is concentrating on:

> "*molding the message of international responsibility for an American audience.*"

It looks like we're being set-up to accept Green values on a global scale and 'responsibility' to protect the international environment.

The purpose of *Sacred Places* is to mold our minds. Meyer Simon's job is to convince us to accept new values to avoid environmental ruin. This fits the plan outlined by Gus Hall. Greens intend to change our values, ethics and principles using the power of suggestion and entertainment to re-educate Americans to think properly. Gorbachev makes his brainwashing goal clear.

> *"A revolution has to take place in people's minds..."*
> *From Red to Green-Audubon-1994*
> Mikhail Gorbachev

The Greens are planning to take advantage of our concern for the environment to literally brainwash the masses by ambushing unsuspecting American minds.

> *"The Gorbachev Foundation is run by Dr. James A. Garrison, a former executive of the Esalen Institute, a mind-control organization involved in conducting experimental psychological techniques in American school classrooms."*
> *McAlvany Intelligence-1995*
> (Bold Emphasis Added)

If you plan to brainwash the American people, it's handy to have a mind-control expert on your team. Gorbachev's goal is to change our principles, values and ethics under the guise of environmental protection by using mind control techniques. The Shevardnadze International Foreign Policy Association, headquartered in San Francisco, is also run by Garrison.

Deliberately planning to use a program like 'Sacred Places' to brainwash Americans to change our morals and mold our opinions is beyond dishonest. This behind the scenes con-job is a shameful violation of the public trust. It may not be illegal, but it is wrong.

President Clinton praised progressives in Hollywood, like Mr. Fleishman, for 'redefining' entertainment and using the behind the scenes approach, as a tool to:

"make the major cultural shifts our world is now experiencing to be as graceful and positive as possible"[1]

Both Gorbachev and Clinton think this behind the scenes approach to brainwash Americans is acceptable. We better think about that.

What about consumer protection? Americans cannot protect our minds without full disclosure. If the label says chicken, we don't expect to get fish. If a car is advertised, we don't expect to buy a bicycle. Americans who sit down to be entertained don't expect to be programmed. No different than expecting news professionals to present facts, professionals in the entertainment industry must be accountable for the products they offer.

The free flow of ideas is critical to the democratic process. This is not a free speech or censorship issue. This is about accountability. Redefining entertainment without disclosing the new rules to the American people is fraud. It is misrepresentation. The viewer expects an entertainment product, not a political soapbox product.

Does freedom of speech extend to ignoring America's national security? If we can say anything we want without regard to national security, why is Aldrich Ames, the spy, in jail? He was exercising his freedom of speech and sharing secrets with the Soviets. Is using entertainment, specifically designed to change our values by using state of the art mind-control techniques a censorship or a national security issue?

Redefining entertainment and using it for political gain is an issue that needs to be debated. Should politics and entertainment be mixed? Politicians are beginning to use entertainment to sell themselves to the American people. Political popularity, generated by which candidate gets on the most talk shows, will change evaluating a candidate. It will make it more and more a popularity contest instead of, an arms length, objective look at their political views. Politics and entertainment ought to remain separate. A television program that focuses on political issues is different than using entertainment to popularize candidates or trick people into changing their values or forming a political opinion due to the appeal of the actor or the power of suggestion. The entertainment industry, government officials and the American people must examine this issue as it relates to consumer protection and national security.

The tobacco industry has to put warning labels on cigarette packages. *Sacred Places* ought to carry a warning label that states: Hazardous to America. Viewer discretion advised. Contains brainwashing material designed to erase our culture.

Larry Abraham, indicates in the book *New Lies for Old* that Gorbachev and others, who plan to create and impose world government, will use this approach:

> *"Perverting of the soul is far better accomplished by liberalism than it is by totalitarianism."*

Sold Out

Abraham correctly predicted how Mikhail Gorbachev and his cohorts would approach the subject of world government. Gorbachev is using the appeal of progressive ideas mixed with the fear of environmental disaster to convince us to change our values and submit to his ideas. Gorbachev is currently working on the Earth Charter The Earth Charter looks like Gorbachev's 'shot' at quietly imposing world government.

Beyond changing our values, Gorbachev claims the only way to protect the environment is via:

> "*the development and implementation of an Earth Charter, a body of international ecological laws that would guide the actions of individuals, corporations and governments...the time has come for a code of ethical and moral principles that will govern the conduct of nations and people with respect to the environment.*"
>
> *Grassroots*
> (Bold Emphasis Added)

The Earth Charter will contain a new set of vague environmental 'principles' designed to control the actions and behaviors of people and nations around the world. Global Green along with the Earth Council has a three-step plan in place to promote, and then implement the Earth Charter in America. The Green plan is to get the Earth Charter passed in each country, then ratified as international law.

Global Green is working on a joint campaign designed to get Americans to support the Earth Charter. The United States is expected to support the Earth Charter so other countries will follow. Global Green plans to foster public support for the charter by using leaders in these sectors of society:

- Environmental
- Literary
- Educators
- Performing arts
- Philosophers
- American Indian
- Political leaders
- Youth
- Religious
- Non-Government Organizations

Some people are already pushing global government.

> *"David Rockefeller recently addressed the Business Council of the United Nations and warned that the 'window of opportunity' for installing the New World Order is very...*
> *...narrow, and that is because of opposition to it that is building (i.e. from U.S. conservatives and traditionalists) that if the opportunity is not realized quickly, it could be lost forever."*
> McAlvany Intelligence Advisor-March 1995

Gorbachev is working with Maurice Strong, former Secretary General of the United Nations, now Chairman of the Earth Council. Gorbachev and Strong developed a draft of the Earth Charter by the end of 1995. The final draft was to be ready in 1997. Gorbachev planned on the United States being the first to sign it into law. His goal was to see the Earth Charter ratified by all nations and decreed 'global law' in 2000. The Earth Charter USA campaign is now in full swing and has the support of major environmental groups.

> *"When the Communist Party of the Soviet Union met for its 27th Congress in February 1986, it passed on a program of 'ideological and educational work' which provided guidelines for 'the struggle against bourgeois (Capitalists) ideology, to be valid toward the year 2000. The program said: The most acute struggle between the two world outlooks on the international scene reflects the opposition of the two world systems - socialism and capitalism."*
> The Soviet Propaganda Machine
> Martin Ebon

Gorbachev was in power, in the Soviet Union, when the above plan was approved. The battle between Socialism and Capitalism has been taken to the international level. Gorbachev is directly involved in the 'ideological struggle' between the two world systems. The question of Capitalism or Socialism is being presented as an environmental question by the Green movement. The communist program to win their struggle against Capitalism was to be completed towards the year 2000, the same year Gorbachev plans to have the Earth Charter ratified into international law.

The mass media was identified by the Communists as their key tool to persuade people to accept Socialism. Gorbachev's GCI and Global Green are using mass media to reshape our values. The Earth Charter will be based on new Green ideas for how people of the world must live.

Why is Gorbachev targeting the United States to take the lead on the Earth Charter instead of Russia? If Gorbachev has a desire to protect the environment, he ought to be expected to prove the ideas of the Earth Charter work. Cleaning up the globe seems to be a big step, even for Mr. Gorbachev. Expecting the United States to agree to new values and global law with no track record is arrogant and ridiculous. Is Gorbachev's goal, global environmental protection or, control of the globe? Gorbachev's goals include:

- a new civilization based on a new governing paradigm
- new Green laws for citizens to live by
- new international environmental laws
- a World Court. (Judge Gorbachev presiding?)

The title of the *Grassroots* article is interesting:

"Green Cross International...Steering a course for global environmental reform with Mikhail Gorbachev at the helm."

Mr. Porritt indicated the vision for the Green future went 'beyond world government'. It looks like the Earth Charter is the vehicle to gain legal control over the lives of the American people and establish 'compulsory Green living'. One washing machine per 20 people, rationed foods and Green Dictators.

Possible, Probable or Incomprehensible?

"The high office of the President has been used to foment a plot to destroy America's freedom and before I leave office, I must inform the citizens of their plight."
President John F. Kennedy
McAlvany Intelligence Advisor

President Kennedy made the above statement when speaking at Columbia University in 1963.

"Ten days later, John F. Kennedy was assassinated."
McAlvany Intelligence Advisor

We will never know exactly what President Kennedy meant when he warned us the office of the President would be used against us. What we can learn from his warning is to pay more attention to the actions of our government and the actions of our Presidents.

If the President of the United States signs an International Treaty such as the Earth Charter, it becomes the supreme law of our land.

Americans will be expected to comply with the values and laws laid down in the Charter. If we do not comply, the laws would be enforced by our government, from the top-down. If this occurs, the office of the President will have been used to destroy America's freedom.

A new America could be established with the stroke of the President's pen. Although the Senate would have to ratify it, Green Communism could be instituted in America as fast as it supposedly fell apart in Russia. The American way of life, as we know it, could be erased in short order. The Green flag would be flying instead of the Red one and the long-term goal of world Communism would be achieved.

If Americans accept the Earth Charter, Mr. Krushchev will have correctly predicted:

> *"The United States will eventually fly the Communist Red Flag ... the American people will hoist it themselves."*

H. Rowan Gaither, Jr., President of the Ford Foundation stated in 1953 that they intended:

> *"to use their grant-making powers to so alter life in the United States that we can be comfortably merged with the Soviet Union"*

Funding for Green groups comes from the Environmental Grantmakers Association. Who funded Gorbachev?

- Ford Foundation
- Pew Charitable Trusts
- Rockefeller Brothers Fund
- Rockefeller Family Fund

These same groups were among the top ten Environmental Grantmakers for 1990. This information was provided by the Environmental Data Research Institute, in the book, *Trashing the Economy*. These groups have and are playing a key role in the success of the Green movement. If the Earth Charter is signed, life in the United States and Russia would be virtually guided by the same rules and the goal expressed by H. Rowan Gaither would be achieved.

The 'Communist Rules for Revolution' stress keeping citizen's minds off their government and on trivial things. Where is the American mind? Are we keeping close watch on the activities of our government? Is this all just coincidence, or are we being *Set Up and Sold Out?*

Like The Man Who Winks In The Dark

The following statement was made by Gorbachev in a 1994 interview in *Audubon* magazine, titled, *From Red to Green*.

> *"Now that we are rid of this syndrome of imposing the communist model on people, now that we've given them the chance to get rid of this dogma.*
>
> *I have to tell you Americans that you've been pushing your American way of life for decades. You thought it was perfection itself, the ultimate achievement of human thought ...There has to be a different approach ... Americans have to be more modest in their desires. We have to stimulate human qualities in people rather than greed."*
>
> Mikhail Gorbachev
(Bold Emphasis Added)

Gorbachev's attitude toward Americans and Capitalism doesn't exactly sound like peaceful coexistence. What Gorbachev said in the first sentence is very important.

> *'Now that **we are rid of this syndrome of imposing the communist model on people,** now that **we've** given **them** the chance to get rid of this dogma,'*

Break it down. Who's we? Who's them? Who gave them a chance to do what?

Gorbachev's 'we' would be himself, the Soviets and the Communist Party U.S.A. The 'them' is 'us', the American people.

The Soviets have given the Americans the chance to get over our fear of Communism and over our fear of the Communists imposing their model on us through a take-over attempt. This is a critical point because the sentence reveals a 'Freudian slip'. A Freudian slip occurs when someone accidentally reveals something they did not intend to reveal. This statement was made by Gorbachev in a 1994 personal interview regarding the newly formed Green Cross International. It focused on his vision for GCI as a global environmental organization.

The 'we' in Gorbachev's statement can't be the environmental community because he has only begun to play a leadership role in the Green movement. It would not make sense for that group to give Americans the time to get over the conviction that Communists were a threat to our nation. What did Gorbachev reveal when he stated Americans had been given the chance to get over their fear of Communism? What does it have to do with his involvement with GCI and the Green movement?

The answer to that question is found in the following statement by a Soviet leader. Note: bourgeoisie means us, the Capitalists.

> *"War to the hilt between communism and capitalism is inevitable. Today, of course, we are not strong enough to attack. Our time will come. To win, we shall need the element of surprise. The bourgeoisie will have to be put to sleep. So we shall begin by launching the most spectacular peace movement on record. There will be electrifying overtures and unheard of concessions. The capitalist countries, stupid and decadent, will rejoice to cooperate in their own destruction. They will leap at another chance to be friends. As soon as their guard is down, we will smash them with our clenched fist."*
>
> *Lenin School for Political Warfare-1930's*
> Dimitri Manuilsky

This explains Gorbachev's use of the terms 'we' and 'them.'

"...we've given them the chance to get rid of this dogma..."

We've been given just enough time to forget Communism is a threat to us.

Have we have been set-up?

- Americans are not on the alert for Communism
- Communists have made a spectacular bid for peace
- Communists have made unheard of concessions
- Americans have rejoiced for a new peaceful Russia
- Americans are cooperating with Gorbachev's Green ideas
- Americans are leaping at the chance to be friends
- America's guard is down

> *"As soon as their guard is down, we will smash them with our clenched fist"*

Coincidence, or the execution of a calculated political effort?

The Green I.Q. Test

> *"A democracy cannot be both ignorant and free."*
> Thomas Jefferson

Take the Green IQ. test. Let's see if we've got this straight.

- our ex-arch enemy and Communist leader
- who, while in power, financed the Communist Party USA
- who has a terrible environmental record
- is now working with environmental groups
- is headquartered at the Presidio in San Francisco
- is in leadership position in subversive Green movement
- is using entertainment to brainwash Americans
- is telling Americans to change all our values
- is urging Americans to support Earth Charter concept
- is urging America to be the first to sign the Earth Charter
- is using Charter to legally impose his values on Americans
- his values can become 'compulsory Green living'
- he can make legal control possible or we can volunteer

International environmental law and a new form of Green Communist world government. We fail the test, if we fail to understand, we are in the:

"war to the hilt between communism and capitalism"

The goal of the Communists remains the same. Golitsyn cautioned us in *New Lies For Old*, that the communist advance on America was in the final stages of implementation, that the goal was world domination and the overthrow of Capitalism.

This is a calculated political effort with national and international support. This is war on America camouflaged as environmental protection. Have we been re-educated to the point we no longer view a Communist revolution as a treasonous threat? Many members of the Green movement are revolutionaries who must face the consequences of their efforts to overthrow our government. Other than calling themselves Watermelons, Green on the outside, Red on the inside, can they make it any plainer? Consider this, straight from the horse's mouth:

> *"I am a Communist, a convinced Communist! For some that may be a fantasy. But to me it is my main goal."*
> Mikhail Gorbachev
> *New York Times – 1989*

If it looks like a Duck, walks like a Duck, quacks like a Duck, chances are, it's a Duck.

The man who winks in the dark knows what he's doing but no one else does. Like the man who winks in the dark, the Greens know exactly what they're doing but the American people have been left in the dark. This is not about environmental protection. The Green movement is about achieving absolute power. It is about setting-us-up to accept Socialism is an ecological imperative.

No American likes a 'them vs. us outlook', but the Greens created it. We must realize this is a war. If we do not stand up and be counted, we will be pressured into Socialism, then forced into Communism, one issue, one law, one company and one person at a time. This is part of the Communist's long-term plan.

> *"Each year humanity takes a step towards Communism. Maybe not you, but in all events your grandson will surely be a Communist."*
>
> Nikita Krushchev
> June – 1956

The Communists have been at this a long time. It doesn't matter what we call it; Green movement, Eco-Socialism, the Earth Charter or the New World Order. The Communists plan to take over America.

The bottom line is, we're being had. These revolutionaries intend to control the conduct of the people of this nation using the environment as the vehicle. 'Compulsory Green living' will be forced on us if we do not take immediate responsibility for our future and respond to the Green threat to our freedom and national security.

The Gorbachev Foundation Directors includes these men who formerly held top security positions for the United States:

- Secretary of State George Shultz
- United States Senator Gary Hart
- United States Senator Alan Cranston

Isn't this a conflict of interest between the American people and the Soviet Union?

When Will We Say: Enough is Enough?

Americans have willingly given the Green movement their trust and hard earned cash. Americans will continue to support the Greens if the American people are not alerted to the political goals of the Greens. Lying to us, using our children, manipulating our political system, ridiculing our traditions and rewriting our history all add up to the Green goal to erase our culture and destroy the country we love. We can take action and challenge this or sit-back and watch the Greens completely transform our society.

We need to understand we've all been used by the Communists to advance their goals, in one way or another. A prime example involves using a hyphen before the word American. The political purpose to begin using the hyphen before American is to change our culture by changing the way we identify with each other. That trendy little hyphen is forcing us to acknowledge differences instead of accepting and feeling our unity. During the research process, the first place the hyphen appeared attached to the word American was in communist literature. Afro-American and Mexican-American were used.

America is the melting pot. That is our culture. People come here to become Americans and melt into this great culture. America is living proof of how all kinds of people can work together and achieve success. That is our connection to each other. The most important word in America is American. It stands alone. American is the term that defines who we are. There is no other culture, no other nation and no other people exactly like us. We are unique. We can be proud of who we are. We are all Americans first. Our other heritage follows. If there was a war, would the Irish return to Ireland, the French to France or Africans to Africa? Obviously not, because America is our country.

The Communists targeted these unsuspecting Americans to manipulate their issues and advance the communist political agenda:

- Indians
- Puerto Ricans
- Asians
- Women
- Entertainers
- Children
- Senior citizens
- Education
- Labor Unions
- Poor
- Blacks
- Whites
- Mexicans
- Gays
- Politicians
- Young Americans
- Healthcare
- Jewish
- Religious leaders
- Homeless

The Greens also targeted those involved in the environmental cause. January 1989, *Political Affairs*, the Communist journal featured the article: *The Environment: A Natural Terrain for Communists.* The author, Virginia Warner Brodine stated:

"A specific Communist program will come from developing a Marxist understanding throughout the Party for the environmental crisis and from participation in environmental struggles which will help us to apply this understanding in local, national and international situations. This can advance the cause of all-people's unity and bring the most advanced environmentalists into the fight for socialism."

(Bold Emphasis Added)

Most Americans involved in the environmental movement are caring, honest Americans who can get off the Green bandwagon as fast as they got on. We need to slow down, step back and reevaluate the entire environmental situation. We need to question every piece of proposed environmental legislation and make distinctions concerning the political agenda of the Green Movement. We must also address the threat that the Greens, Gorbachev and the Communist Party USA pose to our national security.

> *"Yes, we advocate a peaceful, electoral path to socialism. However, we have to be honest and say that **we cannot predict, at this stage, whether a peaceful transition will be possible.**"*
>
> Gus Hall
> *Political Affairs - 1989*
> (Bold Emphasis Added)

Advocating *"a peaceful path to Socialism"* is different than guaranteeing it. This statement indicates the Communists have considered and are prepared to use force and violence to implement Socialism in America. Die Yuppie Scum, Visualize Industrial Collapse, and Subvert the Dominant Paradigm fit the implied idea, if we don't volunteer for Communism, Green dictators will try to force it on us.

Albert Kahn, author of *High Treason*, indicates in 1948 the members of the CPUSA were charged with conspiracy because they:

- formed a political party devoted to Marxist-Leninist ideas
- published and promoted principles of Marxism-Leninism
- set-up schools to teach principles of Marxism-Leninism
- planned overthrow of government using force and violence

Nothing has changed. The Communists have just gotten bolder. There is a fine line between free speech and treason. Julia Johnsen, author of, *Should The Communist Party Be Outlawed?* indicates that according to the Constitution, the founding fathers defined treason this way.

> *"Treason against the United States shall consist only in levying war against them or in adhering to their enemies, giving them aid and comfort.'*

According to that definition the Green Communist ought to be considered traitors because they are:

adhering to or 'devoted' to the enemy
aiding or 'helping' the enemy cause
comforting or 'encouraging' enemy

- fighting against Capitalism and government system
- supporting and promoting Communism
- referring to their cause as a **war** against America
- encouraging terrorist, war-like activities

The Greens are working with Gorbachev. Although the Soviets and Gorbachev have professed to no longer be enemies of the United States, one need only review the plan outlined by Dimitri Manuilsky in 1930 and what has occurred over the last 65 years. Communist's propaganda and disinformation have caught Americans off guard.

Green Communists are twisting environmental issues and using our system to break down our system. They are taking advantage of our trust while they set-us-up for take-over by walking the fine line between free speech and treason. Doesn't feel very good does it? Well, America:

"it ain't over, till it's over"
Yogi Berra

The first Americans rebelled against dictatorship and excessive government control. As Americans, we have an obligation to honor that tradition and protect our liberty and our freedom. We all have absolute freedom until we begin to infringe on the rights and freedoms of others. The Greens have crossed the line.

Americans do not agree on all things, all of the time. That is good. It shows we are independent thinkers. One thing we have in common is that we cherish our freedom and the opportunity to make all kinds of independent choices. From where we live to what we eat, rich, poor or in-between, no American wants to be dictated to.

This is not about environmental excellence. It's not about being a Democrat or a Republican. It is not about being a conservative or a liberal. This is about making a decision to save our country and choose our future.

When Patrick Henry said *"Give me liberty or give me death"* he was not making a casual statement. The first Americans set the standard for what being an American meant. They had the will, the courage and the heartfelt determination to live free.

It is our challenge to protect their legacy and once again show what Americans are made of. We have the will, the courage and the heartfelt determination to fight for America and the right to live free.

The future of a nation stems from a foundation of pride in the past and from that, hope for the future. If we continue to let the Greens butcher our national pride, our foundation slowly disintegrates and our culture becomes replaceable. Love of country and culture is what holds a nation together.

We need to reclaim our patriotism and pride. We need to love and protect our country. It's where we live, where we work and what we pay taxes to support.

Americans Set Us Free and Americans Can Keep Us Free.

Our forefathers and mothers risk it all to be free. They took heart, took a chance and beat the odds. They gave their lifetimes to give us our freedom. Rekindle that spirit. Our freedom is at risk and we don't have time to be timid.

> *"A ship is safe in the harbor, but that is not what ships are built for"*
>
> Shedd

Life is filled with risks. The time to act is now, before we wake up in a society we will not recognize. For too long, we have ranted and raved mainly at home. It's time to go public. We have the power and the opportunity to shape our future. Many Americans have become complacent. We depended on others because we did not realize there was a desperate need for our involvement. It's not that we don't care. It's that we didn't know. Now we know and it's time to show we care.

The Weapons of Choice are Wit and Wisdom

The Green revolution will continue unless we realize it's up to each and every one of us to make the time and effort to stop it. The subversive agenda of the Greens must be challenged. Wherever we live, whatever we do, we can find ways to help. The time has come to pick sides. The war is on. The weapons of choice are wit and wisdom. As the saying goes:

> *"We can not direct the wind but we can adjust the Sails"*

We can't pass freedom on to our children if we submit to Green Communism. How our children and grandchildren live in the years ahead depends on how we respond to the Greens today. The question every American must answer is: Am I willing to let the Greens push Green Communism down our collective American throat?

Don't forget what this Green thinks of us.

I have to tell you Americans that you've been pushing your American way of life for decades. You thought it was perfection itself, the ultimate achievement of human thought ...There has to be a different approach ... Americans have to be more modest in their desires. We have to stimulate human qualities in people rather than greed."

Mikhail Gorbachev
(Bold Emphasis Added)

What's on Gus Hall's wish list?

"The end will not come when the commissars finally haul 60 million hopelessly diseased, capitalistic 'animals' off to liquidation centers or ***when Communist Party Chief, Gus Hall, gets his wish to see the "last Congressman strangled to death with the guts of the last preacher"...***

The battle will be lost, not when freedom of speech is finally taken away, but when Americans become so 'adjusted' or 'conditioned' to 'getting along with the group' that when they finally see the threat, they say, I can't afford to be controversial."

None Dare Call It Treason
John Stormer
(Bold Emphasis Added)

Will the politically correct Green 'thought police' or independent Americans determine our future? If you don't agree with the Green vision for America, join the rest of us and read on.

It is time to call it treason. It is time to be controversial.

7

Just The Facts
and a comment or two

<u>Authors note:</u> *Set Up & Sold Out* was first released in 1995. In 1998, the second edition was released, which included over 70 points that had already surfaced to confirm the message. These points follow from page 295 to page 335. The latest facts to confirm it is Green Communism begin on page 337 in this 2003 updated third edition.

Environmental cause used to conceal Green Communism:

1995 - *The Perestroika Deception* by Anatoliy Golitsyn, former KGB policy planner, was released in the United States for the first time. Golitsyn's editor states, "despite his proven track record of providing accurate, verifiable information to the West (since 1961) and despite his 94% accuracy rating....his warnings have been overlooked by Western policy makers." Golitsyn states the goal is world Communism and warns of this strategy to achieve it.

> *"...in the late 1980's, the KGB despatched its most experienced operatives to the United States to conduct unpublicized Embassy briefings with members of the American political, scientific, intellectual and economic elite. These briefings laid the basis for a rapid expansion of intensive contacts between Soviet/Russian builders of influence and the American elite - an activity which **Gorbachev continued through 'new' structures such as the Gorbachev Foundation/USA (with 'global' initiatives such as the 'Global Security Project') and International Green Cross of which Gorbachev has made himself President and which exploits global environmentalism as a dimension of the strategy. Its ultimate purpose is an attack on private property.**"*

Golitsyn suggests Western policy makers are ignoring his warnings because spy cases like the Aldrich Ames case show, "the Russians won the intelligence war" and they don't want to hear that message.

We are being *Set Up & Sold Out*. American policy makers ought to focus on saving the nation instead of saving face.

1997 - *Western Journalism Center* reports:

> "*Patrick Moore, founding member and former director of Greenpeace for 15 years, testified before a congressional subcommittee in support of logging. Moore said:*
>
> "**much of the environmental movement has been hijacked by extremist activists who use the language of the environment for a movement that has more to do with class struggle and anti-corporatism.**"

1997 - The *Washington Times* (Dec. 14th) "Letter to the editor":

> "**Many of us that were involved in intelligence saw the Green Parties in Europe as a haven for the Communists during the Cold War. Lately, the environmental movement has become the new home for left-wing radicals. Is it any wonder that after Communism has failed all over the world, the environmental movement has us all marching toward Communism's ultimate goal of the redistribution of the world's wealth?** They are doing this by forcing the developed world to pay the heavy price in pollution controls, while the developing world goes unrestricted. The lack of ability on the part of climatologists to predict next weeks' weather should be a clue that they do not possess the means to predict trends in the next century. **We need to reign in our zealots** at the conference in Japan and stick to empirical science when it comes to global warming."
>
> Jamie Thackaberry
> Fort Bragg, North Carolina

We've been Set Up

1987 - November. Mikhail Gorbachev said:

> "*Comrades, do not be concerned about all you hear about glasnost, Perestroika and democracy in the coming years. These are primarily for outward consumption. There will be no significant internal changes in the Soviet Union, other than for cosmetic purposes. Our purpose is to disarm the Americans and let them fall asleep.*"
>
> Speech to Soviet Politburo

Retired USAF Brigadier General Ben Partin, a 25-year veteran, said:

> "*Globalism and the end game of World Communism are identical.*"

Someone forgot to tell the Russians the Cold War is over.

1997 - February. *Associated Press* report titled "Spies haven't come in from the cold just yet...FBI is on the trail of some 200 in US." *AP* quotes a senior bureau official":

> "*The end of the Cold War has brought no slackening in foreign espionage against this country*"

Raymond Mislock, FBI, Chief of National Security, Washington DC said:

- *"it is no accident that the SVRR (the Soviet KGB) and GRU (Russian intelligence) residencies in Washington are the largest in the world*

- *"it's not just the Russians. The threat comes from throughout the world.*

- *"some people in government who should have known better assumed this would die with the end of the Cold War."*

Russia Caught Building Secret Complex

1996 - April 16. *Associated Press* reported:

> *"In a secret project that may have roots deep in the Cold War,* **Russia is building a mammoth, underground military complex** *in the Ural Mountains, The New York Times reported today. The project, which has been observed by U.S. spy satellites, involves a huge complex served by a railroad, a highway and thousands of workers, Western officials and Russian witnesses told the Times. Construction of the project mystifies American specialists, who speculate it may be anything from an underground nuclear command post to a secret weapons production plant, the report said. The Russian Defense Ministry refused to discuss the project."*

1996 - November 19. *NBC News* Anchor Tom Brokaw:

> *"If Russia is so dependent on the United States for economic help these days, for political support, even for security questions, why was it buying a spy in the American CIA? And why would a career CIA officer sell out?"*

NBC's Pete William's reported:

- *"The U.S. State Department called the recruitment of Harold Nicholson as a spy: "unacceptable and inconsistent with the pattern of relations between the U.S & Russia."*

- *"Intelligence officials told NBC News, Russia's spy apparatus still aggressively works to find sources inside the U.S. government."*

- *"Intelligence insiders indicate the U.S. spies on Russia because the Soviets still have the largest stockpile of nuclear, chemical and biological weapons in the world."*

- *"Former Defense Official Graham Allison said 'Russia remains the only country on the globe where decisions and actions by the government could cause our society to disappear."*

- *"Some intelligence analysts think the CIA should pay more attention to the growing nuclear capabilities of Third World countries, like China and India."*

Russia, Red China form Military Partnership:

1996 - December. Moscow. *"Russia, China plan new 'strategic partnership' Moscow -* **Russia and China pledged Saturday to create a stronger new partnership aimed at countering the influence of the United States. The two long time rivals declared their intentions to forge closer military and economic ties** *in a communiqué at the end of Chinese Premier Li Peng's three-day visit to Moscow. Russian papers hailed the 'strategic partnership'. The respected daily Izvestia called it "our reply to the United States" and Nezavisimaya Gazeta said "it will entail changes of a geopolitical nature."*

Clinton-Gore politics mirror Communism:

1997 - During an interview, former Navy Intelligence Operative, David Price, author of the book *Secret* said:

"I produce actual Communist Party USA literature and flyers in the book where they urge voters to vote for Bill Clinton, where they say Bill Clinton's agenda is their agenda, where they outline all the things he plans to do to the United States and how that is congruent with Communist Party goals."

In the book *Secret,* Price points out that Reed Irvine, of Accuracy In Media, reported Jeremy Rifkin worked with a radical left movement and in 1971 "was assigned to sanitize its literature and tone down the socialist rhetoric so it would not drive away the average citizen." This sheds new light on Rifkin's use of big words like 'biosphere' and unique words like 'inimical' to camouflage socialist ideas.

Communism is Not Dead

1996 - December. *The American Bulletin* featured an article by Cleon Skousen, "Bill Clinton's Age Old Christmas List, AKA Communist Aims and Goals". Skousen, a highly respected 16-year veteran of the FBI specialized in the Communist movement. He listed the 45 Communist goals from his book *The Naked Communist*. These goals were entered into the Congressional Record, January 10, 1963. Skousen pointed out many goals have been achieved. A few goals from that list:

#4   Permit free trade between nations regardless of Communist affiliation and regardless of whether or not items could be used for war

#10   Allow all Soviet satellites individual representation in the UN

#24   Break down the cultural standards of morality by promoting pornography and obscenity in books, magazines, motion pictures, radio and TV

#26   Present homosexuality, degeneracy and promiscuity as normal, natural and healthy

#28   Eliminate prayer or any phase of religious expression in the schools

#32   Support any socialist movement to give centralized control over any part of the culture, education, social agencies, welfare programs, mental health clinics, etc.

#40   Discredit the family as an institution. Encourage promiscuity and easy divorce

#42   Create the impression that violence and insurrection are legitimate aspects of the American tradition; students and special interest groups should rise up and use united force to solve economic, political and social problems"

Goal #42 is what the Green Communists are in the process of doing. Review goal #10. The idea was to have multiple communist entities with individual influence at the UN. In 1963 the Soviet Union had satellites. If we bring the goal into the 90's, it fits the Green use of NGOs or non-government organizations to influence UN decisions. Non-government environmental organizations can be accredited with 'observer' or 'consultative' status on UN issues. Communist's wanted to multiply their influence at the UN. Today, multiple Green NGOs have the ability to influence UN decisions. Clinton's Executive Order #12986 gave NGOs 'above the law' status.

An interesting point:

1996 - September. "Al Gore's father (also a Senator from Tennessee) was a close friend, confidante and benefactor of billionaire Armand Hammer who worked as an agent for the Soviet Union from Lenin through Gorbachev. Hammer's father Julius was the founder of the Communist Party USA."

McAlvany Intelligence Advisor

Communists Activities on the Home Front:

1996 - July 4. Los Angeles:

*Press reported fight during two-sided demonstration was over immigration. An eye witness reports citizens were attacked by Progressive Labor Party militants. Flyers at the scene read: **"We need to unite for Revolution.** A system based on racist terror, lies and exploitation must be destroyed. **We need communism."***

1996 - September. *Los Angeles Sentinel* reported:

"Carl Dix, national spokesperson of the Revolutionary Communist Party USA was in Los Angeles to spread the gospel of revolutionary communism to Southern California"

1997 - May 3. "Communism, 1997 style" by Daniel Yovich. Yovich, a *Times* Correspondent, reported:

> *"Purdue students and area residents take to the streets to rally support for the communist fight to abolish the capitalist system".* The event was sponsored by the Progressive Labor Party. James Smith, office manager in the Chicago Progressive Labor Party estimates about 500 marchers will assemble. Smith said, "We don't need white power, black power or Chicano power, *we need to build a Communist Party of several thousand workers prepared to turn the bosses' fascism and wars into a revolution for communism."*

1997 - October 8. Communist Party USA press release states:

> *"The Communist party denounced attempts by the FBI ... to connect the CPUSA with its former youth organization to the arrest of three individuals from Wisconsin ... the FBI ... looks to connect legitimate political views and legitimate political movements as evidence of being "foreign agents."*

Green Movement and Communists share goals:

1992 - Communist Party USA's Environmental Program praised by Hazel Wolf, Seattle Audobon Society. She said it:

> *"presents a viable plan to carry out on the long march to Socialism."*

Green Movement, Green Party work together:

1996 - *Sierra Club Green Guide*, Green Party listed with top 50 of the most powerful and influential environmental groups

1992 - World Coordination of Green Parties position:

> *"The notion of ownership would be replaced by the notion of tenancy, the rent of the land set to accurately reflect its use "*

1992 - U.S. Green Party Program position statement:

> *"Green communities are supported by the implementation of land trust, intentional communities, shared ownership, and other alternatives to traditional individual land and property ownership."*

From the *Communist Manifesto*:

> *"Abolition of private property in land and application of all rents of land to public purposes".*

Greens will use Biodiversity and ecosystem management to seize control of U.S. land base:

1996 - November. *Ecologic* magazine on World Food Summit:

> ***"Land is seen by the United Nations to be a "global commons" that should not be owned by individuals. Land is a public resource which must be controlled by the government...***
>
> *Government should allocate land use to individuals based on their productivity. Private ownership of land is an obstacle to food security*

The *Convention on Biological Diversity* and the *Global Biodiversity Assessment*, the United Nations 1140 page instruction book for implementing the treaty calls for

> *... the conversion of 'at least 50%' of the land area in the United States to be converted to wilderness, off limits to human beings. An additional 25% of the land area is to be designated as 'buffer zones' that are to be managed collaboratively.*
>
> *People are to be relocated into "sustainable communities," the design for which is presented in the President's Council on Sustainable Development report, Sustainable America: A New Consensus."*

1997 - May. *Anza Valley Outlook* news headline, "Maryland passes U.N. Biodiversity Treaty". Author Joan Veon stated:

> *"President Clinton's visit to the Maryland legislature in February was not for tea. At stake was the passing of two radical bills which fulfill the objectives of the UN Biodiversity Treaty. The bills Rural Legacy and Smart Growth will:*
>
> > • *force people to move to 'approved areas'*
> > • *change the meaning of property rights*
> > • *shift from Constitutional to environmental governance"*

A Congressional report provided by the American Policy Center indicates over 51 million acres in the U.S., 68% of our national park acreage, including the Statue of Liberty, is to be placed under U.N. control, all under the guise of protecting the environment.

Greens are planning industrial collapse of U.S.:

1992 - The Earth Charter is Gorbachev's and Socialist UN leader Maurice Strong's pet project. Strong shared their plan to transform America at the Earth Summit in Rio. Strong said:

> *"It is clear that current lifestyles and consumption patterns of the affluent middle class, involving high meat intake, consumption of large amounts of frozen and convenience foods, ownership of motor vehicles, small electric appliances, home and work place air conditioning and suburban housing are unsustainable.*
>
> *... Isn't it the only hope for the planet that the industrialized civilizations collapse? Isn't it our responsibility to bring this about? The United States is clearly the greatest risk to the world's ecological health."*

Sierra Club, industrial collapse and draining Lake Powell:

1997 - Sierra Club plans to drain Lake Powell to restore the visual, the plant and wildlife environment. The Lake, located on the Arizona-Utah border, was established in 1963 at a cost of $515 million. It supplies electric to 6 million ratepayers in 6 western states, 638,000 households. In 1995, 2.5 million people visited the lake, 445,000 for boating. Draining the lake would collapse the lake-based economy. Shutting-off electric services in 6 states could set the stage for industrial collapse.

Greens call for non-consumptive use of wildlife:

1995 - October 11. *Wall Street Journal*. Charles McCoy reports:

> "*The animal rights movement has a new angle, it wants to ban fishing. Not just big commercial operations... all fishing, from the pursuit of the wily trout here in Montana to cane-pole catfishing down at the local pond.*"

Two Faces of Green. 'Set-em-up and sell-em-out.'

1996 - *The Future is Ours, A Handbook for Student Activists in the 21st Century* by John Bartlett features a Chapter titled "Act First, Apologize Later" by Adam Werbach, the 23 year old president of the Sierra Club. Adam had help from the Sierra Club's Board of Directors. Sierra and Werbach share this manipulative strategy:

> "*bad guys that we already know, like the National Rifle Association, continually lobbies Congress to allow hunting in all our national parks ... I will never say don't work with those who oppose you... Hunters, for example can be powerful allies of environmentalists. Both groups share the goal of preserving our natural resources for the future. I will say, however, that there comes a point when you know who your friends are and don't owe anything to anyone else.*"

Werbach indicates the Sierra Club believes their role is:

- *to form public opinion, not follow it*
- *to show what being 'green' really means*
- *to take broad visionary strokes*

Greens get more support from the Clinton Administration:

1997 - January. *Property Rights Update* newsletter reports:

> "President Clinton issued Executive Order 12986. The E.O. was written to protect members of the United Nations committee on International Union for Conservation of Nature and Natural Resources. It reads: I hereby extend to the International Union for Conservation of Nature and Natural Resources the privileges and immunities that provide or pertain to immunity from suit."

> "The report states 'this E.O. was intended to protect the non-government organizations from suit... when we obtained a copy of the membership of this UN organization, we were shocked to see the list included several U.S. government agencies'... No wonder Bruce Babbitt is running amuck and getting away with it."

A list of members was provided. A few are listed below. Why would Clinton-Gore give these groups 'above the law' status?

Environmental Protection Agency	U.S. Forest Service
Department of Interior	National Park Service
National Audubon Society	Sierra Club
Natural Resource Defense Council	World Wildlife Fund
National Wildlife Federation	World Bank
Nature Conservancy	UNEP
World Resources Institute	UNDP

There is hope. According to the report:

> "attorney Karen Budd-Falen states Presidential proclamations and executive orders do not have 'full force and effect', it means they could be disputed in a lawsuit."

Environmental Grantmakers calling the shots:

1997 - February. Notes from the Environmental Grantmakers Association meeting, provided by the National Center for Public Policy Research, included these points:

- *"Sorting out what to do administratively (by Executive order) and legislatively. We want to maximize the **executive order** approach and use that as a template for legislative action."*

- *"Nader suggests we speak of pollution in terms of violence. Pollution should be a law and order issue."*

- *"Watch out that the media become tired of us and stops believing our stories."*

- *"With the resurgence of **the labor movement the time is right for their collaboration with the environmental movement.**"*

Greens building a 'progressive', revolutionary movement:

The Green- labor or 'workers' alliance is already in motion. One of the independent parties will be the umbrella to unite the masses in revolution. The environmental-labor alliance is a goal outlined in the Communist Parties environmental program. Gus Hall was a founding organizer of the AFL-CIO1997 - Jane Perkins, environmental liaison of the AFL-CIO was the keynote speaker for the Ancient Forest Conference. She advocated building the labor-environmental alliance. Prior to the AFL-CIO, Perkins was the President of Friends of the Earth, a group identified in *Target America* as an affiliate of NLG. NLG affiliate groups promote communist ideas.

Gloria LaRiva, Vice Presidential candidate for the Worker's World Party was also invited to speak at that conference. Her Party's primary goal is a socialist revolution.

'Compulsory Green living' from the top-down:

1994 - Clinton-Gore create the President's Council on Sustainable Development. The PCSD has since developed Task Force reports that lay the groundwork to transform America to a 'sustainable society'. These 'all-encompassing' reports will affect every sector of our society. Reports include:

- Sustainable America, A New Consensus
- Energy and Transportation
- Population and Consumption
- Natural Resources
- Sustainable Agriculture
- Eco-Efficiency
- Education for Sustainability (includes 'Green schools')
- Public Linkage, Dialogue and Education

1996 - *PCSD Task Force* reports include a disclaimer indicating that the ideas presented do not 'necessarily' reflect administration policy. Yet the Clinton-Gore Administration has already directed the Council to implement these ideas as policy. A September, 1996 letter from the PCSD states:

> *"As requested we are sending you our report, Sustainable America: A New Consensus, which was transmitted to President Clinton in March of this year. At that time,* **President Clinton asked the Council to continue its work and begin the process of implementing the report's recommendations...** *As we proceed with the implementation phase, we encourage you to stay in touch and to inform us of progress your community is making in pursuing a sustainable future."*

Karen Anderson, a California educational activist, points out on page ii of the "Public Linkage, Dialogue and Education" report (PLTF) it states: "for practical reasons the Task Force **did not seek to provide policy recommendations"**. On page iii, it states:

*"PLTF's mission is to: **formulate policies** on how to integrate sustainable development into the nation's formal and non-formal educational systems."*

Clinton-Gore promote socialist ideas for private property:

1996 - The Center of Excellence for Sustainable Development web site, handled by the Department of Energy and recommended by the PCSD featured the article "Owning and Belonging, The private landowner as an Ecosystem Member" by Eric Freyogle from the Spring '96 issue of *Sustain*. Freyogle outlines his strategy to achieve sustainability. He states:

*"**serious environmentalists need to express their support for private property as a general idea ... the more vocal this support the fewer fears that will arise.** The fewer fears, the more feasible it will be to undertake long-term ecological education.*

*... Once Americans understand the ecological roles of particular lands ... **they can support new land-use limits. Step by step, they can embrace new ownership norms***

*... **as more and more privately owned acres become subject to land use restrictions and conservation easements, the line between private and public land will diminish in importance** and rightly so. In years to come shared control will become more common on private and rural lands... **What counts ultimately is not whose name is on the deed but how the land is put to use and who makes the land-use decisions.**"*

Greens will push 'village concept' of 'community children':

1996 - Hillary Clinton's book *It Takes a Village* is released.

'Village concept' will be used to glorify Green Communist's ideas for 'Eco-Villages', communes and co-housing:

1995 - *Asking for the Earth* by James George - forward by Maurice Strong. George's vision for a better world includes:

> *"What was perceived in the 60's as weird counter-culture has already ripened into a more stable and responsible proto-culture."*

1996 - Jonathon Porritt is featured in book titled:

> *Eco-Villages and Sustainable Communities, Models for the 21st Century*

1996 - *Utne Reader Almanac*, featured article:

> *"Enjoy what's best about both village life and modern living...Eco-villages update the 60's communal farm for the 21st century."*

1991 - *Communes and the Green Vision, Counterculture, Lifestyle and the New Age* by David Pepper

1997 - Center of Excellence for Sustainable Development web site recommended by the PCSD, offers many ways to create a sustainable community including Eco-villages, co-housing or housing cooperatives and links to the global eco-village network.

Americans are famous for innovative ideas. What is wrong is the approach our representatives are taking to transform America. Open debate vs. no debate. We need a healthy public debate. Every American does not have access to the Internet to discover these plans. The American people ought to be informed in one way or another of what is being considered, why it's being considered and then have an opportunity to support or decline the idea.

Greens know what they're doing but no one else does.

Top level Green strategists gathered for the annual Ancient Forest Activists Conference. The "Election Review and

Planning Political Strategy" panel featured Marty Hayden, Sierra Club Legal Defense Fund, Chad Hanson, Earth Island Institute, Connie Stewart, Northcoast Environmental Center and former Congressman Jim Jontz, Western Ancient Forest Campaign. Panelists shared ideas, tactics and goals. Stewart told participants:

> *"Big trees motivate them. Historical issues motivate them. Public access motivates them. It's great to talk science among ourselves but I'll never forget, I was in an Earth First! Rally and these 17 year olds were talking about microorganisms. I'm thinking, nobody wants to hear this stuff, you're talking to the media, just talk about the special-ness of the place. We don't have to die of virtue or justify why we want to protect things ...* **JUST GET THE LAND!"**

We've been Set-Up:

1997 - August. The *Free American* features an excerpt from a 1991 speech by David Rockefeller said:

> *"We are grateful to the Washington Post, the New York Times, Time Magazine and other great publications whose directors have attended our meetings and respected their promises of discretion for almost forty years. It would have been impossible for us to develop our plan for the world if we had been subject to the bright lights of publicity during those years but the world is now more prepared to march toward world government."*

1953 - The Ford Foundation President said:

> *"we will use our grant-making power to so alter life in the United States that it can be comfortably merged with the Soviet Union."*

1977 - Rockefeller Brothers book, *The Unfinished Agenda,* a citizen's policy guide to environmental issues. The last chapter is titled 'A Question of Values'. It states:

> *"this book is about a world transition from abundance to scarcity, a transition that is already well underway".* A *'sustainable society'* is referred to and the alternative energy-policy path is oriented not toward the supply of abstract economic services but **toward the satisfaction of human needs"**

1972 - Gus Hall outlines the same idea in his book *Ecology*:

> *"The means of production, factories, mines and mills become the property of the people. They operate and produce only to 'fulfill human needs'."*

Gorbachev to target U.S. elite to support his Earth Charter:

1995 - September. State of the World Forum, 500 of America's most influential people were invited to Gorbachev's event. He was seeking assistance for building a new civilization with new spiritual values to guide society.

Gorbachev's Earth Charter is designed to control the lives of individuals and businesses worldwide. These are vague ideas that can be easily twisted into more and more rules:

1997 - Earth Charter speech, Rio+5 Forum. Gorbachev said:

> **"I believe the Earth Charter opens a new phase not only in the ecological movement, but also in the world's public life.** We must do everything we can so that this Charter is accepted exactly as it was designed, **a set of vitally important rules."**

The goal was for the U.S. to sign it before the year 2000. The Rockefellers hosted the 1997 Earth Charter Conference.

Green Communists are using TV to brainwash Americans:

Gorbachev's Green Cross International programs include:

> *"Education through Entertainment in the USA ... Encouraging leading Hollywood Directors, producers, writers and other performing artist to incorporate environmental themes into entertainment is an effective way to reach millions of people.* Cooperating with the Environmental Media Association and Global Green USA, GCI promotes the use of film, television and music as a **persuasive channel** to inform audiences about living environmentally responsible lives."

Rockefeller's also recognized the potential of using entertainment as a tool. It states in *The Unfinished Agenda*:

> *"very clearly television is a major influence on the American value system, the basic ideas that inform all actions and choices. This value system has enormous implications for the environment"*

Rapidly approaching stage three. Control of the Airwaves:

1998 - February. *Citizens' Intelligence Digest* quote:

> *"After you witness ('60 Minutes' producer) Don Hewitt BRAGGING that he doctored the news and provided needed 'medicine' for a sick candidate (Bill Clinton), you will NEVER watch '60 Minutes' the same way again."*
>
> Jim Quinn
Pittsburgh Radio Host

1998 - February. *Free American* reported the following:

> *"Richard M. Cohan, Senior Producer of CBS political news said: 'We are going to impose our agenda on the coverage by dealing with the issues and subjects we choose to deal with'."*

"Richard Salant, former President of *CBS* said:

> *'Our job is to give people not what they want but what we decide they ought to have'.*"

The *Free American* reports:

> *"the recent curious proposal for a special UN 'jam- squad'... a special UN team that could be dispatched to crisis points around the globe carrying equipment to jam or block harmful radio and TV broadcast... Writing in the current issue of 'Foreign Affairs' magazine, Jamie M. Metzl, a former United Nations human rights officer, proposes the creation of what would be officially called an 'independent information intervention unit' at the UN. It's goal, he writes, would be 'countering dangerous messages that incite people to violence'."*

Entertainment promoting Communist messages:

'Working' is a good example of 'behind the scenes' TV programming with a comic facade. The show opens with what appears to be a film-clip of Russian peasants marching 'drone-like' off to work. The messages from one episode included feminists are superior; employees are mistreated 'workers' up against a Boss who is a monumental Capitalist pig. The communist term for 'workers', proletariat, was used. The story line has the Boss pursuing a temporary employee, a feminist who tells him, **"This company stands for every discriminating business practice there is. What ever happened to Revolution in this country?** The Boss quickly dumps his position and says his name is 'Fidel'. He doesn't know what feminist values are so he has the employees make him a 'crib sheet'. He reads it and says, **"I'm for hand gun control?"** Next, Boss and feminist are in an employee's apartment when the employee comes home and catches them. Boss quickly says, "This is my roommate, Poncho, **he just got back from Northern California where he's been spiking redwood trees."** Feminist says: **"Good for you Poncho!"** Final words, **"Fight the Power!"**

Promoting Eco-Terrorism is unprofessional and irresponsible.

Hollywood Honors Communists:

1997 - October 30. AP reports Paul Jarrico, a Hollywood writer blacklisted in the 40's died in a car accident after he "received a standing ovation when Hollywood looked back at its darkest days 50 years ago and honored 'blacklist survivors'."

Greens will target religious leaders for political gain and to change the religious focus from creator to creation. Communist goal #27, "infiltrate the churches...."

1995 - November. Washington, *Associated Press* headline:

*"Religious groups speak up for the animals. Several churches and synagogues are wading into the congressional fight over the Endangered Species Act, arguing God is on their side. 'Over the past 30 years, the Endangered Species Act has served as un ark for imperiled American wildlife, said Rabbi David Saperstein, of the Reform Jewish Movement and the **"National Religious Partnership for the Environment."***

1997 - December. CFACT, Washington, D.C. reports:

*"If the new politically correct church litany being widely circulated by the **National Religious Partnership for the Environment** catches on many pulpits may elevate saving the planet right up there with saving our souls. In the opening the leader offers sacred adoration for rocks, rivers and sky while people call on the Almighty to heal our water, land and air. Later, the congregation begs forgiveness for our wanton greed, careless waste and polluting ways. Apparently, some think Moses' Top 10 list isn't sufficient without a Green commandment of their own."*

Greens have no respect for traditional religious beliefs or they would not mock them nor arrogantly suggest a Green replacement.

Gorbachev thinks he ought to replace Moses:

1997 - May. *LA Times*, topic Earth Charter, Gorbachev stated:

> *"My hope is that **this charter will be a kind of 'Ten Commandments', a 'Sermon on the Mount' that provides a guide for human behavior** toward the environment in the next century and beyond".*

Communist goal #27: "replace revealed religion with social religion". The social religion is Green spirituality and the Earth Charter.

1995 - Winter edition, *Creation Spirituality*. Letter to the editor:

> *"I'm deeply disappointed to realize that 'Creation Spirituality' is a political front magazine. I have taken it as a source for spiritual inspiration and awe -- not to join a radical movement, which the Autumn 1995 issue indicates...*
>
> A. McCarry, Calif

1995 - Autumn edition, *Creation Spirituality*. Editor Matthew Fox, "Creation Spirituality: Here Come the Postmoderns" exposes the political purpose. Fox indicates Creation spirituality is:

- the opposite of fundamentalism
- the tradition of pre-patriarchal Europe, goddess worship
- creating a 'new story' of our origins and culture
- committed to social and ecological justice
- sides with movements waging these struggles, like postmoderns

Charles Jencks, author of the *'Postmodern Reader'* is quoted. He describes postmodern as:

> *"together under a very large ecumenical umbrella, are many of the current liberationist movements, feminism and post-feminist are essential to it... the green and ecological movements have contributed important values and ideas, especially inter-*

connectedness and holism and particularly connect-up with...
other post-modern religious trends..."

Fox indicates *Creation Spirituality* is a political front. He said:

"... the very fact the Newts have so much power is
evidence the more green and progressive forces have not
done our job well enough, a job of educating and of
making coalitions...we hope Creation Spirituality will
link up with other postmodern movements... to influence
our culture more profoundly."

Guilty man flees when no one pursues? Fox stated:

"... the Christian Coalition, active in the Republican Party...
used its power to "ban the word imagination" from a school
district. Fox goes on to say:

"One reason why imagination is replacing Communism as the
new 'bete noire' of the right wing is that the post modern age is
an age of new images."

Fox speaks of influencing our culture, our interconnectedness with nature and of new images for a new age.
Hitler also used the earth connection, hailed a new age and
used new images to erase a culture.

Green philosopher Murray Bookchin also promotes post-
patriarchal, communist values. S.S.D.D. Same stuff different
decade.

According to *Webster's* dictionary, a 'bete noire' is 'a person or
thing especially disliked or dreaded'.

Why do the Greens consistently identify themselves with
Communism? Guilty man flees when no one pursues.

'Fellow Travelers' term used to identify closet Communist:

A minister wrote to Fox asking, "*What role can Protestant Evangelical churches play in realizing the vision of creation spirituality and its vision for the world.*" Fox ended his reply with: "*Best wishes on your journey and that of your fellow travelers in faith!*"

Creation Spirituality
Spring 1997

Communist Goal #24 Break down the cultural standards of morality. Goal #27, "Discredit the Bible"

'Hitler went to Heaven' **by Neale Donald Walsch:**

1996 - December. *AP* reports "His 'Conversations' paid off."

"Neale Donald Walsch has a hit with Conversations With God, a book he says virtually wrote itself in early morning discussions with God during which She revealed Herself as a benign deity... and according to Walsch said that, 'good and evil and right and wrong don't exist because God judges no one... there are no rules, restrictions, taboos or sin... God told him, Do what you want to do... I do not love good more than I love bad... Hitler went to heaven. When you understand this you understand God...."

The reporter asked, **"How does Walsch know the conversation is with God, not his own imagination?** Walsch replies:

*"the thoughts that were coming through me were thoughts I never had... **the ideas that came to me were ideas I had never entertained.**"*

The reporter then points out, **"the message is strangely similar to an obscure book written in 1982... called *Hitler Went to Heaven*.** The author? A Neale Marshall Walsch, who later changed his name to Bob White, then Neale Donald Walsch:

*...**It's the same ideas, Walsch says. But I had forgotten all about that book.**"*

Communist Goal #11, "promote the United Nations as the only hope for mankind... demand it be set-up as a one-world government"

1997 - May. *Magical Blend* magazine. Article titled "What is God telling this man now? Neale Donald Walsch's *Conversations with God, BOOK II*" Quotes from the article:

> God: "I am suggesting your codes of behavior be based on a Higher Understanding... **Whenever CommonGood or CollectiveGood is mentioned everyone yells 'Communism!...** you have failed miserably... your society is profit driven..."

> Walsch: "How can we eliminate... the pain... the suffering?"

> God answers: "by eliminating all separations between you. By **constructing a New Model of the World.** By holding it within the framework of a **new idea...** which is a radical departure from the present world view... this will only happen if you reconstruct your global reality and govern yourselves accordingly..."

> **Walsch: "Are you talking about a One World Government?"**

> **God: "I am."**

It is important to remember, one of Hitler's key principles was placing the 'common good before individual good'. It's also interesting the communist term 'Model' is used to describe this 'new idea' for One World Government. It's the same term Gorbachev used when he indicated Americans had been given enough time to get over the fear of Communists forcing their **model** on us. It looks like another way to justify World Communism.

Under the Communist model, people are dispensable:

Golitsyn, in the *Perestroika Deception*, reminds Americans there is good reason to reverse our position with Russia. He states:

"The moral basis for a reversal of the American response and for recommending a rejection of cooperation with the Soviet Union is simple: A system which has murdered 20 million of its own people (50 million, if the loss of life in China under Communism is included) which has raped its intellectuals and has brought suffering and misery to the peoples of the Soviet Empire does not deserve to be renewed. The American people are under no obligation to help with the resurrection of such a plainly evil system."

Green leaders express same idea and numbers for drastic population reduction. Share idea to 'eliminate' people:

"In order to stabilize world population, we must eliminate 350,000 people per day."

Jacques Cousteau
1991, UNESCO Courier

March 1996, it was learned that Jacques Cousteau was the number one promoter of Communism and raising money for the Communist Party worldwide.

"Right now there are just way too many people on the planet. We need to cut the world's population from the current 5 billion to no more than 250 to 350 million."

Ted Turner, 1996
Last Trumpet Newsletter

Reducing the population to 250 -350 million would mean that over 4 billion people would have to be eliminated.

"one of my three main goals would be to reduce the human population to about 100 million worldwide."

Dave Foreman, Earth First! Co-founder
Sierra Club - Board of Directors

Make control possible by making control legal:

Earth Action, a network of 1600 Green groups pushing the U.S. to sign the Climate Change Treaty advocate *improving*

*energy use by "shifting from the private car to public transport"
and the creation of **"an environmental decision-making
body be established at the UN, able to set binding
standards for protection of the planet without waiting for
unanimous agreement".***

Could binding standards include population reduction?

Green Police, Eco-cops emerge to protect the environment:

1997- June 7. *San Francisco Examiner:*

> *"U.S. Soldiers going on nature watch". Report states "U.S.
> soldiers gearing up to take on new duties...as warriors for the
> environment...will be asked to help protect jungles and
> endangered species..."This is a legitimate military issue" said
> Timothy Wirth, undersecretary of state for global affairs..."this
> is not a bunch of trendy greenies".*

**Communist goal #11 Promote UN...demand it be set-up as
one world government... with it's own, independent armed
forces.**

1997 - London. *Associated Press* reports:

> *"UN Secretary General Kofi Annan says he had to reassure
> some members of Congress that they need not fear a UN
> takeover of the United States." Kofi said, "As I said, we don't
> have the means to take the U.S. and even if we did take it, I
> wasn't sure we could hold it. Not that we would want to do it in
> any case."*

Is this a 'Freudian Slip' or is the UN making plans? Americans
ought to take this 'slip of the tongue' seriously. It's not probable the
UN Secretary General would say "even if we did take it, I wasn't
sure we could hold it" unless they were considering taking that
action.

Greens use 'chicken little' plan to scare us into submission:

This quote from the book, *The Holes in the Ozone Scare, The Scientific Evidence The Sky Isn't Falling*:

> *"Witch doctors operate on the basis of asserted supernatural powers that they use to scare and awe their devotees. Climate catastrophe doomsayers use the same kind of psychological manipulation to achieve their goals. This was revealed by the leading climate modeler in the United States, Stephen Schneider, in an interview with the October 1989 issue of 'Discover' magazine. Schneider, who works at the National Center of Atmospheric Research at Boulder, Colorado, said:*

> ***"We need to get some broad-based support to capture the public's imagination.** That of course entails getting loads of media coverage. **So we have to offer up scary scenarios, make simplified, dramatic statements and make little mention of any doubts we may have... Each of us has to decide what is the right balance between being effective and being honest."***

1992 - Environmental Program, Communist Party USA.   It states:

> *"Move forward rapidly on international environmental treaties"*

Global Warming is a lot of 'Hot Air':

1997 - December 12. *Mail Tribune* headline: "Local scientist cool on warming" by Paul Fattig. Fattig reports:

> *"Arthur Robinson says the international hue and cry over global warming is a lot of hot air... and warns the accord reached in Japan will cause more harm than good... Robinson said, 'Global temperatures go up and down with the solar activity.... a small fluctuation in the sun's activity causes global changes". Fattig reports this "conclusion was published in the Wall Street Journal on December 4. 'Robinson said, 'There are lots of scientists who have looked at global warming and know it's nonsense'.*

"One is Sallie Baliunas, an astro-physicist at Harvard who read the essay and said: 'His (Robinson's) facts are so straightforward: There is no evidence for catastrophic warming. It astonishes me that people haven't bothered to read his data'.

"It's all fact, he's dead on target, offered physicist, Robert Jastrow, director of the Mount Wilson Observatory near Los Angeles. Jastrow is also a senior scientist at the George Marshall Institute, a think-tank of scientists in Washington, D.C..

"You'll notice we're still below the average and that it's been warming for 3,000 years, Robinson said, pointing to a chart, things were warmer in the Middle Ages 1000 years ago than they are today... there were no global disasters associated with these higher temperatures. "Robinson argues, 'mankind's use of hydrocarbons is helping the environment by increasing vegetation, including trees', but he says, 'his voice is being drowned out'." Robinson said, What gets more attention? The guy who says the sky is falling or the guy who says everything will be fine?"

Robinson is the founder of the Oregon Institute of Science and Medicine; he has a BA from the California Institute of Technology and a doctorate in chemistry from the University of California at San Diego.

Green goal to control the auto industry includes promoting bicycling to reduce the use of private automobiles:

1997 - May 3. The *Oregonian*, headline "Bike Month gets rolling with politicians push...Four U.S. representatives speak about efforts to encourage Oregonians to ride a bicycle instead of drive a car". Kathryn Tongue reports:

"Rep. James Oberstar D-Minnesota joined reps. Peter DeFazio, Earl Blumenauer and Darlene Hooley, all Democrats to celebrate bicycling... Oberstar, a proponent of federal financing for bicycling and walking said:

'as we take people out of cars and into other modes of transportation including bikes, we'll have cleaner air and a better quality of life'."

Another goal outlined in the *Communist Manifesto* is:

*"Centralize the means of communication and **transport** in the hands of the state"*

1992 - Children's book *For the Love of Our Earth*. Author P.K. Hallinan, explains to children that if we love the earth:

"We'll stop using engines that sputter and spark"

Other Green goals on the way to being achieved:

1991 - *Trilogy* magazine. More from the list of "50 Difficult Things You Can Do To Save The Earth", based on a survey of environmental groups and compiled by the editors of *Earth Island Journal*. Other goals on the list the Greens are working toward:

11. Stop the sale, distribution and export of cigarettes

24. Replace majority rule with proportional representation

33. Redirect military budget... retrain soldiers for ecological restoration

43. Travel by bus, never by air

Earth Day is a front for the Green Communist Movement:

Earth Day 1970 - Dennis Hayes stated:

*"We are building a movement with a broad political base which transcends political boundaries, that values people more than technology, people more than political boundaries and **people more than profit."***

The Green Party, Communist Party slogan: People Before Profit.

Communist goal #41 Emphasize the need to raise children away form the negative influence of parents..." Education reform includes teaching communist values:

Carolyn Steinke, founder of PIE, Parents Involved in Education says Polytechnical Vocational Education is:

> *"nothing more than training your child for a job and calling it education. It's the Soviet educational system in America."*

Gorbachev supposedly fell from power in 1991. In 1990, the U.S. Dept. of Education spent $4 million to study changing our educational system to match enemy Communist Russia? Why, in 1997, are government officials pushing the educational system developed by the Soviets designed to train their children to be Communist? The Greens, like Mrs. Clinton, believe 'it takes a whole village' to raise a child.

1996 - September 16. *New American* article "Target: Total Government, sheds new light on the village concept":

> *"A forthright endorsement of the Marxist perspective on the family was offered by Dr. Mary Jo Bane, the Clinton Administration's Asst. Secretary of Admin. for Children and Families. According to Dr. Bane:*

> *"If we want to talk about equality of opportunity for children, then the fact that children are raised in families means there's no equality...we must take them away from families and communally raise them...'"*

The article went on to point out that "the following directive was issued to Russian Communist Party educators in 1918:

> *'We must remove the children from the crude influence of their families. We must take them over and, to speak frankly, nationalize them'."*

Green teachers cross the line, lie to officials and violate the public trust to teach children away from their parents:

1996 - Educators attended the Ancient Forest Activist Conference to discuss environmental education. John Borowski, a teacher and ancient forest activist was a facilitator. Borowski said:

> "I've been bringing kids up to Opal Creek for years. **My whole gig here is to get teachers in traditional situations K-12 and higher to incorporate whatever they're teaching into environmental topics.**
>
> My first year at Dayton, I thought how can I get the kids to Opal Creek? I'm teaching Chemistry. **I want to give field trips to this forest so I tell the administration "it's to do water studies and it has nothing to do with the forest".** At least that's what I told them.
>
> **...We did do nitrate and phosphate tests but it lead into "What's a water shed?" It became very easy for me to bring in these other aspects and I could defend it quite easily.**
>
> ...The following year I said, I would like to take all our ninth graders to Opal Creek, integrate a bunch of studies, creative writing, map drawing and compass work...
>
> ... That's the reason we were able to reach kids. **You don't take a group of kids to the forest, walk around and then it's done because they don't sense seriously why they were there.**
>
> **...The President of the Board of Education was irate we were turning the kids into 'Tree Huggers' when they go to Opal Creek. His son is a sophomore who went last year and now his goal is to save old and native forests.**
>
> **...I can't tell you how powerful education is.** If we're ever going to teach the **right way** to our kids (K-12) we will teach them in a creative fashion. That's the ticket. **There's a hook for every**

there. Get on your Boards of Education. Then you could direct Curriculum."

Communist Goal # 36, Infiltrate and gain control of more unions. The Communist Party is happy:

1997 - August 30. *People's Weekly World,* Gus Hall states:

> *"We can roughly define the beginning of a new era as the militant rank and file upsurge of the 1990's the radicalization of the working class that changed the leadership and direction of the AFL-CIO. The new level of prestige of our Party is evidence that anti-communism is on its way out."*

The president of the AFL-CIO is John Sweeney. In 1990, the *Eco-Socialist Review,* newsletter for the Democratic Socialists of America, listed Al Gore and John Sweeney as speakers for the DSA conference. Sweeney is a DSA member. Greens have connections to the AFL-CIO, DSA and 'progressive' groups.

1997 - October 4. *Peoples Weekly World,* Fred Gaboury said:

> *"AFL-CIO takes out old anti-Communist clause....delegates to the 21st Constitutional Convention unanimously repealed language in the federation's constitution barring members of the Communist Party from full participation in the AFL-CIO or subordinate bodies"*

1997 - November 22. *Peoples Weekly World,* "A new day for reds". Reporter Scott Marshall quotes Gus Hall:

> *"For over 50 years, our party has had to deal with the biggest of all lies - anti-communism. The removal (AFL-CIO removal of communist clause from constitution) has ramifications way beyond the trade union movement. It is a historic event I have been waiting almost 50 years to celebrate."* Hall's final comment was: *"it offers hope for a better life through united struggle today and a vision for winning a socialist USA tomorrow."*

Green goal: Transform society and change our values:

1995 - Bioneers Conference, San Francisco. Topics: A Green Political Future and Values, Politics and Culture - to reformulate our societies core values.

Greens: "If we can't get the vote, we'll import the vote."

1996 - October 28. *New American.* "Insider Report", states:

> *"Documents provided by the Immigration and Naturalization Service to a congressional subcommittee suggest the Clinton Administration has encouraged massive immigration fraud as a way to increase its potential constituency. Citizenship USA, an administration initiative plans to naturalize a record 1.3 million citizens by the end of the year."*

Reports indicate Vice President Gore's office lead the push. As a result, 5,000 or more people became citizens despite criminal records that included rape and murder.

Greens will call for Proportional Representation:

1996 - February. *Humanist* magazine reports that in 1995 Rep. Cynthia McKinney proposed HR2545, a bill that would:

> *"lift the 1967 federal law that mandates one seat per congressional district, allowing states the option of electing their congressional delegation by multi-seat 'proportional representation'...where 10% of the popular vote wins 10% of the seats. The success of the German Green Party demonstrates the potential for third parties"*

1997 - October 30. *Mail Tribune* headline reads "Activist want to change 'winner-take-all' elections". Paul Fattig reports:

> *"Blair Bobier is leading an initiative drive to establish proportional representation in the Oregon House of Representatives"...Blair said, "if the party gets 10 percent of the*

votes, that party gets 10 percent of the seats in the House." Blair
then stated, *"more and more people are refusing to identify with
the old major parties."*

After creating chaos, Greens will emerge on national scene:

1995 - Ralph Nader ran for President on Green ticket.

Communist will run Greens, Independents or Democrats:

1996 - March 4. *Associated Press* headline reads, "Communist
Provokes Council." Report indicates Kevin Hornbuckle ran
for the city council position as a registered Democrat:

> *"constituents didn't know what they were voting for when they
> cast their votes. Hornbuckle never disclosed his membership in
> the Communist Party of Oregon when he ran in 1992."
> Hornbuckle stated: "I'd simply point out that Communists in
> the United States are fighting for health care, housing and jobs
> as a human right, I'm proud to be a Communist."*

1996 - November, 1996 *Associated Press*, headline reads, "In
Arcata, it's easy to be Green". Martha Irvine reports:

> *"Pro-environment party attains control of council... Greens are
> hoping to make their victory in Arcata the start of a trend...
> Hanan, one of the new Green city council members said:*
>
> *"We need to find towns in the Midwest where industry is
> broken down and say, "How can we turn this into a really neat
> town?"*
>
> *"The rise of the Greens with their far-left, German-born
> philosophy is unsettling to some members of Arcata's old guard,
> 'It'd scare you to death. You've got anarchists and socialists in
> this town" said Nancy Barnes...who is planning to move."*

Gorbachev and the Soviet's Green con job:

1995 - August 16. 'Interview by Bill Jasper, editor of 'The New American', with Christopher Story, editor of the 'Soviet Analyst', published as an occasional paper by the 'International Currency Review'. Regarding Gorbachev's supposed fall from power and the Soviets concern about being exposed, Christopher Story said:

"Gorbachev hinted on several occasions the 'Break with the Past' was imminent. On May 17, 1990, he remarked 'we have entered the last lap', one year later, at a press conference with President Mitterrand (May 6, 1991) he said, 'the dangers lie in the fact that someone, analyzing at some private moment or other, this or that instance or episode or event, including a dramatic event, should not make hasty conclusions and cast doubt on all that has been acquired and what we have created in putting international relations onto new rails, entering as all of us have said, a period of peaceful development'...

*... **Gorbachev... hinted at continuing anxiety in Soviet strategic circles about the possibility Moscow's devious Leninist strategy of 'convergence' with the West on Communist terms, facilitated by the forthcoming false 'Break with the Past', might be exposed by someone like Golitsyn in the West who had done his homework on the strategic deception tradition of Lenin."***

As stated throughout this work, Americans share a commitment to create a healthier environment. Environmental issues are being twisted to justify Socialism then impose Communism.

1992 -Environmental Program, Communist Party USA

"Socialism makes the change in property relations which provides a sound basis for bringing the production system into harmony with nature. Socialism can end both the exploitation of labor and the exploitation of nature. It can make possible the

planning of production for the needs of the people and for sustainable ecosystems in a sustainable economy..."

"...the environment that sustains us can be saved only by changing our economic system... The Communist Party of the United States sees the capitalist ruling class as the enemy of both workers and the environment... we need socialism"

Green means 'a radical political movement' with goals such as economic conversion and revolution:

1998 - Green Empowerment Resources web site. (www.empowermentresources.com/) The Greens are getting bolder and are starting to reveal the scope of the movement. The following statement is from that site. It states:

"The term 'Green' could be defined as 'environmentalist' but there is a lot more to it than that. The Green movement includes green politics, green ecological living, green businesses and green ecological products. Green politics runs the gamut from dedicated Green Party members and Green movement political activists worldwide to the major environmental organizations to the majority of Americans who consider themselves pro-environment. Then there is the left-green political movement, the deep ecology spiritual political movement and the environmental justice movement. When I use the term Green I am referring to a holistic 1960's style world view that includes ecology, peace, feminism, social justice, the human potential movement, the counterculture, etc."

The majority of Americans who consider themselves pro-environment probably do not realize they are also supporting the radical left-green. This web site outline reflects an overview of the Green movement, not the subversive political agenda, the rapid rate of advancement or the powerful political support the movement has to achieve their goals by the year 2000.

This is not about personal expression or differing political opinions. It is about violating the public trust and using our love of nature as the emotional hook to advance a political agenda Americans know little or nothing about. It is about abusing classrooms to create a cult-like political following.

A list of Green buzzwords for personal reference:

Consensus	Decentralization	Grassroots Democracy
Social Justice	Smart Growth	Community visioning
Social Equity	Land Trust	Post patriarchal Values
Co-housing	Multiculturalism	Global Responsibility
Collaboration	Social Rights	Conservation Easements
New Paradigm	Biodiversity	Sustainable Communities
Co-operatives	Progressive	Proportional Representation
Eco-Village	Deep Ecology	Creation Spirituality
Eco-Feminist	Human potential	Social Potential
Ecosystem	Social Change	Integral Culture
Stewardship	Cultural Creatives	New Politics of Meaning

The latest piecemeal terms to manipulate Americans into joining the Green Movement are: 'Cultural Creatives', 'Politics of Meaning' and 'Social Potential'. New words but the same goals: social change and making the environment our 'central organizing principle'. How can the Greens change the rules and the laws that guide our nation or our economic system? Very quietly. The *President's Council on Sustainable Development (PCSD)* has a unique set of goals and guidelines centered around:

- a collaborative decision making process (not majority rule)
- social equity, new values, land ethics or stewardship
- government involved in monitoring performance
- a sustainable economy and people to do meaningful work

The *PCSD Task Force* Report: "Principles, Goals and Definitions". The following ideas are presented in the "Intra-Generational Equity" section:

"In economics, 'equity' is studied in terms of the distribution of income and wealth. While command over resources is a major aspect of equity, it is not the full story. The principle of equity embraces the interrelated notions of fairness, impartiality, justice, non-discrimination, human rights and social rights...

*... **the environmental equity question can only be addressed by exploring the issue of income equity...***

*... economic forces are at work that governments cannot and should not seek to control... in whatever way government decides to approach equity questions, intragenerational equity has 2 important consequences for economic policy...first is that lessening of **economic inequality will have to be seen as a primary goal of economic policy** ... in other words **measures to reduce income inequities will need to be integrated with policies aimed at improvement in economic efficiency and structural reform...***

... second... evaluation of policies aimed at other aspects of sustainable development will need to take explicit account of equity impacts as part of the overall assessment of policies."

It is clear the way the term 'equity' as it is used, suggests government involvement in economic reform and income distribution. Redistribution of the wealth? The key to understanding why the term 'equity' is important is how it is defined. Equity generally means fairness and justice. Two out of three dictionaries also define equity as:

"any body of legal doctrines and rules similarly developed to enlarge, supplement, or override a system of law which has become too narrow and rigid in its scope."

Justice-Equity is defined as:

"in ordinary use justice implies the strict and judicial rendering of what is due, 'equity' emphasizes rather the idea of fairness or even-handed impartiality"

Behind the desired 'warm-fuzzy' affect of creating a more fair, just and impartial society lies the 'other' meaning. **The development of 'a body of legal rules to override a system of law'.** From that angle 'sustainable development' appears to be a clever way to disguise changing the rules we operate by and shaping a planned society where the government is involved in managing the economy and income structures. Everyone would be equal, the income fairly distributed and citizens would do **'meaningful work'.** Communists use the term 'socially useful' work. It looks and sounds like Green Communism. Is the PCSD term 'equity' being used to carefully override existing rules and mask imposing Green Communism on unsuspecting Americans?

Section 2 of this Task Force report is "Key Reports & Extracts". Obviously, these are important tutorials. This quote from Vice President Gore's book *Earth in the Balance* is included:

> *"Adopting a central organizing principle -- one agreed to voluntarily -- means embarking on an all-out effort to use every policy and program, every law and institution, every treaty and alliance, every tactic and strategy, every plan and course of action -- to use, in short, every means to halt the destruction of the environment and to preserve and nurture our ecological system."*

Is this what is happening? Has the environment become our 'central organizing principle' without our knowledge? The PCSD report "Sustainable America, A New Consensus" is misleading. If the American people have not been consulted and are not aware of these plans then there is **no consensus** or voluntary agreement. Do we want to follow Hitler's lead and make the environment our 'central organizing principle' for public life and public policy? It certainly appears the Greens, members of the Clinton-Gore Administration, the Communist Party USA, DSA, NGOs and Gorbachev are all working hard to impose that agenda. It also appears the Greens are achieving their goals by imposing little pieces of 'compulsory Green living' from the top-down. The Greens are using multiple minority issues, the PCSD, international treaties, biodiversity protection, ecosystem management, Executive Orders, Proclamations and any other means to accomplish their mission to control the American people.

Remember, in 1990 the Democratic Socialist of America, DSA, sponsored a conference featuring John Sweeney and Al Gore. "Building Eco-Socialism in the 90s" and "Watermelon Activist" were key topics for DSA at the time. The following excerpts are from a DSA fundraising letter from Ed Asner:

"DSA knows... this country needs new leadership... that exposes the real enemy of unemployed and underpaid working people as the same enemy of women, gays, environmentalists and people of color... we need to talk plainly about the fundamental redistribution of the wealth and power in this country... Our strategy centers on forming coalitions among all constituencies for social change, building a majority movement that can democratically transform American society... thousands of DSAers work in every progressive cause, the women's movement, African-American, Latino, gay, lesbian, union and environmental movements... We are part of an international movement..."

The writing is on the wall and it reads, 'world Communism'. The time to sit-back has come and gone. It's time to take losing our freedom seriously. We stand at the crossroads; the choice is a Green Communist dictatorship or continued freedom. The future is in our hands. If we choose freedom, we must insist upon accountability from our political leaders and a public debate of these issues immediately if not sooner.

Krushchev predicted, they would "take us over, from within, without firing a single shot". Are we going to stand-by and let that happen?

8

ALL TRUTH PASSES THROUGH 3 STAGES

1. It is ridiculed.
2. It is violently opposed.
3. It is accepted as self-evident.

Author unknown

The environmental cause may have started out with reasonable goals but that is no longer the case. The facts prove the Greens, the Party and the movement, are twisting environmental issues to implement an elitist, subversive, political agenda that mirrors Communism.

It is easy to understand why the Greens hijacked the environmental cause. The wonders of nature inspire and touch us all. The Greens know 'these feelings' are powerful motivators. They are using 'these emotions' to blind the American people to their political end game and unscrupulously manipulate children into their political ranks.

The facts in the following pages will reveal the Green's covert plans to use the idea of sustainability, the Earth Charter and their version of 'systems thinking' to:

- teach America's children Green political values, K-12
- control individual behavior, limit human potential
- change and control business and the economy
- change our government system

- change property rights and socialize the land base
- change America's core beliefs and values

These charges are not made lightly and are backed up in the following pages with fact, after fact, after fact. The Greens think we are just too stupid to figure this out and too lazy to take action to protect our children, our nation and our freedom.

In 1999, *E magazine* reporter Tracey Rembert interviewed CNN's, CEO Ted Turner about his leadership role in the environmental movement. In the article "Billionaire, Media Mogul and Environmentalist", Ted Turner said:

> *"I think we're smarter than the opposition"…"We're better educated and I put my money on the smart minority rather than the dumb majority…"*

This statement tells us, there *is* an elitist, minority group that *is* working to impose their environmental agenda on the American people, which they consider the "dumb majority". This statement tells us; this minority group thinks they know what's best for the rest of us.

We are not stupid but we have been too trusting. The Greens are a revolutionary, minority, political movement that is using the environmental cause to hide steps to take control of our lives and our nation.

60's Revolutionaries: Alive, Well and Green

Fritjof Capra is a long-term leader in the Green movement and the co-author of the 1986 book, *Green Politics*. The following excerpts are from Capra's December 1, 2002 article "Where Have All the Flowers Gone? Reflections on the Spirit and Legacy of the Sixties". Capra states:

"What happened to the cultural movements of the sixties?... Our subculture was immediately identifiable... It had its own rituals ... fascination with spirituality and the occult ... Rock music and psychedelic drugs were powerful bonds ... casual communal nudity and freely shared sexuality..."

*"**Green Politics** - In the sixties we questioned the dominant society... we lived ... our protest rather than ... **systematizing it ... During the 1980's and 1990's, the Green movement** became a permanent fixture of the European political landscape ... **They are the political embodiment of the core values of the sixties."***

*"At the turn of this century, an impressive global coalition of nongovernmental organizations (NGOs), many led by men and women with deep personal roots in the sixties, **formed around the core values of** human dignity and **ecological sustainability.** In 1999, hundreds of these grassroots organizations ... prepared for the joint protest actions at the ... World Trade Organization (WTO) in Seattle. ... This new form of alternative global community, sharing core values ... is one of the most important legacies of the sixties. "*

*"**If it succeeds** in reshaping economic globalization ... to make it compatible with the values of human dignity and ecological sustainability, **the dreams of the 'sixties revolution' will have been realized:** Imagine no possessions, I wonder if you can ..."*

This Green leader made it clear, the revolutionary goals of the 60's will be achieved if the Greens achieve their plans for sustainability. The Green movement exemplifies the revolutionary goals of the 60's. The 60's activists are leading the Green movement and revolution is still the goal.

Green leader Mikhail Gorbachev said "a revolution had to take place in people's minds" and that's the Green plan in a nutshell. The Greens know exactly what they're doing. The

Green's plan to overthrow America from within hinges on their ability to use fear of environmental doom to change America's values and replace them with Green values.

A special brainwashing campaign, designed just for the American people, is underway. Sustainability, the Earth Charter, the Green's version of 'systems thinking' and environmental education are key parts of their strategy.

Gorbachev's predecessor said, "We will take you over from within without firing a single shot". If the Greens succeed, Krushchev will be right. The choice is ours. The Greens can only change America if we let them change our beliefs and let them brainwash our children. Remember, Gorbachev has brainwashing experience.

Fritjof Capra pointed out in his article "Where Have All the Flowers Gone?", that the reason they were not successful in the 60's was because they did not have a 'systemized' approach.

Well, now they do and it's called 'systems thinking' and 'education for sustainability'. It is straight out of Capra's 1986 book, *Green Politics, How the Greens are transforming the political culture of Europe and inspiring a worldwide movement that can change the course of America's future.*

The Green version of 'systems thinking' is the core value and the guiding principle of the Green Party. Green ideas about 'systems thinking' are the opposite of America's founding values and principles. The following definitions of America's founding principles are from the book, *We The People,* by Thomas E. Patterson. The Green Party and movement principles are this author's summary.

AMERICA'S PRINIPLES OF FREEDOM & GOVERNMENT

LIBERTY - INDEPENDENCE
"Is the principle that individuals should be free to act and think as they choose, provided they don't infringe unreasonably on the freedom & well-being of others."

SELF-GOVERNMENT
"Is the principle that the people are the ultimate source of governing and their general welfare is the only legitimate purpose of government."

EQUALITY
"Holds that all individuals have moral worth, are entitled to fair treatment under the law and should have equal opportunity for material gain and political influence."

INDIVIDUALISM
"Is a commitment to personal initiative, self-sufficiency, and material accumulation. This principle upholds the superiority of a private enterprise economic system and includes the idea of the individual as the foundation of society."

UNITY – THE MELTING POT
"Is the principle that Americans are one people and form an indivisible union."

GREEN PARTY & GREEN MOVEMENT PRINCIPLES

INTERDEPENDENCE
Green systems thinking: Man is part of nature, not a steward, above nature. Idea to control individual actions and limit human potential.

GREEN COMMUNISM
Control of production and distribution of goods and services. Resources held in common. Control growth. Classless society.

SOCIAL JUSTICE
Socialize land base. Eradicate poverty by redistributing the wealth, within nations and among nations, to meet basic needs of all people: job, food, home, healthcare, education.

SUSTAINABILITY
Interdependent, group focus. Planned society, controlled economy. Community is the foundation of society not the individual. Work for the common good not individual gain. Lands as commons, end private property ownership.

EARTH CHARTER VALUES
World unity. Erase melting pot. Change values. Divide & conquer the American people.

Green's Define 'Systems Thinking'

Green Party leader Fritjof Capra is also the founder of the Center for Ecoliteracy, which promotes:

> *"Foster ecoliteracy through a network of schools ... Being ecologically literate means understanding basic patterns of how nature sustains life ... applying this knowledge requires* **systems thinking,** *thinking in terms of connectedness ...* **seeing the world as an interconnected whole ... grounding in systems thinking ... ecoliteracy offers a powerful framework for ... school reform."**

Ecoliteracy and school reform equal teaching Green political values in schools. Capra's book *Green Politics* explains the political meaning behind 'systems thinking'.

> **"Western culture** *has been dominated for several hundred years by a conceptualization of our bodies, the body politic and the natural world as hierarchically arranged ... "*

> *"...* **systems view** *involves looking at the world in terms of relationships and integration..."*
>
>

Green Politics, 1986
> Fritjof Capra and Charlene Spretnak

The above statement indicates that Western culture believes there is a natural order and man is a step above the animal kingdom.

To clarify the Green 'systems view' of nature, the authors of *Green Politics* quote a leading Green Party spokesperson and philosophy professor, Manon Maren-Griesbach. The following statement is from Griesbach's book the *Philosophy of the Greens:*

> *"... let yourself be guided by the meaning of ecology, that everything is interwoven,* **there is no such thing as first or second.**

"The emphasis is on relations and interconnections – in Gregory Bateson's words,

"the pattern which connects the crab to the lobster and the orchid to the primrose and all four of the them to me *– is the foundation of Green thought and being, whether it is called grassroots democracy or something else. This consciousness is simply there in the Greens....*

*"***We define ecological politics** *as those measures that* **understand human beings and our environment as being part of nature.** *... In particular,* **ecological politics presents and all-encompassing rejection** *of an economy of exploitation and plundering of natural resources and raw materials, as well as the destructive intervention into the cycles of nature's household."*

Translation:

- Everything in nature is equal. Humans are equal to lobsters and flowers

- *"Call it grassroots democracy or something else"* but 'systems thinking' is the root of Green political values

- Greens reject the use of natural resources and intervention into nature's household

No one wants to see all natural resources plundered. The Green version of 'systems thinking' is a political strategy, a tool, to change Western values and replace them with Green values. Greens are targeting public education to teach their political values.

Ecoliteracy, ecological wisdom, interconnectedness, grassroots democracy and sustainability all stem from the Green's political interpretation and use of 'systems thinking'.

A 'Conflict of Values'

The Green version of 'systems thinking' is rooted in the idea man is part of nature, not above nature. Greens teach that man is a species, no different than a plant or an animal. Earth Day uses all-species parades to get children to accept this idea. In contrast, America's core values, are rooted in the belief man is a step above the plant and animal kingdom and charged with good stewardship.

This is the 'conflict of values' Gorbachev is talking about. To be controllable and accept sustainable Green Communism, American's self worth must be diminished to that of an insect. The idea, man is part of nature, is the tool to lower our expectations and condition us to accept total control. Gorbachev emphasized his Green political view:

> *"The idea that ... humanity is the king of nature is the psychological prerequisite of the current environmental crisis."* ... *"humanity is just part of nature."* ... *The greening of politics is the return of humankind to the awareness humanity is part of nature. The moral improvement of society ... is inconceivable without this."*
>
> The Search for a New Civilization 1995
> Mikhail Gorbachev

The Green Party and the Earth Charter values are the same. A key part of the Green's strategy is to plug into public schools and use 'education for sustainability' and 'systems thinking' to teach every child in America Green political values. If the Greens control America's children they control America's future.

> *"The future of our Nation will be determined, more than anything else, by the character of our children."*
> *President Reagan's Quotations*
> Ronald Reagan
> September 23, 1982

As Capra said, if the Greens achieve their goals for 'ecological sustainability' they win, revolution happens. Capra's, Center for Ecoliteracy, is already teaching Green 'systems thinking' in several California schools.

The Greens have support for teaching 'education for sustainability' and 'systems thinking', from government agencies, educators and business leaders who may, or may not understand their political agenda.

The best way to understand where the Greens are now, where they are headed and what we can do to protect our children and our freedoms is to break their strategy down into parts and connect the dots.

The Earth Charter

The purpose of the Earth Charter USA campaign is to get the American people to support Gorbachev's Earth Charter, which is:

> "... a body of international ecological laws that would **guide the actions of individuals, corporations and governments...**
>
> ... the time has come for a code of ethical and moral principles that will govern the conduct of nations and people with respect to the environment."
>
> Grassroots magazine

Again, it's a 'conflict of values'. The Earth Charter is a political tool to change and replace America's values with Green Communist values to control the American people.

The following statements on Socialism and Greening politics are from Mikhail Gorbachev's 1995 book, *The Search for a New Beginning: Developing a New Civilization.*

On page 59, Gorbachev states:

> *"the future of human society will not be defined in terms of* **capitalism versus socialism"**

On page 61, Gorbachev states:

> **"we must return to** *the well-known human values that are embodied in the ideals of the world's religions and also in* **the socialist ideas** *that inherited much from those values"*

The above statements reveal a blatant contradiction. On one page Gorbachev says it's not *"capitalism versus socialism"* then he says, *"we must return to ... socialist ideas..."*

Gorbachev, like the Greens, is pushing Socialism because, as even young Communists know, Socialism is the stepping-stone to Communism.

> **"Socialism is the society that will pave the way for a communist society** *by setting a foundation of co-operation and sharing of all things in common. Communism is the realization of these goals."*
>
> Young Communist League

Co-operation and sharing all things in common are goals of the Green Party. In 1998, the Socialist Party of Oregon merged with the Green Party to become the Pacific Green Party. The Green revolutionaries are working together.

In his book, Gorbachev outlines his goals for a new sustainable civilization. He said that:

> **"Economic, political, class, interethnic, or ideological wars will have to be abolished"**

Does this mean all ideas that don't match Green ideas will have to be abolished? Sounds like a new Soviet Union. Gorbachev's political goals for a new civilization are definitely Green. He states:

"The greening of politics is a new view of the problem of consumption and its rationalization..."

"The greening of politics affects approaches to tackling many social problems connected ... to the environment."

"The greening of politics means maximum support for scientific research and fundamental disciplines that study the biosphere and its ecosystems."

"The greening of politics is an affirmation of the priority of values common to humanity, enriching education and upbringing with ecological content from childhood onward and developing a new modern attitude toward nature."

"The greening of politics is the return of humankind of the awareness of humanity as a part of nature."

The Search for a New Beginning
Developing a New Civilization

There is no question Gorbachev is pushing the Green Party agenda. Sugar coating the ideas in 'Green speak' does not change the bottom line political objectives.

Notice Gorbachev made a strong plea for "maximum support for scientific research" regarding the environment.

Not a bad idea, except the Greens are not above using bio-fraud and lying to achieve their political goals.

This is why we cannot base all our environmental decisions on science alone.

Gorbachev, in his previous statements, makes it clear Green political goals include:

- using education to influence children's upbringing
- teaching ecological values from childhood onward
- developing 'new modern attitudes' in children

Greens are using Earth Day and environmental education to reach and teach America's children their beliefs. Gorbachev's use of the term "upbringing" ought to cause American families serious concern. In America, parents usually decide how their children will be raised.

Under Communist rule the government is heavily involved in a child's life. It certainly sounds like this is what Gorbachev has in mind.

In the last chapter of his book *The Search for a New Beginning: Developing a New Civilization*, Gorbachev states:

> **"I do not believe in imposing models and schemes on society**. *I believe in the individual, in the potential of intellect and conscience."*

The above statement reveals another blatant contradiction. If Mr. Gorbachev does "not believe in imposing models and schemes on society" then why is his pet project the Earth Charter?

The Earth Charter is a 'set of rules' for the entire world to obey. That's definitely imposing his will on people. Gorbachev has also said that he sees the Earth Charter as a new Ten Commandments.

The Earth Charter is an international treaty, written by Gorbachev and friends and, it is an attempt to use the environment to conceal imposing Green World Communism.

"We must build on the Earth Charter that came out of the 1992 UN environmental Earth Summit. New definitions of what constitutes real security between nations must be debated and adopted by the foreign policy community."

Green Party Program 2000

The Greens will use the events of September 11th to garner support for the Earth Charter as a path to world peace. We all want world peace. The Earth Charter cannot guarantee world peace.

The Earth Charter USA Campaign

Richard M. Clugston, the Director of the Earth Charter USA campaign describes the Earth Charter this way:

"I invite you to become involved in the Earth Charter USA Campaign … Change your lifestyle, your profession and our government to support a sustainable future.

Become an Earth Charter Facilitator and guide your community, church or school groups through an education and advocacy process. We want individual citizens to weigh in on behalf of those values, policies and practices necessary to redirect our politics and economy toward sustainability."

According to Richard Clugston, and he ought to know, the Earth Charter's goals for a sustainable future require that Americans:

- Change our government
- Redirect our politics and economy
- Change our values, policies and practices
- Change our lifestyles and professions

The scope of the Earth Charter is staggering but it is right in line with the Green's goals to change our government and economy to sustainable Communism. According to Steven Rockefeller, chairman of the Earth Charter International drafting committee, the Earth Charter:

> *"is designed to serve as a **universal code of conduct to guide people and nations toward sustainability."***

The code of conduct is a Green set of rules for us to obey. Gorbachev's Earth Charter includes the Communist's goal to redistribute the wealth, "within nations and among nations" to meet the basic needs of all people.

The Earth Charter reads:

> *"We must realize that **when basic needs have been met,** human development is primarily about being more, not having more."*

Citizens living under Communism don't have to worry about having more because working for the common good makes all slaves equally poor.

Sustainability is the catch phrase and the environment is the shield to hide their planned shift to Communism. The Greens have worked carefully to build blind trust so Americans will not question their goals for sustainability.

The last thing the Greens want the American people to see is the simple truth. The Director of the Earth Charter USA campaign, Richard Clugston, said:

> *"**change our government** to support a sustainable future"*

Please read the next sentence out loud.

We must change our government to create a healthier environment.

It sounds ridiculous because it is ridiculous. Yet, this is the stated goal of the Earth Charter USA campaign.

Remember, the Greens think we are so-o-o-o stupid we will fall for their claim that we must change our government to save the earth.

Green groups that have already endorsed the Earth Charter or are working to implement the Earth Charter goals include:

- Sierra Club
- National Wildlife Federation
- Friends of the Earth
- Natural Resource Defense Council
- Wilderness Society
- Wildlands Project
- Rain Forest Action Network
- World Resource Institute
- Earth Council
- University Leaders for a Sustainable Future
- Student Environmental Action Coalition
- The Earth Day Network

FYI – The Student Environmental Action Coalition (SEAC) works directly with:

- Young Communist League
- Campus Greens
- Young Democratic Socialists
- Young People's Socialists League

The Earth Day Network's *Teach Out Guide* recommends the Student Environmental Action Coalition to students right along with the *Earth First! Journal*.

Partners in the Earth Charter USA campaign include:

- Global Education Associates
- Citizen's Network for Sustainable Development
- Baha'is of the United States
- The Interfaith Center of New York
- American Association of Engineering Societies
- The Humane Society of the United States
- Institute for Ethics and Meaning
- Soka Gakkai USA
- The Earth Council
- Boston Research Center for the 21st Century
- The Earth Day Network

All these groups are Partners in the Earth Charter USA campaign and according to campaign organizers that means:

"Earth Charter USA Partners are organizations that are committed to promoting Earth Charter values and using the Earth Charter in their education and advocacy work.

"Through the Earth Charter USA Partners, the ideas of the Earth Charter are spread more quickly and national support for the Earth Charter becomes stronger."

All these groups are promoting the Earth Charter "in their education and advocacy work". We must realize, these groups, however well intentioned, are advocating revolutionary change in our government and our lives. A strategic goal of the campaign is to get the Earth Charter taught in schools.

The Earth Day Network is using its political, financial and public appeal to *quickly* build national support for the Earth Charter. The Earth Day Network includes the leaders of every major environmental group.

A few of the groups listed on the Earth Day Board of Directors included leaders from:

- Sierra Club
- Natural Resource Defense Council
- Wilderness Society
- League of Conservation Voters
- Environmental Working Group
- Earth Voice
- National Environmental Trust
- Center for Environmental Citizen
- Earth Day New York

A few of the groups listed on the Earth Day Network 's U.S. Council, *the people behind Earth Day*" include:

- National Wildlife Federation
- Urban Habitat Program
- Friends of the Earth
- Rails to Trails Conservancy
- World Wildlife Fund
- Planned Parenthood
- National Audubon Society
- The Natural Step
- Izaak Walton League
- Zero Population Growth
- Physicians for Social Responsibility
- Earth Justice Legal Defense Fund
- Union of Concerned Scientists
- Defenders of Wildlife
- American Rivers
- Children's Defense Fund
- Environmental Defense Fund
- The Wilderness Society
- Oregon State University

- Stanford University
- Dartmouth College
- University of Virginia
- National Parks and Conservation Association
- National Religious Partnership for Environment

Green Party Vice Presidential candidate Winona LaDuke, and Earth First! tree-sitter Julia Butterfly Hill were also on the Earth Day Network's U.S. Council.

The stated goal of the Earth Charter USA campaign is to "change our government." That statement is on the first page, first paragraph, in the "Message from the Director," Richard Clugston. It stands out. No one could miss it.

Major environmental groups and the Earth Day Network are promoting the Earth Charter and the goal to change our government.

No matter how well intentioned the individuals involved may be and no matter how much we care about the environment, we must get it through our heads, the Green movement is promoting revolutionary change.

Our government system allows citizens to advocate change but that is not what is happening here. This is a sting operation. The Greens are not being up front.

How many people on the street corner know that environmental groups are supporting the Earth Charter and the goal to change our government?

How many Americans know the Earth Day Network is a Partner in the Earth Charter campaign?

Another goal of the Earth Charter campaign is to:

"... increase the participation of young people in utilizing the Earth Charter as a guideline in their work as active agents of change."

Communists teach young people to sacrifice their dreams and work for the common good. Although the following youth activities sound like what America's children have been asked to do to save the earth, the following is what is expected of young Communists.

"More is expected of students than that they believe the official doctrine. They must also become 'active builders of the Communists society'... in addition to study they must participate in the life of the community...they are asked to volunteer for special community projects, such as construction or beautifying the city, harvesting crops, or working on a virgin lands project. Participation in socially useful work forms part of the students record."

Communism, What It Is and How It Works
Schlesinger and Blustain

It's interesting Communists use the term "active builders" of the communist society and Gorbachev's Earth Charter campaign stresses that youth must be "active agents of change" and build support for the Earth Charter. Same concept.

Getting the Earth Charter and sustainability principles taught in classrooms is the Green's top priority. Many of the groups involved in supporting the Earth Charter and the Earth Day Network distribute materials to schools.

Earth Charter goals for education include:

> *The Earth Charter is to be "contemplated, applied and internalized."*... *"* To this end, the Earth Charter needs to be incorporated into both formal and non-formal education. This process must involve various communities that continue to *integrate the Charter into the curriculum of schools and universities..."*

Teaching the Earth Charter's political values as part of the school curriculum sounds like brainwashing. The Earth Day Network is a partner in the Earth Charter campaign and distributes free materials to over 75,000 schools.

Our children, preschool through graduate school, are the targets. Richard M. Clugston, Director of the Earth Charter USA campaign said:

> *"Become an Earth Charter Facilitator and **guide your community, church or school groups** through an education and advocacy process."*

The Baha'is of the United States are Partners in the Earth Charter campaign. The Baha'i International Community participated in developing the Earth Charter. The Earth Charter and a statement from the Baha'is are featured in the "Reorienting Education" section in "Education for Sustainable Development"(ESD) materials. Part of the Baha'i statement is:

> *"World Citizenship: A Global Ethic for Sustainable Development. The Baha'i International Community has articulated a statement of ethics, which follows, that supports sustainability.*
>
> *"The greatest challenge facing the world ... is to **release the enormous financial,** technical, human and moral **resources required for sustainable development. These resources will be freed up only as the peoples of the world develop a***

profound sense of responsibility for the fate of the planet and for the well-being of the entire human family. ... World citizenship ... encompasses the ... principles, values, attitudes and behavior that the people of the world must embrace if sustainable development is to be realized ... World citizenship encompasses the principles of social and economic justice ... and the willingness to sacrifice for the common good ... "

Source: www.esdtoolkit.org/discussion/reorient.htm

Although not reprinted in its entirety, this statement by the Baha'is reveals the basic elements of Green Party goals for a sustainable society and match Communist Party goals.

Green Ideas	Baha'i Ideas
Share the wealth equally	Release resources, share with world
Meet basic human needs	Well-being of entire human family
Work for common good	Sacrifice, world first, person last
Indoctrinate behavior	Teach values, attitudes, behavior
Change government	Change government, world citizens

A livable, sustainable world is a necessity. Implementation of a global cooperation to save the air and oceans, the habitats, wildlife and human populations from environmental degradation and corporate plunder."

Communist Party USA

The American people are generous and kind and, already voluntarily give millions to help those in need. The goal to help those in need and create a healthier environment does not require, changing our government, becoming world citizens or supporting Green Communism.

"And it is no accident that the very worst environmental tragedies were created by communist governments, in which the power of the state completely overwhelms the capabilities of the individual steward."

Earth in the Balance, 1992
Al Gore
Former Vice President

Education, The Earth Charter and Eco Terrorism

Partners in the Earth Charter USA campaign include the Earth Day Network, the Baha'is of the United States, the Humane Society of the United States and others. Partners in the Earth Charter campaign are committed to using the Earth Charter *"in their education and advocacy work."*

December 9, 2002, the Center for Consumer Freedom reported:

> *"the Humane Society of the United States (HSUS) has been quietly funding an Internet service used by the violent criminals of the Animal Liberation Front (ALF). HSUS has been widely criticized for hiring ALF-affiliated J.P. Goodwin in 2001.*

The Human Society contributing to the ALF is a problem. The following statement is from a November 23, 2002 report, "Rounding the Curve on Eco-Terrorism" by Kelly A. Stoner, executive director of Stop Eco-Violence. Stoner said:

> *"According to the FBI, ELF and its cohort the Animal Liberation Front (ALF) alone have caused about **$43 million in damage through more than 600 attacks since 1996**" ... "In the fight for the freedom of these animals, all is justified."*

The Green Party 1989 program sheds light on where the idea to free all the animals from human domination comes from:

> *"**Ecological Wisdom** teaches us to view ourselves as a part of nature rather than as on top of it or dominating it. Intrinsic to this view is the concept of the interconnectedness of all living beings. ... **When we view ourselves as part of the web of life, rather than as masters of the natural world**, it is apparent that we should relate to other animals as kindred individuals, not as resources to be exploited. **If other animals are viewed as kindred individuals ... it follows that they**

have an intrinsic right to live out their natural lives free of
human domination and interference."..."Voluntary
relinquishment of tyrannical human power over other animals is
essential to the realization of a Green and just society."

This is the Green Party version of 'systems thinking'. Humans and animals are equal. The Greens are behind the push to make people 'guardians' instead of 'owners' of their pets. The following statement from ELF, the Earth Liberation Front, was reported by Scott Westcott, *Times News*, November 2002:

"...Where it is necessary, we will no longer hesitate to pick up the gun to implement justice and provide the needed protection for our planet...

"Wescott wrote "Bob Rudge, special agent in charge of the FBI office in Erie, said the e-mail marked the first time in the United States that **ELF has threatened violence against humans in its quest to halt activities it deems harmful to the environment and animals.**

"The Earth Liberation Front is the heir to the radical group Earth First!, which gained attention in the 1980's and 1990's for driving spikes into trees in the Pacific Northwest to thwart efforts of loggers and timber companies."

However well intentioned these groups and their members may be, the bottom line is, they are promoting revolutionary change. The Green's political messages do not belong in school. We are duty bound to take immediate, responsible, courteous and effective steps to protect our children and our government system. We cannot afford to lose either one.

Every parent, teacher, student, community and political leader needs to be aware of the Green's ulterior political motives. Seemingly innocent materials from the Humane Society, the Baha'is, the Earth Charter, Ecoliteracy, Education for Sustainability, the National Wildlife Federation, the Earth

Day Network and other Green groups need to be evaluated before hitting the classroom.

Professional educators ought to be appalled once they understand the Greens are using education to indoctrinate students for political gain. Educators ought to be among the first to say using schools and classrooms to advance personal or political beliefs is not acceptable.

Lessons learned from Hitler's abuse of education for political gain stands as a stark reminder of the psychological, emotional and political dangers of allowing anyone to teach their personal or political agenda in school.

Eco-terrorism, violent mass protests and the political agenda of the Green movement match Communist Party goal #42 on the list of the 45 Communist Party goals entered in the Congressional record January 10, 1963. Goal #45 is:

> *"Create the impression that violence and insurrection are legitimate aspects of the American tradition;* ***that students and special interest groups should rise up and use "united force" to solve economic, political and social problems."***

The goals are from the book *The Naked Communist* by Cleon Skousen, who served in the FBI for 16 years. Skousen compiled the list based on his study of Communism in America.

The Green movement is the umbrella movement for multiple, anti-American groups. These groups are hiding behind the environmental cause, and using "united force" to push their revolutionary political agenda on the American people.

"America Under Siege" was the title of a January 21, 2003 article by David Horowitz about the peace demonstrations in Washington D.C. and San Francisco. Horowitz reported:

> "America's enemies within turned out in force on Sunday in Washington D.C., and San Francisco under the auspices of the Communist Workers World Party operating under its front organization A.N.W.S.E.R. Once again demonstrators pretended to be peace activists.
>
> "Imam Mussa ... said ... 'We're calling for a system change"... "Revolution. We won't get any justice as long as that criminal Congress is up there... We're calling for revolution. It's revolution time brothers and sisters."

Profs Who Hate America

"Profs Who Hate America" was the title of an article in the *New York Post*, November 12, 2002 by Daniel Pipes. Pipes wrote:

> "What is the long-term effect of an extremist, intolerant and anti-American environment on university students?
>
> "The time has come for adult supervision of the faculty and administrators at many American campuses. Especially as we are at war, the goal must be for universities to resume their civic duty
>
> "This can be achieved if outsiders (alumni, state legislators, non-university specialists, parents of students and others) take steps to create a politically balanced atmosphere, critique failed scholarship, establish standards for media statements by faculty and broaden the range of campus discourse"

The Greens have gained an unprecedented foothold in education. Green politics don't belong in school. The only educators who will not welcome parent and citizen help to rid our schools of the Green's political influence are those who either support the Greens or those who support teachers injecting their personal political bias in the classroom.

The following statement is from the 1964 book, *Communism, What It Is and How It Works* by Schlesinger and Blustain:

"Teachers in the United States refrain from interjecting political bias in their classroom work, and would be severely criticized if they used their teaching to promote personal political views."

"In the USSR, however, only one point of view – Marxism-Leninism – is permitted, and teachers are expected to present it to their pupils. For this reason, even sentences used to teach principles of grammar, word problems in arithmetic and many others, all serve to reinforce Communist ideology..."

That was in 1964 when classrooms were safe havens instead of indoctrination centers for the Greens. Just like the Communists in the USSR, the Greens intend to use every subject area to teach children to follow the Green Party line. It's high time to get Green politics out of America's schools and return to a high quality, basic education instead of the present social indoctrination.

Tampering With Nature

"Tampering with Nature" was the title of an ABC report by John Stossel. Although the Greens launched a major campaign to stop Stossel's report about how environmental education and Earth Day were being used to indoctrinate children, it aired anyway. The Greens did not want this segment to air. The level of effort to stop Stossel's program, is the level of concern the Greens have to keep the American people from finding out they are indoctrinating children.

Stossel's report included an interview with a group of young children. Stossel asked the children:

"Is America getting more polluted?"

All the children replied with a loud and extended, *"YesYesYessssss!"* Stossel said, *"Why don't they know the facts?"* then he stated:

"The EPA says, over the past 30 years the air has been getting cleaner. Smog days, even in Los Angeles, are now rare. "

"Nitrogen Dioxide, Sulfur Dioxide, Carbon Monoxide, Lead, and every major pollutant the government measures is decreasing and, the EPA says our lakes and rivers are cleaner now too. … But these kids don't believe it."

Stossel then told the children, *"The government says over the past 30 years its been getting cleaner."*

All the children yelled, *"NoNoNoooooo!!! They're lying!!!"*

Stossel concluded: *"You say you're educating these kids, I think you are indoctrinating them."*

Babies Can't Read

Now is the time to think about the negative psychological impacts the Greens are having on our children.

For instance, the National Wildlife Federation (NWF) website features "Earth Tomorrow, Where Green Teens Get Informed and Get Involved". The tag line reads: *"Teenagers can help make a difference in their own communities and gain environmental leadership experience."* Although the content is tame, this is a conditioning process to grow political support. The NWF is making it 'cool' to be Green.

The National Wildlife Federation website also features "Kidzone" an action site for infants and toddlers 1 to 3 years old. A NWF magazine called *Wild Animal Baby* is, according to the promotion, *"Perfect For Kids 0 to 3"*.

Perfect for kids 0 to 3 years old? How many newborn babies and toddlers have you seen reading up on the environment? For heavens sake, most 1-year-old babies can barely walk.

What's the point of activities and magazines for babies? Votes. Babies grow up. If America's children are conditioned to identify with being Green from birth on, they will vote Green. The magazine *Wild Animal Baby* serves to Green both parent and child.

In 1995, (see page 139), the concern was raised that children were being used to boost the Green's political influence. In a 1998 speech, Mark Van Putten, President of the National Wildlife Federation admitted:

> *"we count over 4 million members and supporters. **That includes I admit ... all those kids reading Ranger Rick magazine.** But I think they are some of the most important constituents we have ... **because that's the leadership of the next generation."***

The NWF also has special sections for children 3 and up. All is not warm and cuddly here. Hitler and Lenin targeted children and began political conditioning at a very young age. This is what the Greens are doing.

If the Greens respected children and this had nothing to do with conditioning them to identify with being Green, then why produce a magazine for babies? Why spend time and money on a magazine for babies? Babies can't read.

The National Wildlife Federation has endorsed the Earth Charter and the goal to change our government. It's time to cancel that subscription to *Ranger Rick* and get it out of schools.

Using Earth Day to Build the Green Movement

"Learning From History" is an Earth Day 2000 article by the director of the Earth Day Network, Denis Hayes. Hayes states:

> *"The **environmental movement is the most successful social movement** in American history."*

> *"**We need to re-convince America** that **the environmental movement is not an elitist** crusade, but a struggle to ensure a **sustainable** future for everyone."*

> *"**We have to** re-commit ourselves to **building a Green majoritarian movement to lead America** into the 21st century."*

Important points to note:

- The Green movement is an elitist movement
- Earth Day shares Green's goal of sustainability
- Earth Day is a tool to build the Green political movement

Earth Day Event Ideas include:

> *"**Greening Politics... Use Earth Day to work for ongoing change** in your community by organizing a **political project.** Here are some ideas on **how to use Earth Day to work for political change.**"*
>
> Earth Day Network 2002
> Source: www.earthday.net/howto/greening.stm

Earth Day is a Green political event focused on revolutionary change. Earth Day does not belong in school.

Turn that Kid into an Earth First!er

The Earth Day Network recommends the *Earth First! Journal* to students and promotes the actions of Earth First! Earth First! is well known for tree sits, spiking trees to stop logging and other acts of sabotage and eco-terrorism.

The headline, on the Earth Day Network website, to promote the child's book, *Fighting for the Forest*, was "Turn that Kid into an Earth First!er". The book was about a young boy who failed to save a forest from being clear-cut. Obviously, the Earth Day Network is promoting the actions of Earth First! and encouraging students to follow their lead.

The *Earth First! Journal*, May 2001, dedicated a full page to honor ELF for burning down the Vail ski resort. A "How-to Guide on the Sport and Science of SUV Mischief" was also featured. It outlined how to damage SUV's without getting caught. The March 2000 *Earth First! Journal* promoted the Global Day of Action, a mass protest:

> *"against the social, political and economic institutions of the capitalist system."*

These are anti-American protests. The Earth Day Network, which includes every major environmental group, is aware of the tactics and goals of Earth First!. The Earth Day Network is glorifying Earth First! to recruit young people. The Earth Day Network promoted Earth First!'er Julia Butterfly Hill for her 1997-1999 tree sit by making her:

- a member of Earth Day Network's U.S. Council
- a featured speaker at youth events
- a star in the Earth Day television special co-starring teen idol Leonardo DiCaprio

This Earth Day presentation, starring DiCaprio, was intended to influence students. Special note was made that it would be available to schools through Channel 1. The subliminal message to students is, risk your life to save the environment, sit in a treetop and meet a movie star.

A former Earth First!er called in during a radio interview and made the following statement to alert the listening audience:

> *"I'm glad you're exposing this Holly, especially the children school thing is so biased. **They're fostering a profound hatred for this country** and I know about this personally. In 1985 **I was deeply involved in Earth First!**, Dave Foreman and I, he's one of the founders, Mike Roselle another anarchist. All we talked about was blowing stuff up...There are thousands of people in this community that are not only anti-technology, they are anti-business, they want anarchy. They want business to be shut down. **They are completely anti-America."***
> KUGN Radio Interview

In November 2000, the Sierra Club featured a series of articles promoting student activism and tree sits. The article by Heather Miller was titled "Generation Green, Young rebels with a cause are taking to the streets, the parks, and the treetops to fight for the planet". Miller's article included the following statement about a young man, whose code name is Lorax.

> *"I've changed a lot." The 25-year old has spent a total of 13 months in the trees. In a simple ceremony, he even "married" a big tree they've named Grandma."*

Miller reported that most tree sits "have sprung up since 1997" after "Julia Butterfly Hill scaled Luna". The young man's nick name, Lorax, is likely based on *The Lorax* by Dr. Seuss, a story about a forest that was wiped off the face of the earth due to imaginary greed and logging. All the forest creatures had to move away because the area was completely devastated. It's a compelling tale that leaves the reader sad and remorseful.

In real life trees are replanted and, although logging isn't pretty, trees do grow back. A healthy appreciation of nature is good. Using this story to plant a political opinion is unethical and a political foul.

Political Foul Play

An example of using the Lorax story to unfairly influence children is found on the Native Forest Council website, in the section for "Teachers and Parents". The heading reads: "Build Science Fluency in the Classroom and at Home With These Classics". *The Lorax* by Dr. Seuss is listed and is described as:

> "*An all-time classic, perfect for all ages. **The Lorax is a poignant tale of industrial society's lack of regard** of natural things.*"
>
> Source: www.forestcouncil.org/learn/teacherbooks.php

The word poignant means emotional, sad or distressing. Children are being manipulated. John Borowski is the Native Forest Council's "environmental education coordinator" who advocates using *The Lorax* in school. In March 2002, the Native Forest Council launched the "Honest Education Campaign". Listed under the campaign's funding needs is this statement:

> "*For K-5 students, we would like to distribute copies of the Lorax, Dr. Seuss's timeless treasure on protecting our environment and especially our forest. An accompanying guide would provide a primer on forests, their structure and value. The primer would also provide fun activities and labs for a hands on approach.*"

A fairy tale is science fiction. *The Lorax* is not a true story. It is not a science book. The idea to use it as a lesson plan is manipulative. Using sadness and fear of loss to shape a child's real life opinion on how to protect the "environment, especially the forest" is wrong. Borowski's outline suggests linking bad feelings to logging and "fun activities" to protecting the forest. This isn't education; it's manipulation leading to indoctrination.

Although this may be an effective teaching method, using schools to teach personal political views is unfair and unethical. These teaching methods can lead to students becoming political activists, as we learned from Mr. Borowski himself (see page 326).

Using public education to lure children and students into the political ranks of a revolutionary movement is a supreme violation of ethics and the public trust. It is a monumental offense with serious consequences.

So Sad, So Unnecessary

The Sierra Club and the Earth Day Network glamorize tree sitting but our young people pay the price. America's young men and women are being used as propaganda tools and are dying needlessly.

In October 2002, an Earth First! activist, a young man, just 22-years-old, fell to his death, during his first tree sit.

The *Associated Press* reported in April, another tree sitter, a young woman, also just 22-years-old"… "died after falling from a tree..."

Why are young people sitting in trees? Why aren't they out playing softball or having a picnic at the beach? They are sitting in trees and risking their lives because the Greens have invaded classrooms with their doom and gloom message and an agenda to push students into political activism. Remember this from page 122?

> *"to what do we owe this recent surge of environmental responsibility among today's children? ... Many people believe that it begins with more activist-oriented ecology and conservation programs taught in schools...*
>
> *Kids are not only being trained to recognize potential environmental hazards in the home and their neighborhoods, but also are being taught to go out and do something about it..."*
>
> 1993 Earth Journal
Buzzworm magazine –Editors

The Greens are targeting America's best and brightest. Many of our idealistic, sensitive, passionate young people are not focused on their dreams with hope and inspiration. Instead, they are sacrificing their lives because the Greens have led them to believe the world is coming to an end.

Movement Has Lost its way

April 13, 2002, the front page headline in the *Mail Tribune* read, "Founder of Greenpeace Says Movement Has Lost Its Way". Tribune reporter, Paul Fattig, interviewed Dr. Patrick Moore, a co-founder of Greenpeace. Fattig's article included the following statements:

> *"Patrick Moore wanted to make one point clear from the outset, "I'm still a very strong environmentalist." said Moore, 54, one of the founders of Greenpeace. "I believe we did a lot of great things to raise public awareness."*
>
> *"Having said that, Moore, who spent 15 years with Greenpeace, took issue with what he believes is today's environmental extremism."*

"Dr. Moore said: "The environmental movement has shifted from being politically centered and science based to having a fairly strong left-wing rhetoric that has more the do with politics than science."

"There is no reason why environmentalists should be left-wing."

"A hallmark of people who aren't able to argue with you is to put you down as a person, rather than deal with the issues."

"The point is that the world is not coming to an end as some would suggest"

The Greens are the leftist political force that has hijacked the environmental cause to conceal their revolutionary agenda.

The Greens are also exploiting our children's love of the cute-and-furry to convince them to become vegetarians as part of their duty to build a sustainable future.

"Voluntary relinquishment of tyrannical human power over other animals is essential to the realization of a Green and just society."

Green Party Program 1992

The Earth Day Network actively promotes eating lower on the food chain and vegetarianism. The Earth Day Network's November 26, 2002, issue of *Grist* magazine, featured "Flipping the Bird, Sage Advice on Vegetarianism, organic foods, and more" by Umbra Fisk. Umbra is the 'Dear Abby' of the Earth Day Network's magazine, *Grist*. The article began with the reprint of a letter from Laida who had written to Umbra asking for advice. Laida was "confused" about how to answer her Uncle who said: "If humans are not supposed to eat meat, then why do we have teeth?"

The advice Umbra gave to Laida sheds more light on who's teaching our young people to be unkind, rude and intolerant.

Umbra's advice included the following points:

- Review and rehearse the following
- Refuse to play: He's poking you, don't take the bait ... tell him it's an interesting question, then act distracted
- Ignore the obnoxious question or say "You seem uncomfortable with my vegetarianism"
- Gross'em Out: Say, "I'm just not comfortable eating cannibalistic animals raised on human sewage and the fingers of slaughterhouse workers."
- Caustic Retort: say, "Well, if you're not supposed to breastfeed, why do you have nipples?"

Laida's Uncle asked her a simple question, which Umbra turned into a mean-spirited family fight. Instead of suggesting a respectful, loving conversation between family members, Umbra gave Laida a lesson from the 'Green's nasty school'.

Where is the compassion, respect and tolerance? Revolutionary political movements are not tolerant.

Herding the Masses

Earth Day goals for sustainability and social transformation match Green Party goals. The Earth Day Network held a special session, August 30, 2002, at the World Summit on Sustainable Development on "Education for Sustainability". The session outline states:

> "Additionally, **teaching the world's youth** to live within the means of the planet is an important part of **implementing sustainable development."**

This statement leaves little doubt, implementing sustainable development, involves Earth Day and teaching children to live within the means set for them by the Greens.

The Greens use Earth Day as a political tool to "herd" the American masses and our children, in whatever direction they want us to go. An April 21, 1999, *TIME.com*, featured an article about Earth Day, by David S. Jackson. Jackson said:

> *"Where do you go when you need someone to rally 200 million people? ...* **Whenever the environmental movement needs someone to gather the troops worldwide it turns to"** *... an activist who"* has the "ability to herd the masses toward a common goal. *His name is Denis Hayes but you can call him* **Mr. Earth Day."**

The Earth Day Network is using Earth Day to advance the goals of the Greens, both the Party and the movement. Here are a few identical terms both groups use.

Earth Day Network Principles	**Green Party Goals**
Transformation	Transformation
Social	Social
Economic	Economic
Personal	Personal
Political	Political

These groups share the political goals to transform America, our culture, our economy, our government and our lives.

> **"We are building a movement**, *a movement with a broad base, a movement which transcends political boundaries. It* **is a movement that values** *people more than technology, people more than political boundaries and* **people more than profit."**
> Denis Hayes, April 22, 1970

> *"We will work to promote alternative economic structures that* **put human needs ahead of profits**...*natural resources should be held in common for the common good."*
> Green Party Program 1992

The Green Party and the Communist Party use the slogan "People Before Profit".

Earth Day is a political event for the Greens. The Earth Day Network was a sponsor of the Econference 2000. The goal of this conference was to "make Earth Day 2000 and Election Day 2000 the springboard for a Green millennium".

Obviously getting the Green vote out is part of Earth Day's political agenda. Green Party Presidential candidate Ralph Nader was the keynote speaker at Econference 2000. Conference sponsors included:

- Campus Ecology, National Wildlife Federation project
- Campus Green Vote
- Center for Environmental Citizenship
- Free the Planet
- Sierra Student Coalition
- Student Alliance For Reforming Corporations
- University Leaders for a Sustainable Future

The Shadow Curriculum

The University Leaders for a Sustainable Future (ULSF) role is to add Green values to the curriculum and teach sustainability in all disciplines. Without realizing it, students will:

"... integrate values, knowledge, skills and behavior leading to environmentally responsible citizenship".

ULSF calls this the "Shadow Curriculum". Another term for this is brainwashing. This is what Green 'systems thinking' is all about. This is an underhanded way to instill Green political values in primary, secondary and university students.

It's interesting the executive Director of the University Leaders for a Sustainable Future is Richard Clugston.

Clugston is also the Director of the Earth Charter USA campaign.

ULSF works closely with the Earth Day Network and is actively promoting the Earth Charter and the Green's political agenda under the banner of academic excellence. Educators and universities involved with the University Leaders For a Sustainable Future may not be aware of the underlying political agenda.

What other groups work with the Greens and endorse the Earth Charter's goal to change our government? The Alliance For Democracy for one. What are their political goals?

> *"We want to build a movement that will be stronger than the political parties and eventually will take control of the country."* ... *"We're ready to change the system..."*
>
> Ronnie Dugger
> Founder, Alliance For Democracy
> October 5, 1998

> *"The mission of the Alliance for Democracy is to free all people from corporate domination of politics, economics, the environment ... to establish true democracy and create a just society with **a sustainable, equitable economy.**"*
>
> Source: www.afd-online.org/splash.htm

The Alliance for Democracy is also one of the endorsers of the Pro-Democracy campaign. Goals of the Pro-Democracy campaign include abolishing the Electoral College and replacing it with majority rule.

Instant run-off voting and proportional representation, a Green Party goal, are also part of Pro-Democracy's campaign agenda. Who else do the Greens work with?

Groups working together and endorsing the Pro-Democracy campaign include:

- Communist Party USA
- Green Party of the United States
- The Greens/GPUSA
- Campus Greens
- Alliance for Democracy
- Alliance for Sustainable Jobs and the Environment
- Rainforest Action Network
- Ruckus Society
- Democratic Socialist of America
- The Socialist Forum
- Socialist Party USA
- Rainbow Coalition
- International Socialist Organization
- Independent Progressive Politics Network
- National Lawyers Guild
- Progressive Challenge (Institute for Policy Studies)
- We the People
- Z Magazine
- SPEAK OUT!
- Rock the Vote
- International Libertarian Network
- Coalition to Save the Urban Forest
- Labor Community Strategy Center
- Voice of the Environment
- Save the Redwoods/Boycott the GAP
- Global Exchange
- Multiple state Green Parties

Source: www.greenparty.org/press/12202000.html
(or) www.ippn.org/unsorted/Endorse.htm

All these groups are part of the Green movement.

Sustainability, Communism With a Facelift

Sustainable development, as defined by the Environmental Literacy Council, is:

> *"an attempt to link conservation of natural resources with economic development. Although widely accepted by many governmental and non-governmental agencies as a goal, concerns about what the concept means in practice have been raised by many."*
>
> Source: www.enviroliteracy.org

The 'attempt' to link sustainability to the economy comes from the Greens, the Party and the movement. Sustainability is a crucial part of the Green's 'fast track' plan to take control. Sustainability is a primary Green Party goal.

John Resenbrink, Green Party spokesman and political science teacher, outlined the strategy to link sustainability to the economy in 1992. He said:

> *"The Green Policy of uniting the concepts of ecology and economy and applying the principle of sustainability to society as a whole,* ... *adds community as an integral feature of the good life. The good life of the future is the sustainable life of temperate, balanced growth."*
>
> The Greens and the Politics of Transformation
> John Resenbrink

Sustainability is not simply a new, progressive or fashionable term. Sustainability is a core principle of the Green Party and a main goal of the Green movement. Sustainability means changing our government, economy, culture, behavior and lifestyle.

If our elected representatives continue to blindly embrace the Green idea of sustainability, and use the Green's definition to guide public policy, then the Greens, as Capra said, will achieve their goals of the 60's revolution. The Greens know they don't have to own the car to drive our nation into a Green future. This is part of the Green's strategy.

A quick reference is found in the book, *Earth Rising* by Philip Shabecoff, published in 2000. The Pew Charitable Trust and Rockefeller Financial Services funded the book. Pew and Rockefeller have also funded Gorbachev.

The purpose of *Earth Rising* was to define the future agenda of the Green movement based on interviews with leaders of major environmental groups, the Green Party and a host of individuals.

To define future goals of the environmental movement, the author interviewed Green Party leaders right along with the leaders of the Sierra Club, the National Wildlife Federation, Friends of the Earth and others, because the Green Party and the Green movement work together and are one in the same.

Shabecoff quotes Green Party spokesman John Resenbrink and Karl Grossman, a teacher and author, in sequence. It was Grossman who called attention to the fact:

> *"alternative political movements have changed national politics* without winning control of the political apparatus."

The American people would be better served if Green ideas about sustainability were scrutinized, dissected and debated before any further action is taken.

According to John Resenbrink, *"Sustainability demands a society"* where public policy dictates that:

> *"nature's substance, and the investment decisions that transform it into goods and services, be used for the nonpostponable needs of all citizens"*

According to the Greens, basic needs include:

- *housing*
- *clothing*
- *food*
- *water*
- *air*
- *physical security*
- *transportation*
- *education*
- *energy*
- *other goods and services such as healthcare*

The Greens and the Politics of Transformation

Lenin promised, *Peace, Bread and Land for all*. Controlling the resources to meet the basic needs of all is a Communist Party goal. Review the above goals and the following statement by Resenbrink:

> *"sustainability is a central and guiding philosophy for action by private and public persons."*
>
> *The Greens and the Politics of Transformation*

Green ideas for a sustainable society affect all of us. These ideas would apply to every aspect of our lives, public and private. According to these guidelines, what would it take to achieve a sustainable society in America? As Gorbachev said, a revolution would have to take place in our minds. We'd have to change our values.

First, we would have to change the way we think and operate. Our economy would have to be changed to the point where our resources (financial, natural and work product) were pooled and held in common to meet the basic needs of all people.

Second, we would have to put the interests of society before our personal goals and work for the good of all. The principles of sustainability would guide all our actions, public and private.

Regardless of what sustainability started out to be, it is has been turned into an ideological, political weapon.

Take a good look at the following goals set by the Communist Party in the Soviet Union.

> *"Party Goals. The program mentions **two important tasks** which must be accomplished before Communism can be introduced: **the economy must be developed to a point where the needs of all** can be satisfied, and the nature of the **Soviet citizen must be remade** to make him fit to live in a communist society. This **'new man' must** learn to **work** voluntarily and **gladly for the good of all** and to put the interests of society **before his personal wishes."***
>
> Communism, What It Is and How It Works
> Schlesinger & Blustain

Green Communism

It's the same plan. What the Greens say we must do to achieve a sustainable society, is what the Communist Party said the Russians needed to do, before Communism could be introduced. Sustainability is Communism with a facelift. Sustainability is Communism in a skillfully designed Green costume to hide the political goals from the American people.

> *"The means of production, factories, mines and mills become the property of the people. They operate and produce only to **'fulfill human needs."***
>
> Ecology, 1972
> Gus Hall,
> Chairman, Communist Party USA

This 1972 quote and book title, *Ecology*, show the environment was part of the Communist's strategy 30 years ago. The Communist plan to 'fulfill basic human needs' is the same as the Green's plan to 'meet basic human needs'.

The 1997 *Sustainable Communities Task Force Report*, prepared by Clinton's, *President's Council on Sustainable Development* (PCSD), outlines the exact same objective. The PCSD's, Policy Recommendation #1, includes the plan to:

> *"draft an economic development strategy that will fulfill basic human needs"*

The Greens are pushing Communism disguised as steps to save the earth. The similarities are unmistakable. This is not a coincidence. This is a long-term, calculated political effort.

> *"It's bad if your enemy is quick. But it's worse if he is patient."*
> *Parade* magazine, June 24, 2001
> Marilyn vos Savant

Marilyn vos Savant is a regular contributor to *Parade* magazine and is listed in the *Guinness Book of World Records*, Hall of Fame, for "Highest IQ."

Another confirmation on what sustainability means is found in the 1999 report on the PCSD from the Tahoe Center for a Sustainable Future. "The Principles of Sustainable Development" report states:

> *"sustainable development requires fundamental changes in the conduct of government, private institutions and individuals"*

Sustainability means changing America and abandoning the values, principles and freedoms we cherish. The Greens hope we will 'leap before we look' and embrace sustainability.

Setting Us Up For Sustainability, Socialism Then Communism

Lenin's Plan	Green Plan	*PCSD Plan	Earth Charter
Planned society	Planned society	Planned society	Planned society
Small Societies	Cooperative Communities	Cooperative Communities	Cooperative Communities
Local economic exchange	Local economic barter	Local, regional economic focus	Sustainable world economic order
Public, group decision making	Public, group decision making	Public, group decision making	Cooperative, public problem solving
Socially Useful work	Meaningful work	Meaningful work	Meaningful employment
Share wealth equally	Share wealth, redistribute	Share wealth social equity	Equitable wealth distribution, within nations and among nations
True Democracy	True Democracy	True Participation	Truly Democratic
Meet basic needs	Meet basic needs	Meet basic needs	Meet basic needs
Abolish commercial secrecy	Public right to know	Transparency business public information	Transparency, public disclosure
Socialize economy Liquidate market Unify central economic plan	Sustainable economy, interfere with market produce what is needed	Sustainability redefine commercial activity, services not products	Rules to control U.S. business and citizen actions to impose sustainable, planned economy
Change values Revolution transform society	Change our values Revolution transform society	Change values. change the way people think and act	Change American's values, behavior and government. Redirect US politics Equals revolution
Atheist	Deep Ecology Wicca, Gaia, Mother Earth Spirituality	Align human activities with natural cycles of the earth	Gorbachev sees Earth Charter as the new Ten Commandments

*The PCSD is former President Clinton's, President's Council on Sustainable Development. Established in 1994

'The only task that remains is to organize the population into cooperative societies, with most of the population organized in cooperatives, socialism will achieve its aim automatically...the system of civilized cooperatives is the system of socialism"
Lenin

Competition Is A Sin

We need to get our eye off the Green's doom of the minute and focus on the Green's political agenda. The Green movement is financed by some of the wealthiest families and foundations in America including the Rockefellers.

"Competition is a sin"
John D. Rockefeller, Sr.
The Rockefeller File by Gary Allen

Obviously, Mr. Rockefeller does not like competition. This statement might explain why the Rockefeller's are involved in the Earth Charter. If you wipe out every American's opportunity to accumulate wealth, which is one of the foundations of freedom this nation was built on, then there would be no competition. The Greens would own it all. Then, as in a communist country, elitists live in luxury while the rest of the people live like slaves, working for the common good.

The more we compare Green goals for sustainability to Communist goals, the more obvious it is they are the same. We are being manipulated, big time. The following statement is from a March 30, 2002, *WorldNetDaily*, article by Joan Veon, titled "Sustainable Development".

"In the interests of the present and future generations, the necessary steps are taken ... to protect and make scientific, rational use of the land and its mineral and water resources, and the plant and animal kingdoms to preserve the purity of air and water, ensure reproduction of natural wealth, and improve the human development."

These ideas sound reasonable but we can't judge this book by its cover. This warm and thoughtful portrayal of taking care of the environment for future generations is actually the description of land use under Communism. This statement is from the 1977 *Constitution of the Union of Soviet Socialist Republics*.

Freedom Is The Key

The Greens are using our love of nature to turn the evaluation process upside down. An example of this is found in a question posed by the Greens several times, *"doesn't talking about the Green's political agenda and Communism take away from environmental issues?"*

The answer to that question is NO. It would be *completely irresponsible* for us not to evaluate environmental demands as they relate to the Green Party and Communism. The Greens want the environment to be the only focus of the discussion but that is not a good plan. Remember what Al Gore said:

> *"And it is no accident that **the very worst environmental tragedies were created by communist governments**, in which the power of the state completely overwhelms the capabilities of the individual steward."*
>
>

Earth in the Balance, 1992
Al Gore
Former Vice President

One of the environments leading advocates, former Vice President Gore, confirmed, *"The very worst environmental tragedies were created by communist governments"*. A healthy environment absolutely depends on protecting our individual freedoms, property rights and government system. America has a better environmental record because we live in a free republic and not under a communist dictatorship.

Questions to consider before supporting any environmental proposal ought to include the following:

1. Does it violate citizen's rights and freedoms?
2. Do the people affected support it? If not, why not?
3. Is it based on sound science? Is it to control the land?
4. Is it a Green Party goal?
5. Does it help the environment?
6. Do the benefits outweigh the costs?
7. Does it erode Constitutional principles?

These questions need to be answered *before* any more laws, lawsuits, species listings or court rulings force more innocent people to suffer.

The Motive Matters

Mark Van Putten, President of the National Wildlife Federation said multiple times in a 1998 speech to the National Press Club, that the Endangered Species Act had created an 'unheralded revolution' in land use (an unheralded revolution is a 'quiet' revolution). He said:

"This shift in just 25 years is nothing short of revolutionary."

Van Putten also said:

"most endangered species rely on private property for their habitat."

Most species reside on private lands because landowners take good care of their land. Van Putten had this to say to the groups, like the American Farm Bureau, who expressed concern about the many Endangered Species listings:

"Now, to those who often oppose us, *especially those who fight nearly every species listing, my message to you is simple:* **Get over it."**

When asked, *"Do you support the use of the Endangered Species Act as a surrogate to block development?"* Van Putten replied:

*"I said before in my comments in terms of protecting prairie dogs, the **motive doesn't matter.** What matters is species recovery. The issue isn't what motivates those who brought spotted owls to the public's attention and brought the lawsuits..."*

The Green's political motivation behind using the ESA to block development or put farmers and others out of business does matter. The Greens are using our system to bring down our system.

*"The establishment of an American Soviet government will involve the **confiscation of large landed estates** in town and country, and also, **the whole body of forest, mineral deposits, lakes, rivers, and so on."***

William Z. Foster
National Chairman Communist Party USA 1932

Control the Resources, Control the People

A tragic example of the abuse of science and misuse of the Endangered Species Act is outlined in this July 12, 2002, *Capital Press* report, titled "Sound Science Proposal Opposed" by Larry Swisher. Swisher wrote:

"...the use and misuse of science in implementing the Endangered Species Act. The designation of the spotted owl, numerous salmon and other species as threatened or endangered has led to restrictions on Northwest private land owners as well as on timber, grazing, mining and other use of federal resources.

*"Rep. Greg Walden, R-Ore. ... urged requiring endangered species listings and other major decisions by federal officials undergo "peer review" by independent scientists. **He said such a review would have prevented last year's tragic cut-off of***

irrigation water to more than 1,000 farmers in the Klamath
Basin of southwestern Oregon and adjacent California.

**"The Department of Interior's decision was 'based on an
incorrect interpretation of scientific data** *relating to the
endangered shortnose and Lost River sucker fish and coho
salmon', Walden said."*

*"The loss of crops and income caused farmers to go bankrupt and
cost the local economy $100 million to $200 million, he said...a
follow-up draft report by* **the independent National Academy
of Scientists concluded that "the science that led to the
government's decision did not support the water shut-off"**
and the suffering was unnecessary' Walden said."

Farmers and others in the Klamath Basin had been sharing
water since 1902 and, even in drought years, had managed
just fine. Then the Greens got involved and the farmer's
irrigation water was shut off. There was no water for crops,
hay, livestock or the 433 species in the nearby Klamath
National Wildlife Refuge.

The Greens would have kept the water off had it not been for
the iron will of the farmers who stood-up for their water
rights and won.

The Greens are out to change America's economic system and
that involves justifying taking control of production and
distribution. The battle over land and water is not over.

Abusing laws like the ESA is just one of the tactics the Greens
are using to take control of the land, the people, production
and distribution.

Here are a few more Green goals for land use:

- *"We oppose ...private ownership of natural ecosystems, such as water..."*

- *"We promote policies that limit the amount of agricultural land that can be owned or controlled by any given person."*

- *"We encourage the social ownership of the land..."*

- *"We believe in discouraging and eventually eliminating land speculation that is the purchase of land to sell in the future for profit..."*

Green Party Program 1992

The Greens are using the environment as the excuse to abolish private property ownership. America's founding fathers created our government based on respect for individual rights, property ownership and freedom. They created a carefully designed check and balance system to protect those rights. We are the guardians of those rights and freedoms.

Who's Minding the Store?

Science is an important part of environmental decisions but what if the data has been manipulated to advance the Green's political goals? Environmental decisions ought to be made with consideration of scientific data, common sense and a healthy respect for Constitutional principles.

We cannot entrust the entire future of our nation to science alone because scientific data can be manipulated. Relying strictly on science has already created some BIG problems that hurt innocent people and the environment. The future of our nation is far too important to base our decisions about the environment on science alone. Recently, scientific results seem to depend on who's minding the store.

Case in point, bio-fraud is increasing. Bio-fraud is a new term to describe the act of manipulating scientific data relating to environmental issues.

Following are a few examples that make us wonder, just how many other times have the Greens lied and used bio-fraud to trick us into submitting to their demands?

On January 24, 2002, the article "The Missing Lynx, the latest Clinton scandal has fur flying in Washington" turned heads. The article, by Kimberly Strassel, a reporter for the *Wall Street Journal*, included the following points:

> "In December, a scandal broke over a high-profile survey to count threatened Canada lynx. **Seven employees** from the Fish & Wildlife Service, the Forest Service and a state agency submitted hair samples from captive lynx and tried to pass them off as wild. When caught, the employees claimed they were testing the DNA identification process."

> "Strassel wrote "The lynx scandal underscores everything that's wrong with Fish & Wildlife and the Forest Service. **It shows how the agencies succumbed to a Clinton-era culture that puts ideology ahead of science.**"

> "It demonstrates the undue influence environmental groups hold over these departments. It also shows how vaguely written laws like the Endangered Species Act can be used to further political agendas, even in the complete absence of hard science."

If the employees were actually testing the DNA process, why didn't they report the 'glitch in the process' after the 'planted' lynx hairs were not detected? Instead, they let it slide until they were caught.

On March 14, 2002, *Washington Times* reporter, Audrey Hudson, exposed another example of bio-fraud. Hudson reported in her article "Owl data knowingly faulty" that:

> *"Forest Service officials knowingly used faulty data of spotted owl habitat to block logging in a California forest, according to court documents obtained by The Washington Times. The Forest Service did not have a "rational basis" for halting the timber sale to Wetsel-Oviatt Lumber Company, said the previously undisclosed ruling by Federal Claims Court Judge Lawerence S. Margolis."*

The thousands of honest, hard working government employees are not the problem. Our government is not the problem. The problem is, there are people in positions of trust who are using their influence to deceive the American people and advance the Green's political agenda. The problem with lies is that people believe them.

Green Claims of Mass Extinction Rates Meaningless

Thomas Bray is a columnist with the *Detroit News*. The following quote is from Bray's article "A Paler Shade of Green" published November 19, 2002:

> *"Some dissenting voices are beginning to be heard. They include the Danish statistician Bjorn Lomborg, whose recent best selling book; "The Skeptical Environmentalist"… takes direct issue with many of the premises of the green land grab. In particular he disputes alarmist scenarios that a global "silent spring" is in the offing."*

> *"In researching the commonly used estimate that **40,000 species a year are going extinct, he found the source is a 1979 book that provides no documentation of the claim."***

*"Indeed, Mr. Lomborg notes, even **scientists identified with the environmental movement confess they have no idea how many species even exist;** so far, only about 1.6 million species have been identified, mostly insects, ... **Estimates of extinction rates thus are meaningless.** "*

Lomborg is not alone in disputing the Green's claim about global warming.

Richard Lindzen is a professor of meteorology at MIT and a member of the National Academy of Sciences panel on climate change. Mr. Lindzen's, June 11, 2001 article "The Press Gets It Wrong, Our report doesn't support the Kyoto treaty" includes the following important points. Mr. Lindzen said:

"Last week the National Academy of Sciences released a report on climate change, prepared for the White House, that was depicted in the press as an implicit endorsement of the Kyoto Protocol."

*"**CNN's Michelle Mitchell was typical of the coverage when she declared that the report represented "a unanimous decision that global warming is real, is getting worse, and is due to man.** There is no wiggle room."*

*"**As one of the 11 scientists who prepared the report, I can state that this is simply untrue.** ... Our primary conclusion was that despite some knowledge and agreement, the science is by no means settled. ... "*

*"But — and **I cannot stress this enough — we are not in a position to confidently attribute past climate change to carbon dioxide or to forecast what the climate will be in the future.** ... We simply do not know what relation, if any, exists between global climate changes and water vapor, clouds, storms, hurricanes, and other factors."*

How could *CNN* make such a big mistake?

Bio-fraud, exaggerated claims about species extinctions and false reports about global warming indicate the Greens think the American people are just too stupid to see through the smokescreen in time to save America and our way of life.

> "*The press is our chief ideological weapon.*"
> Nikita Krushchev
> *Washington Post – 1957*

There is a difference between an honest mistake and squelching the truth. Half-truths and innuendos are not the way to a healthy environment. Our decisions are only as good as the facts we base them on.

9

Operation Green Out!

The Green's believe American's support for a healthy environment has given them the authority to use that support to:

- change our government
- change our economy
- take unprecedented control of our lives
- impose Gorbachev's values and the Earth Charter
- use public education to indoctrinate America's children with Green political values and spiritual beliefs

This is what the Greens have in process now. We do not need to change our government to protect the environment. These goals are political, not environmental. This level of extremism is only necessary if the goal is to take control of the country.

The co-founder of Greenpeace, Dr. Patrick Moore, detached himself from the environmental movement, because it had been hijacked by leftists and extremists.

Frijtof Capra said in his article "Where Have The Flowers Gone" that if the Green movement achieved their goals for 'ecological sustainability' the revolution of the 60's would be achieved. Capra also noted the groups that organized the WTO protest in Seattle had formed a global alliance to achieve these goals. One of the main groups involved in organizing the WTO protests was the International Forum on Globalization, (IFG). Capra's Center for Ecoliteracy is one of IFG's associate groups. The authors of IFG's book *Alternatives to Economic Globalization* share Capra's goal. They state:

"If the planet is to support generations to come, it is vital that an **alternative economic system be built that is rooted in the principle of ecological sustainability"**

The book, written by the leaders of the IFG's associated groups, outlines their goals for a sustainable society. IFG's goals mirror Lenin's goals for cooperative societies and natural resource management. The term the IFG uses to take control of our natural resources is 'common heritage resources' which they define as:

"common heritage resources ... *of the whole species to be shared equally among all. We believe there are three categories of common heritage resources. The first category includes the* **water, land, air, forests and fisheries...** ...*The second includes the culture and knowledge that are* **collective creations of our species.** *Finally, more common resources are those of public services that governments perform* **on behalf of all people to address such basic needs** *of public health, education, public safety."*

This and multiple other points in the book essentially outline Green Party goals for localized, cooperative communities which hold resources in common and use those resources to meet the basic needs of all. The statement above also shows the IFG aligns with the Green Party's version of 'systems thinking' that man is a species.

The joint authors of *Alternatives to Economic Globalization*, hail Fritjof Capra's book *The Hidden Connections*, and point out their success in promoting the Green Party agenda:

*"In Europe, **calls by the IFG members** and others that globalization be replaced by greater emphasis on protecting and rebuilding local economies has **had its first political success. United Kingdom Green members of the European Parliament were elected in 1999** on a manifesto that called for a "protect the local, globally" route to localization."*

The authors of *Alternatives to Economic Globalization* emphasize IFG helped elect Green Party candidates. IFG groups have been promoting Green Party goals for years. The authors define IFG's goal for a new democracy, a living democracy, as one which comes before an 'ecologically sustainable' society:

"... when a community democratically decides how to manage forest immediately around its home ..."

This means the public decides how to use the natural resources not the property owners. Public control (Socialism) is the step before an 'ecologically sustainable' society is achieved. Socialism is also the step before Communism.

A few Green groups and leaders of IFG include:

• The Institute For Policy Studies*	John Cavanagh
• Public Media Center	Jerry Mander
• The Ecologist Magazine	Edward Goldsmith
• Rainforest Action Network*	Randall Hayes
• Public Citizen	Ralph Nader
• Friends of the Earth	Brent Blackwelder
• Center for Ecoliteracy	Peter Buckley
• Earth Island Institute	Dave Phillips
• Sierra Club	Carl Pope
• E.F Schumacher Society	Kirkpatrick Sale
• People Centered Development Forum	David Korten
• Project Underground	Danny Kennedy
• Foundation on Economic Trends	Jeremy Rifkin
• Global Exchange*	Kevin Danaher
• We the People*	Jerry Brown

The (*) indicates the groups that are also involved in the Pro-Democracy campaign and working with the Green Party, the Communist Party, multiple Socialist parties and multiple state Green Parties. Green Party presidential candidate Ralph Nader is also involved with IFG. Green revolutionaries work together.

IFG lists David Korten with the People Centered Development Forum. Korten is also the President of the Positive Futures Network, which is actively promoting the Earth Charter. Korten is also on the Earth Charter Summits Advisory Board along with Richard Clugston. Clugston wears many hats. He is the:

- Director, Earth Charter USA campaign
- Director, University Leaders for a Sustainable Future
- Director, Center for Respect of Life and Environment
- On the planning committee for the 2003, National Center for Science and Environment (NCSE) Conference

All these groups are promoting the Green goal of 'ecological sustainability', which mirrors Communism and the revolutionary goals of the 60's. If they achieve their goals, we will all live within the boundaries set for us by the Greens and in a society where:

- People work for the common good, not individual gain
- Economy, production and distribution are controlled
- Resources are pooled, used to meet basic needs of all
- Government system is changed to Green Communism

Another Green leader confirming these are the goals and that achieving sustainability means taking unprecedented control of our lives, is David Korten. In his book, *Globalizing Civil Society,* Korten makes the following points:

"Sustainable societies will need to discourage incomes larger than necessary to support a modest sustainable lifestyle, advertising that encourages unnecessary consumption and the concentration of financial assets ... The over-consumers --- the people whose lifestyles are unsustainable ... are those whose lives are organized around automobiles, airplanes and meat-based-diets ..."

In his book *Globalizing Civil Society*, Korten indicates, 20% of the world's people are over-consumers, 60% live by meeting basic human needs (sustainers) and 20% (the excluded) live in poverty. The Green plan to achieve a sustainable world is to:

"move the over-consumers and excluded into the sustainer class."

'Ecological sustainability' means changing our individual lifestyles and conforming to a lifestyle where basic human needs are met. Society would function according to the rules and limitations set by the Greens. Green goals to control our behavior, income, diet, financial assets and natural resources are *not* about saving the environment. This is a clever con-job to take control of our country and our lives.

Anatoliy Golitsyn, an ex-KGB officer who defected to the United States, warned in his 1984 book *New Lies for Old* that world Communism was still the Soviet's goal. Larry Abraham, who wrote the book's epilogue, indicated the Communists plan to merge the United States with the Soviet Union so our resources can continue to support them. Abraham said:

"There is only one way: Increase their standard of living, while drastically reducing ours."

Golitsyn's warning was issued 19 years ago and it certainly fits Gorbachev's current Earth Charter plans for the redistribution of the wealth "in nations and among nations".

The Earth Charter would allow Gorbachev to use America's resources to meet the basic needs of all people including the Soviets. The Earth Charter equals Green World Communism.

Green buzzwords to watch for include:

- systems thinking
- ecological sustainability, localized self-determination
- equity, redistribution of the wealth within and among nations

How do the Greens plan to convince the American people to go along with Green Communism? One way is using the idea of 'self-determination' to localize food production and change our food supply system. Another way is a brainwashing campaign designed to change our values and beliefs.

Green Party leader Frijtof Capra knows 'systems thinking' is the way to reach children. The Greens plan to use this process and public education to indoctrinate every child in America. The 1989 Green Party Program states:

> *"We can incorporate ecological wisdom, sustainability, respect for diversity and social justice in our classrooms."*

'The end justifies the means' is the way experts describe the mentality of dedicated Communists. There is no other reasonable explanation for the methods the Greens plan to use to pressure children into adopting their political beliefs.

It's interesting the Greens say we must change our government and our lives because the environment all over the world is in ruin and on the edge of collapse. An article in the *San Jose Mercury News*, December 4, 2002, titled "46 Percent of the Earth is Still Wilderness, Researchers Report" by Paul Rogers, sheds new light on that subject:

"Despite population growth, logging and other environmental threats, nearly half of the land on Earth remains wilderness, undeveloped and nearly unpopulated, according to a study released today" ... *"A lot of the planet is still in pretty decent shape"* said Russell Mittermeier, a Harvard primatologist and president of Conservation International, an environmental group in Washington D.C., that organized the study."*

This is good news. This validates what Greenpeace co-founder Dr. Patrick Moore pointed out; the world is not coming to an end. Our children do not need to live in constant fear. The following statement is from a teenage Earth Day Network volunteer who, thanks to the Greens, is distressed:

"The Earth is being destroyed faster than ever, and the problems we face are becoming increasingly complex. As teenagers, we're about to inherit the planet. We will need to come up with ways to propel human progress forward without destroying the earth in the process."

Emily, 18, an Earth Day Network Volunteer

Living a Sustainable Lifestyle

Living a Sustainable Lifestyle for Our Children's Children is the title of a 2001 book by R. Warren Flint and W.L. Houser. The authors offer a clear look at 'systems thinking' and the goals for an 'ecologically sustainable' society. The authors also provide a disturbing but revealing look at the thought process behind 'systems thinking'. The authors outline how this can be used to shape and teach sustainable values.

The Greens have reinvented themselves. Instead of being environmentalists they are now conservationists. The political strategy behind the name change is to use the 'giving nature and concern for others' that is characteristic of conservatives, to get conservatives to endorse sustainability. Greens plan to use this support to achieve sustainability, without disclosing their definition of sustainability includes denouncing God.

Flint and Houser wrote *"The **seven most harmful** consumer purchase activities could include the following:*

- cars and trucks
- meat
- fruits, vegetables, and grains
- home heating and cooling
- household appliances
- home construction
- home water and sewage"

If fruits, vegetables, grains and meat are all harmful to consume, then what do we eat in a sustainable society?

In a Green society all resources would be held in common and used to meet the basic needs of all. It follows that everyone would receive a designated amount of food to survive.

'Rationed lentils' was how Green Party leader Johathan Porrit described 'compulsory Green living' back in Chapter 1. Compulsory Green living and sustainability are the same.

Another alternative, which has obviously been considered by the Green Communists, is to grow your own food. Under Communism in the Soviet Union, peasants had this option:

> *"a second source of income is the sale of produce raised on private **allotments ranging from one-half to one-third of an acre**, which the peasant may cultivate for himself."*
> Communism, What it is and How it Works
> Schlesinger/Blustain

Flint and Houser, indicate in *Living a Sustainable Lifestyle for Our Children's Children* that 'allotments' have been researched:

"About 1.2 acres of crop land per person is required to provide a diverse diet ... At present this amount of land is still available in the United States for its current population."

To grant allotments, Greens must control the land. Eco-efficency is a term the authors use to justify more land control.

*"**Eco-efficency** tells us to **restrict industry** and **curtail growth**" ... "limit the **creativity and productiveness** of humankind."*

Eco-efficency means:

- Restricting industry
- Restricting growth
- Limiting productiveness of humankind
- Limiting individual's human potential

According to Flint and Houser:

*"The first step toward reducing our ecological impact is to recognize that the "**environmental crisis**" is less an **environmental** and technical **problem than it is a human behavior and social one** ... Clearly, **most of the required action is on the social side** rather than the science side."*

This statement shows the 'environmental crisis' is less of a problem than our behavior. Our behavior is the latest Green excuse for social transformation to a sustainable society. The authors of *Living a Sustainable Lifestyle for Our Children's Children* make the connection, in the following statement, that teaching sustainability is about shaping political values to increase votes for the Greens:

*"When the majority of community members make sustainability a part of everyday decisions while shopping, building, recreating, working, **and voting**, then these communities will achieve sustainability."*

*"As we develop this society there is a **transformation in our individual attitudes and values.** There is now the opportunity for a **complete transformation of our social structures.... Our problems are moral, spiritual, philosophical and behavioral.** The path towards sustainable development can only be built upon a change in human psyche*

*...**Such qualities as ... cooperation and willingness to sacrifice for the common good** for the invisible yet now essential foundation of human society..."*

The Green's goal is social transformation. The environmental cause provides the necessary cover. One of the authors, R. Warren Flint, is the owner and principle consultant of 5E's, an educational and consulting firm. One of the goals of 5E's is equity, which Flint defines as:

*"**achieving total societal welfare by guaranteeing equal access to jobs (income), education, natural resources, and services for all people.**"*

Source: *www.eeeee.net/sd01001.htm*

This 5E goal matches Communist's goals and Green goals for a sustainable society. Sustainability requires the equitable distribution of the wealth, control of natural resources, control of the economy and control of citizens, who work for the common good in exchange for meeting their basic needs.

The authors of *Living a Sustainable Lifestyle for Our Children's Children*, Flint and Houser promote the Earth Charter and its goal to achieve sustainability by using education to:

*"**Make the knowledge, values,** and skills needed to build just and sustainable communities **an integral part of formal education** and lifelong learning for all"*

Using public education to teach Green political beliefs, disguised as the "values and skills needed to build just and sustainable communities", is how the Greens plan to change students values and mold their political beliefs.

Flint and Houser offer a lesson in how 'systems thinking' can be used to promote sustainable values and change existing values:

> *"Self-centered people tend to be piece thinkers. Other-centered people tend to be systems thinkers. A systems thinker is likely to see himself or herself as an inseparable part of the system, whereas a piece thinker normally sets himself or herself apart from and above the system. Like blind people feeling the different parts of an elephant, each person is initially limited by his or her perspective."*

Teaching the Earth Charter in school is the goal and 'systems thinking' is part of program. If 'systems thinking' is taught in schools in this manner, what choice does a child or student have?

This lesson is specifically designed to offer people only 2 choices. They can either be 'self-centered', 'piece thinkers', who see themselves above nature, or 'systems thinkers', who think of others and see themselves as an 'inseparable part' of nature.

This appears to be the approach to teach students 'systems thinking'. Students do not deserve to be belittled, coerced or intimidated in this manner.

This method of shaping values is unscrupulous. If this is the approach to teaching 'systems thinking' it's eco-child abuse. Eco-child abuse occurs when the Greens use children as political pawns and use environmental issues to intimidate or scare children into being Green.

Psychological Warfare

This is only the first part of the lesson in 'systems thinking'. 'Systems thinking' is designed to get people to accept Green values. These lessons are crafted to intimidate, manipulate and reshape the values of the American people, young and old alike.

The next lesson in sustainable values involves advocating Green Party spiritual beliefs by condemning those who believe in God. The Greens are using psychological warfare.

Using the same manipulative approach, Flint and Houser, compare 'systems thinkers', those who believe they are part of nature, to those who believe they are above nature.

The authors present a choice between the Native worldview and the Western worldview to promote being a 'systems thinker'. If this is taught in school, children would be given the choice between the following 2 world views:

Western: "Spirituality is centered in a single Supreme Being" (God)

Native: "Spirituality is imbedded in all elements of the cosmos"

The authors conclude:

> *"On the one hand there is the self-centered, western view.* And on the other is the more socially sensitive, innocent native world view".

This is not quite *Mary Had a Little Lamb*. This is unfair, but it appears, this is how to use 'systems thinking' to pressure children into adopting the Greens political and spiritual beliefs.

The Greens already have churches lending their political support to the environmental cause. The Greens probably just forgot to mention, erasing the belief in God, is one of their political goals. 'The end justifies the means' is the Communist mentality.

In the book, *Living a Sustainable Lifestyle for Our Children's Children*, Flint and Houser present a long list of comparisons that promote the Native world view and put-down the Western belief in a Supreme Being.

The Five E's, Second Nature, University Leaders for a Sustainable Future, the Earth Charter and the Earth Day Network are just a few of the groups advocating the Native or Green world view and teaching 'systems thinking'.

> *"One of the most important tasks of the cultural revolution affecting the wide masses is the task of systematically ... combating religion, the opium of the people."*
>
> The Naked Communist
> Cleon Skousen

The Green movement and Green Party appear to share this Communist goal. Gorbachev and the Greens see man as equal to a flower or a lobster, just a species, part of nature not a steward above nature. Karl Marx the author of the Communist Manifesto, shared this view of man:

> *"He joined 2 very old ideas:*
>
> *That everything in the universe, whether a blade of grass, a human being, or society itself, is constantly changing...*
>
> *That God doesn't exist and the world is composed only of living matter. Hence, man is walking dust. Without a spark or image of his divine Creator."*
>
> Masters of Deceit
> J. Edgar Hoover

The Green version of 'systems thinking' aligns with this thought process and is designed to get students to accept the Green's political belief that they are no different than bugs or dust. This is part of a long term, calculated, political effort.

The Greens anticipate questions regarding teaching their political values in classrooms and have an answer ready. Brendan Mackey, the Chair and Director of the Earth Charter Education Program, shares the following advice on how to defend teaching the very political Earth Charter in school.

The statement below can be found in the article "Teaching Sustainability with the Earth Charter" by Richard Clugston, Wynn Calder and Peter Blaze Corcoran on the ULSF website:

*"Values education is an often-contested theme in education due to legitimate concerns about "which values" and "whose values" are being promoted. **These concerns can be accommodated** so long as the values represent core values that are life-affirming, promote human dignity, advance environmental protection and social and economic justice and respect cultural and ecological diversity and integrity. **The Earth Charter can validly lay claim to represent such a core set of values"** ... "The Earth Charter provides critical content for development of curricula with the educational aim of teaching values and principles for sustainable living."*

Source: www.ulsf.org

Oops! Someone forgot to mention the Earth Charter is a political document with the stated goal to change our government. This fact alone ought to keep the Earth Charter and teaching sustainability out of America's classrooms. Green leaders told us achieving their goals for sustainability is equal to achieving their goals of the 60"s revolution.

The Greens are executing plans to use the Earth Charter, an international document based on the opinions of a few, to indoctrinate America's children with their political and spiritual values. The Earth Charter goals go way beyond changing our government. Gorbachev refers to the Earth Charter as a new Ten Commandments.

The Earth Charter is an international, anti-American, set of political opinions that the Greens plan to teach our children. The Greens think the American people are so-o-o-o stupid we will let them use our tax dollars to brainwash our children and foster revolution in America. The Earth Charter has no place in school. It has no legal standing or parental approval but it is being taught anyway.

According to the authors of the article "Teaching Sustainability with the Earth Charter", the Earth Charter is already being taught at Florida Gulf Coast University, Michigan State University, Western Michigan University and Hendrix College in Arkansas. A Hendrix College student has already taught the Earth Charter in middle school classes. The authors of the article conclude:

> *"The Earth Charter initiative is catalyzing an integrated movement ... to embody the Earth Charter principles in national economic policy, in the ethics and practices of corporations and professionals, in individual values..."*

The Earth Charter is part of the overall plan to change our government, economy and values. An important point on the Green's agenda for education and religion follows.

> *"A Green educational policy will be based on teaching the following values"* ... *"alternative political perspectives, alternative economic views and unbiased study of religions"*
> Green Party Program 1992

Why do the Greens want to teach multiple religions in school? The following statement is from a lesson on 'how to' teach Earth Charter values. It helps us understand the Greens political motivation:

*"Think of it this way. You have a responsibility for your family. Well, **what if your father were the sky, your mother the earth, your brother the animals, and your sister the plants?** This makes it easier to see how we have a responsibility to care for our entire Earth community because they are each a part of our community."*

This native view is a political tool for the Greens.

"We support the renewal of Native American traditional cultures and practices that embody a wealth of spiritual and ecological teachings for living on this land."
Green Party Program 1992

"Like the Iroquois Indians, Greens seek a society where the interests of the seventh generation are considered to the interest of the present."
Green Party Program 2000

As mentioned in earlier chapters, Green Communists are taking advantage of the spiritual beliefs of the American Indian to advance their revolutionary political agenda. Americans take care of the land. That is why our lands are in better shape than those in communist countries. The political purpose behind taking advantage of Indian beliefs is to align with Marx's belief that there is no God, man is no more than walking dust, and you cannot own the earth or sky.

The Communist Party USA published the article "Remarks on the Environment", by Prasad Venugopal, July 7, 2001. Marx's view of private property ownership was quoted:

*"From the standpoint of socialism, **individual private ownership of the earth will appear just as much in bad taste as the ownership of one human being by another.** Even a whole society, a nation, or all contemporary societies taken together, are not the absolute owners of the earth. **They are only its occupants, its beneficiaries, and have to leave it in improved condition to following generations."***
Source: www.cpusa.org/

Using the Indian belief 'your mother is the earth and 'your brother the animals' helps the Greens pave the way for ending private property ownership and freeing all the animals from domination. These are just more excuses to seize control.

If the earth is your mother, then owning her would be like owning a slave, as Marx said. Marx also said "Communism can be summed up in a single sentence, the abolition of private property." This is one of the Green's objectives.

The Greens intend to teach America's children that owning private property is wrong to turn them away from the principles and values this nation was built on.

This is part of Gorbachev's plan to change American's values. In his book *The Search for a New Beginning, Developing a New Civilization*, Mikhail Gorbachev states:

> *"The time has come for humankind to accept the traditional philosophy of the Native Americans: We do not inherit this planet from our parents, we are borrowing it from our children."*

The Greens are playing our heartstrings, from our love of the great outdoors to our love of man's best friend, to cloud our thinking and judgement. If ever there was a time to keep our wits about us and think straight, now is the time.

If the Green movement was about protecting the environment and not about using the environmental cause to conceal steps to take control of our lives, then why are the Greens going after children, God and country?

Just Below the Radar

The focus of education in America is no longer traditional academics. The Greens and others have transformed education, from teaching traditional academics, to teaching political and social values in school.

> *"We are committed to the transformation of the existing public education school system."*
>
> Green Party Program 1992

The following goals are from the 1992 Green Party program, which states "a Green educational policy will be based on **teaching the following values"**:

- Holistic education, focused on creating a sustainable, just and peaceful society in harmony with the Earth and its life

- Expanding the traditional classroom. Bring in plants and animals. Grow food in schoolyards. Use nearby woodlands and neighborhoods to make the local environment the core of the curriculum

- Use hands-on direct experience so students learn to make connections, see nature as an interactive whole as the foundation for all natural studies and science

- Reverence for life in all its forms, interconnectedness

- Parenting programs. Teach parenting, child development and non-violent discipline

- Diversity, the contributions of each race, culture, religion, sex and sexual orientation

- **Oppose memorization and seeking the "right" answer,** students should be free to make mistakes, fear of failure inhibits a person's ability to learn.

- **Learning should be based** on progress, enjoyment and **creative ability to come up with a new response in each situation,** rather than meet standards and conform

- Histories of movements for social, environmental change

- Consensus, feminine consciousness, personal and political non-violence

- Alternative political perspectives and economic views

The Greens have changed education. January 27, 2003 Dr. Laura Schlessinger's article "Time for public schools to throw in the towel" was featured on *WorldNetDaily*. Dr. Laura said:

> *"Last fall, the Center for Civic Information at the Manhattan Institute published the report of a telephone survey of over 1000 fourth and eighth-grade teachers. Among the not so surprising findings was that only about 25 percent of those surveyed said they most cared about whether a student got the right answers.*
>
> ***More of them most cared that students tried hard or used a creative approach.*** *That absurd state of affairs has come about because this generation of teachers, and probably a generation before, have themselves been raised to believe there are no right answers, anyway. So what difference does it make?*

Dr. Laura hit the nail on the head. It's easier to understand why some teachers think this way, when we realize where creating this mindset comes from. It is part of the Green's agenda. Communists don't want the challenge of thinking Americans. This is why reducing the intelligence level of our children and young people is the Green's political priority.

As Frijtof Capra indicated, if the Greens can convince the American people to accept sustainability, the revolution they've been working toward since the 60's will happen.

It's been 43 years since the 60's riots and calls for revolution. As the SDS and others were winding down, the attitude was, if they couldn't change the 'establishment' through revolution they would change it from within. If they teach our children their values, our children will follow.

Capra said many of the 60's revolutionaries were part of the Green movement. Capra and others, involved in promoting Green ideas, are educators, who are using schools to teach their personal, political values.

The Green movement is about politics and power not pollution and peace.

Double-Crossed

> "...Communist leaders stressed the importance of education and regarded it as a tool for the transformation of society"
> Communism, What It Is and How It Works
> Schlesinger and Blustain

Just like the Communists, the Greens see public education as a political tool and children as political pawns. The Greens plan to make teaching sustainable values a priority in environmental education so they can use classrooms to indoctrinate students.

> "Greens see education as a transformative agent in ...primary, secondary and higher education..."
> Green Party Program 1989

'Education for sustainability', 'systems thinking' and the Earth Charter are part of the Green's strategy to make teaching their political values a national educational priority.

The book, *Earth Rising,* by Philip Shabecoff, published in 2000, confirms the Green's plan to use public education to teach their values to children.

The purpose of *Earth Rising* was to outline the goals of the Green movement. It's no accident Green Party leaders were interviewed along with the leaders of major environmental groups. These groups work together and share the same revolutionary political agenda.

According to Shabecoff, his conclusions and recommendations were based on those interviews and his understanding of the movement. A few of the Green groups and individual leaders interviewed for *Earth Rising* included:

- Friends of the Earth   Brent Blackwelder
- Natural Resource Defense Council   John Adams
- Second Nature   Anthony Cortese
- Earth Day   Denis Hayes
- Environmental Defense Fund   Fred Krupp
- World Resource Institute   Jonathan Lash
- National Religious Partnership for the Environment   Paul Gorman
- The Wilderness Society   William Meadows
- National Wildlife Federation   Mark Van Putten
- ALF-CIO, Environmental Liaison   Jane Perkins
- Sierra Club   Carl Pope
- League of Conservation Voters   Deb Callahan
- National Environmental Trust   Phillip Clapp
- World Wildlife Fund   Katherine Fuller
- Native Forest Council   Tim Hermach
- Land Trust Alliance   Jean Hocker
- Southwest Network for Environmental and Economic Justice   Richard Moore

Some of these groups and individuals may not share all the goals outlined by Shabecoff. He indicates in the preface, he based his conclusions on his understanding of the goals discussed during the interviews.

The following is this author's summary of the Green movement's goals and strategy outlined by Shabecoff in *Earth Rising*.

- Use public education (preschool, K-12 and college) to shape children's beliefs and teach students Green values

- Focus on science. Guide projects and use the results

- Reform education. Get on school boards. Control standards and curriculum. Get on college and university boards

- Use support for the environmental cause to change America's political, social and economic systems

- Get churches to embrace a new theology (a new spirituality)

- Sustainability. Change the economy to *fulfill human needs*

- Use American's support for the environmental cause to build the Green Party and elect Green Party candidates

Shabecoff quoted Green Party spokesperson John Resenbrink:

*"He concluded that **the current political system will not be able to address our ecological problems**, and therefore, **"we need a new constellation of power"**.*

The political goals of the Greens include changing our government system. Shabecoff outlined the strategy to use America's support for the environmental cause to promote the political agenda of the Green Party and to elect Green Party candidates.

In 2000, the author of *Earth Rising,* indicated the Greens knew public education was the way to reach and teach America's children their beliefs and values.

In 2003, these Green groups are promoting the Earth Charter and getting Earth Charter values taught in America's schools.

Many of these groups are working with government agencies and the National Center for Environment and Science (NCSE), to make teaching Green politics in our schools an immediate, national priority.

The Green's version of 'systems thinking', 'ecoliteracy' and 'education for sustainability' are the core concepts being promoted as the new 'essential learnings' for a sustainable future.

It may sound unbelievable but these ideas are on-the-table and on their way to being forced into public education from the top down, nationwide.

Following is what the Greens have set-up and how they plan to use classrooms to, take your pick, indoctrinate, socially engineer or brainwash students into adopting their political values.

The following facts ought to move the American people to take immediate action and stop the NCSE plan dead in its tracks.

Brainwashing for a Green Future

Education for a Sustainable and Secure Future was the theme for the "3rd National Conference on Science, Policy and the Environment (NCSE), held January, 2003, Washington, D.C.

Some of the groups on the NCSE conference planning and advisory committee included:

- University Leaders for a Sustainable Future
- 5 E's
- The Biodiversity Project
- Second Nature
- National Audubon Society
- National Park Service
- Disney's Animal Kingdom
- Center for a Sustainable Future
- US Geological Survey
- US Department of Agriculture - CREES
- National Environmental & Education Training Foundation
- Earth Force
- The Sustainability Education Center
- National Science Foundation
- Global Environmental Alliance
- Mary Kay Holding Corporation
- North American Association for Environmental Education

Some of these groups probably don't realize the Green's political motivation behind pushing 'education for sustainability', 'ecoliteracy', 'systems thinking' and the Earth Charter. Some do.

Denis Hayes, the director of the Earth Day Network was a featured speaker at the NCSE conference, which suggests Earth Day will play a leading role in 'herding' the American people and our children toward the NCSE educational goals.

The chairs of former president Clinton's, President's Council for Sustainable Development, Jonathan Lash, President of the World Resource Institute, and Ray Anderson, Chairman and CEO of Interface Flooring, were also featured speakers. The involvement of the former chairs of Clinton's PCSD strongly suggests, the revival of Clinton's agenda for education, which stressed 'systems thinking'.

As Gorbachev indicated, the Green way to change America is to change the way we think and act. The NCSE conference "Education for a Sustainable Future" included a K-12 session. The description of the K-12 session follows.

"K-12 Content
Identification of Essential Learnings at the K-12 Level:

*K-12 education is a major shaper of the **truths, attitudes, ethics, concepts and behaviors** of American society.*

*By **reshaping K-12 education** in the US, so that it systematically and effectively fosters sustainability, we will be able to make great progress towards the achievement of a sustainable world …**Changes in thinking and behavior that foster sustainability are already underway** in our society…*

*…**Our schools need to prepare students** to join this quest **by giving them** the knowledge, skills, **beliefs** and the **'habits of the heart'** that will enable them to fashion a sustainable world.*

*… we need to create a national infrastructure to develop and support the nationwide practice of education for susluinubility in all our schools; and we need to fund the effort and the research need to educate for sustainability broadly and well. If we do this, we may succeed in successfully providing U.S. citizens with the knowledge, the skills and the **attitudes** needed to foster sustainability in their personal, community, and work lives. …*

When the pursuit of sustainability becomes an obvious and **'inescapable goal'** *of all our endeavors, educating for sustainability will necessarily become a primary goal of our school systems."*

Source: www.ncseonline.org

This clearly shows, teaching America's children the same 'Green' attitudes, values and beliefs is the plan. A few of the groups involved in the NCSE conference that are also promoting the Earth Charter include:

- University Leaders for a Sustainable Future
- The Biodiversity Project
- World Resource Institute
- 5 E's

The "K-12 Implementation" session focused on hands-on learning to connect students with nature and their communities. This is the same concept outlined by Fritjof Capra for his Center for Ecoliteracy projects. The K-12 implementation panel included representatives from the National Audubon Society and the National Wildlife Federation.

The Earth Day Network, the Earth Charter, 5E's, Education for Sustainability, University Leaders for a Sustainable Future and the North American Association for Environmental Education are all promoting teaching 'systems thinking'.

The North American Association of Environmental Education (NAAEE) helped plan the NCSE conference. According to NAAEE materials the principles of environmental education include the following:

- "Environmental education includes the affective domain of the **attitudes, values** and **commitments necessary to build a sustainable society**"

- **"Interdependence ...Humans are part of** the natural order. We, and the systems we create – **our societies, political systems, economics, religions, cultures, technologies** – impact the total environment. Since we are part of nature rather than outside it, we are challenged to recognize the ramifications of our interdependence."

Source: www.naaee.org/

Teaching 'systems thinking', which is the guiding principle of the Green Party and teaching the Party's core values of sustainability and interdependence, is how Greens plan to change students values. It is also how the Greens plan to change our government, economy, society, religion, culture and our lives.

There are political connections between the NAAEE and Green goals for social transformation. The eelink website is a Project of the NAAEE. New links featured on the site as of December 30, 2002 include the 'Echoing Green Fellowship Program', which is described as:

> "The Echoing Green Fellowship Program **gives social change** entrepreneurs **tools and resources** to start public service projects in fields including education...youth service"

The 'Echoing Green' website repeats their purpose is:

> "supporting public service fellows as **catalysts for social change"** ... the program was created to provide ... "ideas for driving social change"

Source: www.Echoinggreen.org/

Once again the connection between environmental education and the Green's hidden political agenda for social transformation rears its ugly head.

The National Academies Press 2002 book titled *New Tools for Environmental Protection: Education, Information and Voluntary Measures*, was recommended by the NCSE conference organizers. The authors of *New Tools for Environmental Protection*, are well aware, teaching America's children a uniform set of values, attitudes and beliefs is social engineering. On page 340 of the book, under the heading, "Some Reasons to Be Cautious" it states:

> "... *in our society, we tend to believe that government roles in shaping human behavior should be quite limited. Any indication of social engineering by government, for example, by "experimentally manipulating social norms" ... is likely to be considered a threat to true democracy.*"

Social Engineering

The Greens are manipulating social norms and this is a threat to national security. NCSE goals and Green goals for education amount to Soviet-style indoctrination. Social engineering is not the American way. It's the Communist's method to keep the population in line by training children to be passive, cogs in a wheel. Greens intend to use education to erase individualism and replace it with interdependence and group-think.

The recommendations in the reports following the National Center for Science and Environment Conference (NCSE) confirm their goals for education parallel Green political goals and include the following:

> "*K-12 policy must include education for sustainability as a core priority and should be infused and integrated across all disciplines.*"

The goal is to 'infuse' sustainability lessons into every subject area. Infuse means inculcate. Inculcate means indoctrinate. Indoctrinating America's children is the plan. Our children are in serious trouble.

Other recommendations from the NCSE conference on 'education for sustainability' that mirror the Green's political goals include:

- Use the Earth Charter to teach new ethics for sustainability

- Use 'systems thinking' to teach sustainbility in all subjects

- Use the seventh generation test (Native worldview) as a strategy to teach sustainability

- Connecting sustainability to student's personal core values, stress interrelatedness to nature and their communities

- Encouraging corporate transparency (Lenin called it ending commercial secrecy)

- Linking sustainability to national security:

  *"in communication to the public, (we) need to make it **clear the US is perceived as a threat to world sustainability because of consumption and lifestyles** that go beyond just a few national values."*

  Source: www.ncseonline.org/

Linking national security to sustainability to build support for the Earth Charter is a Green Party goal. Please see quote, top of page 349. The Green plan is to use guilt and fear to push Americans into supporting the Earth Charter.

The NCSE conference recommendations include the idea:

"schools should provide opportunities for students to develop their own values about these issues"

If America's children are taught Green values in every subject area, all day long, week after week, year after year, they will not be able to escape indoctrination.

The NCSE conference recommends brainwashing children and the American people. One of the conference session was:

> *"**Public Communication:** Strategy for a National Public Communications Campaign on Sustainable Development: **How do we transform national public opinion?"***

Recommended resources for this NCSE session on 'how to' transform public opinion included the book *Ethics for a Small Planet: A Communications Handbook on Ethical and Theological Reasons for Protecting Biodiversity"* by the Biodiversity Project.

Ethics for a Small Planet is an interesting but subversive, 144 page book, focused on making social change a moral imperative in the battle to save the earth. The book outlines multiple ways for the Greens to defend their extremist political agenda. Carefully crafted talking points are presented to address predetermined objections along with calculated ways to 'sell it' to the American people.

The authors of *Earth Ethics* anticipate questions about 'systems thinking' being taught in school. They also anticipate questions about private property rights, patriotism and their obvious anti-people, anti-progress and anti-God agenda. The guiding principle of the Green Party is 'systems thinking' and it is #2 on the *Earth Ethics's,* myth-busters list. Following is a summary of the planned response to objections to the idea that man is part of nature not a steward above nature.

Myth-Buster #2 - "The Human Superiority Argument"

The myth: Humans are superior to nature …

The response: The idea of 'superiority' is an outmoded argument that has no practical meaning… "

This statement in *Earth Ethics* confirms 'systems thinking' is a key part of the Green's political strategy to change America's core values. The *Earth Ethics* handbook is a contradiction in ethics. The book offers multiple unethical ways to coerce Americans into submitting to the Green agenda.

For instance, the authors of *Earth Ethics* promote the Green Party version of 'systems thinking' and explain 'how to' use it to manipulate people and keep the focus off their political agenda. The author's state:

> *"Hence, a yellow-bellied flycatcher, a marsh marigold, and an alder swamp – as possessors of intrinsic value – can be said to occupy the same general moral space as a human being. Granting intrinsic values to non-human living things shifts the burden of proof on to those who would despoil the natural world and away from those who wish to preserve, protect, and defend it."*

On the same page the author's highlight the following point:

> *"Non substituteable value is important to keep in mind because it offers a way of capturing the powerful and complex emotional responses that people have toward nature..."*

A key part of the Green's political strategy is to use our emotions as a tool to mask imposing their political agenda.

The purpose of *Earth Ethics* is to teach Green activists 'how to' frame the debate to take advantage of American's emotions and concern for the environment.

The strategy is to get the American people to help them achieve sustainability before people realize sustainability means Green Communism.

The Green plan includes tapping into all-American attributes such as our:

- sense of responsibility
- respect and appreciation for nature
- duty to future generations, stewards of nature

The author's of *Earth Ethics* make it clear the strategy is to:

- make every message personal to build trust
- talk slow, tell stories, use conservative language
- frame all the issues as a question of ethics
- infer Americans are not responsible enough
- put Americans on the defensive
- shift the burden of proof

Earth Ethics is another lesson in psychological warfare designed for adults and students alike. The Green plan is to insult our integrity so we will react and 'show them' how much we care about the environment by supporting sustainability.

It's interesting *Earth Ethics* also focuses on 'Theology'. The Greens are stretching theology so they can use the belief in God as a hammer to get Americans to support sustainability. The following statement is from *Earth Ethics*:

> *"Hence to discount the future is to deny the sovereignty of God.* ***Living unsustainably then becomes a crime against God*** *and against generations yet to come. "*

This is not a religious debate. This is part of the Green's political strategy to change American's values and achieve power. The Greens plan to use American's belief in God to trick people into supporting their political goals without disclosing their anti-God political position.

The book *Earth Ethics* has a section on 'Divine Command and Natural Law'. It states:

> "*Divine command theory suggests that ethical precepts are the product of divine or revealed dictate (ethical rules are dictated by God or Krishna or Allah).*"

This section includes 'how to' respond to this 'divine theory':

> "**Adherents of these theories** *must be prepared to consider several questions. First can we accept certain presuppositions in order to believe this theory? For instance,* **do we accept the existence of a divine being** *to give us instructions or a clear idea of what is natural? Second,* **how do we know what is and what is not the will of God** *or what is natural?* **Who's to say,** *and how do we know we have it right? Third,* **how do we decide which messages** *or dictates ...* **are the right ones to adhere to?**"

Green Communists are at the point of being exposed for their atheist views. The political purpose behind these questions is to muddy the water. The Greens are using theology to justify and mask their political goals. They are twisting theology to get Americans to accept that we are just another species, a part of nature, not a steward of nature. This value-shift would pave the way for the social religion embodied in the Earth Charter. The following is from the list of the 45 Communist goals entered into the Congressional Record, January 10, 1963. Goal #27 is:

> "**Infiltrate the churches and replace revealed religion with social religion. Discredit the Bible** *and emphasize the need for intellectual maturity which does not need a religious crutch*".

Sounds like the Green's political agenda.

> "**Consumerism and other addictions, religious escapism, rigid adherence to dogmatic beliefs** *... are all indicative of a social failure to meet our spiritual needs...*"
>
> Green Party Program 1992

Green goals presented in the book *Earth Ethics* range from condemning private property ownership to advocating sustainability, biodiversity and the Earth Charter.

Churches Beware

The March 26, 2002, 'Politics & Policy' section of the *Wall Street Journal* featured the article "Greens' and Churches Join Hands in Environmental Mission, Sometimes-Uneasy Alliance, a Decade in Making, Fights Alaska Drilling, Global Warming". The article by John J. Flalka included the following important points:

> *"The "greens" haven't suddenly got religion. Rather, they have begun working ... with the nation's major churches"* ...

> *"Sierra Club President Carl Pope" said **"This is the kind of impact you'll never be able to measure in terms of classic lobbying"**, he adds **"Churches set the moral tone for the whole country."***

America's churches "set the moral tone for the whole country". Where would a movement go to change the moral tone (the values) of the country? This is why the Greens went to church. In 1992, Green Party leader, John Resenbrink laid out strategic plans, to build support for the Party, by getting churches to support the Greens. He stated:

> *"Greens are a catalyst for the coming into being of a broad and sweeping movement for transformation. Such a movement is centered on the idea of community and has many parts. At least nine are critical ...*

> *"And ninth, is the exploring of vision and values, for example Green spirituality, and the **development of linkages with churches and religious bodies."***
> *The Greens and the Politics of Transformation*

The Greens went to church to Green the congregation, get votes and to use the power of the Church to advance political goals. Changing values starts with making friends and getting adults and children to identify with and feel good about being Green. Before churches identify with the Greens they ought to study the Green Party program.

The Green movement is a ruthless, political movement that employs the 'end justifies the means mentality'.

We Can't Trust The Greens

The Green's track record is not impressive. Multiple cases of bio-fraud, false claims about species extinctions and global warming all point to serious issues regarding competence, honesty and violating the public trust. If an error happens once or twice, forgive and forget, but this has been going on for years.

The following excerpts are from a December 2002, article in the *Intellectual Activist,* by Keith H. Lockitch. The article is about Bjorn Lomborg and the "Battle of the Skeptical Environmentalist":

> *"To environmentalists, their desire to 'save the planet' from human activity* **supercedes any concern for the facts, and they have no compunction about inventing the imaginary threats** *from which it supposedly needs to be saved."*

> *"The figure that is quoted repeatedly is that species are vanishing at a rate of 40,000 per year, with 25 to 100 percent of all species on earth allegedly doomed to disappear within our lifetime. (Lomborg finds that the actual figure is closer to 0.7% over the next 50 years.) The 40,000 number turns out to be pure fiction, invented by acclaimed environmentalist Norman Myers, in his 1979 book, The Sinking Ark."*

"... Myers himself openly acknowledges that it was "advanced primarily to get the issue of extinction onto scientific and political agendas..."

"... Yet environmentalists and the media continue to trumpet this figure as though it were an actual, scientific estimate of the rate of species extinction. After grudgingly admitting that Myer's number was pulled out of thin air, one of the reviewers for Scientific American says: "Nevertheless, he deserves credit for being the first to say that the number was large and for doing it at a time when it was difficult to make more accurate calculations."

No one can make intelligent decisions about the environment without the facts. False claims and blatant misrepresentations ought to disqualify the Greens from positions of leadership and trust regarding the health and well being of the environment.

The Green's subversive political goals demand that environmental education be put on hold until curriculum materials can be examined from a political standpoint. The health and well being of our children and our nation requires this immediate action.

Social Justice

The steps outlined by the Greens to create a sustainable society establish the values, conditions and standards of a communist society.

This is why 'sustainability' is the goal of the Green Party, the Communist Party, the Earth Charter, the 60's revolutionaries and other extremists. Sustainability, as defined in ecological terms, equals Green Communism.

We refer to Democrats as Democrats and Republicans as Republicans and it's time to refer to Communists as Communists and Green Communists as Green Communists. This is a political issue, not an environmental issue.

Green goals to eradicate poverty, end all oppression of man by man and create a classless society, that provides for the basic needs of all citizens, is identical to Communism. Under Communism every citizen is guaranteed a job, food, housing, healthcare and education, in exchange for working for the common good. This is the Green agenda.

The facts show Green goals for social justice and sustainability match Communism. The Earth Charter and social justice both require the redistribution of the wealth, in nations and among nations, to meet the basic needs of everyone on the planet. This equals Green world Communism.

This is why the goals of the Earth Charter include changing our government. To achieve these goals our government would have to be changed into a dictatorial force that controlled the economy, the resources and the American people. This is what the Greens have in mind. Social justice and sustainability are just two of the excuses to get the job done. To achieve these goals, a revolution would have to take place, on the ground, or in our minds.

We have learned that the wild claims about species extinctions and global warming are false, yet the Greens continue to use them to scare people.

Fear creates the perception that change is unavoidable and sets-the-stage for Gorbachev's goal to create a 'revolution in people's minds'. The Greens are using environmental doom to try and scare us into accepting the absurd idea we must change our government to save the environment.

Insiders, like Dr. Patrick Moore, a co-founder of Greenpeace, have confirmed the environmental movement:

- has lost its way
- has more to do with politics than science
- has been hijacked by leftists and extremists

The Greens are the 'leftists and extremists' that are hiding behind the environmental cause to impose Green Communism. We've been set-up and so have our children.

Sneak and Teach

The Green's plan to reform education includes, 'sneak and teach', which means, sneaking Green Party values into schools. Greens are using schools to teach group-think and interdependence instead of self-reliance and independence. Greens teach their political values in many ways, including cooperative play.

> *"We condemn the ... focus in our schools on team sports, which divides our children into winners and losers... We propose ... a sports program that emphasizes cooperative play..."*
> Green Party Program 1992

"School Says Game of Tag Is Out" was the title of a FOX News report, June 20, 2002, by Anita Vogel. Vogel reported:

> **"A Santa Monica elementary school has banned the game of tag,** *once synonymous with youth and innocence,* **because** *they say* **it creates self-esteem issues among weaker and slower children.** *... Tamara Silver, a parent of a fifth-grader at Franklin Elementary School, said the school sent her two letters informing her of the new rules.*
>
> **The second letter cited safety concerns,** *not issues of self-image,* **to justify the tag ban. I want my child to know that he can have some freedom,** *Silver said.* **"**

The game of tag is out because it's part of the Green's political agenda to eliminate competition, individualism, and the thrill of success at an early age. If children learn to play cooperatively there are no winners. If the Greens eliminate the opportunity to excel they dampen the desire to excel. This is why the Greens stress cooperation, not competition.

The Greens are very close to getting all their political values taught in public schools nationwide through social education and environmental education programs. Earth Day celebrations, that last a day, a week or a month, serve to cement the Green's political values. The Greens are after our children because they know little people don't understand the difference between freedom and servitude. If the Greens are successful, they never will.

> All Who Have
> Meditated On The Art
> Of Governing
> Mankind Are
> Convinced That
> The Fate Of Empires
> Depends On The
> Education Of Youth.
>
> Aristotle
>
> *The Rebirth of America*

It's up to us, whether or not our children, grandchildren, nieces, nephews, cousins and thousands of other precious children, will inherit an America where they are free to think and reach for their dreams. If we fail, our children, all of them, will inherit an American where the Greens engineer their values, limit their passions and dictate their lives. Greens plan to use education to shape children's values so they can control America's future. It was child abuse when Hitler and Lenin used schools to indoctrinate children into the ranks of their political Parties. It's eco-child abuse for the Greens to indoctrinate children into the ranks of their political Party.

We cannot trust the Greens to educate America's children because the facts prove the Greens intend to indoctrinate our children with extremist, anti-American, 60's revolutionary, Green Party values.

We cannot trust the Greens because they are using America's support for the environmental cause to promote Gorbachev's Earth Charter. Supporting the Earth Charter amounts to supporting Communism and a subversive, calculated effort to change our government and take control of our lives.

We cannot trust the Greens to take care of the environment because they repeatedly misrepresent critical facts. We can't have an honest relationship with a dishonest person and we can't have an honest relationship with a dishonest movement.

The goal to help those in need and create a healthier environment does not require changing our government or giving up our freedom. We need to remember what former Vice President Al Gore said:

> *"And it is no accident that **the very worst environmental tragedies were created by communist governments**, in which the power of the state completely overwhelms the capabilities of the individual steward."*
>
> Al Gore
> Former Vice President

Green Communism is not the way to a healthy environment. Freedom, private property ownership and protecting our system of government is the key to environmental excellence.

Many of the Green groups listed on page 55 are still working together to change America. 'Save Our Environment' is a coalition of the following groups:

- Defenders of Wildlife
- Friends of the Earth*
- National Audubon Society
- National Parks & Conservation Association
- National Wildlife Federation*
- Sierra Club*
- Earthjustice (formerly the Sierra Club Legal Defense Fund)
- Union of Concerned Scientist
- Wilderness Society*
- World Wildlife Fund
- Greenpeace
- American Oceans Campaign
- American Rivers
- Environmental Defense
- League of Conservation Voters
- National Environmental Trust
- Natural Resource Defense Council*
- Physicians for Social Responsibility*
- The Ocean Conservancy
- The State PIRGS

Source: www.saveourenvironment.org

Many of these group's leaders were interviewed for the book *Earth Rising*, whose author, Phillip Shabecoff, indicated the movement's future goals included using schools to teach children their values. Some of these groups (see *) also support Gorbachev's Earth Charter and getting Earth Charter values taught in schools.

The Greens will use Earth Day (April 22nd) to pressure students, citizens and political leaders into supporting their 'undisclosed' political agenda. Green goals for sustainability, 'systems thinking', education (NCSE) and support for the Earth Charter add up to Green Communism and the 60's goals for revolution.

The Greens haven't got the job done yet. The choice is still ours but it's time to move. President George Bush said in his 2001 inaugural address:

> "What you do is as important as anything government does ... I ask you to be citizens: citizens, not spectators; citizens, not subjects; responsible citizens, building communities of service and a nation of character. When this spirit of citizenship is missing; no government program can replace it. When this spirit is present, no wrong can stand against it."

It's time to get off the sidelines. Operation Green Out! is the title of this chapter and it is also a national citizens campaign to get Green politics out in the open and out of America's schools. Everyone can do something to help awaken the 'sleeping giant'.

The Sleeping Giant

> "A defector from the Czech KGB described his organizations secret evaluation of Americans. Josef Frolik, testifying before the Senate Committee on the Judiciary on November 18, 1975, said:
>
> "The American people have a reserve of common sense and patriotism that will withstand the onslaught of the Communist propaganda campaign if it can be unmasked and reversed in time...
>
> The patriotism of the average American is extremely high... The KGB intelligence officer should not permit

himself to be misled by the apparent indifference shown by the average American."

"...The American masses are referred to as 'the sleeping giant', who always requires a shock before he comes to his senses, but thereafter is merciless."

Target America
James Tyson

Our forefathers chose their destiny and in the heart of every American that spirit burns. The will to be free is part of who we are. **'The land of the free and the home of the brave',** is not just a phrase, it's an attitude and a heartfelt commitment. Americans must stand together to reclaim our country and preserve our legacy of freedom. This is our duty and our gift to all future Americans. With a past like ours, we could never explain failure. Think American, Act American and remember:

"Choice, not chance determines destiny"

We can begin by making Earth Day a choice not a mandate. Earth Day is using its influence to promote the Earth Charter and the goal to change our government. Earth Day is a political event, advancing a covert, anti-American agenda. It is inappropriate to continue to allow Earth Day to be celebrated, like a national holiday, in taxpayer-funded, public schools. Parents, teachers, political leaders and concerned citizens can join together and insist Earth Day is no longer celebrated on school grounds or promoted in class. This is a reasonable request and a responsible action. Expelling Earth Day requires no more than a memo from the school board or administration. The same applies to the Earth Charter.

For further information on what you can do to help, see the order form in the back of the book for contact details.

Green References

This resource list is provided as a service for readers who are interested in learning more about the Green Movement and Communism.

Greening America

Alternatives to Economic Globilization	Report	2002
Biosphere Politics	Rifkin	1991
Blueprint for a Green Economy	Pierce and Markandya	1989
Building the Green Movement	Bahro	1986
Continental Conservation	Soule and Terborgh	1999
Communes and the Green Vision	Pepper	1991
From Red to Green	Bahro	1984
Earth in the Balance	Gore	1992
Earth Rising	Shabecoff	2000
Ecology	Hall	
1972		
Ecology and Socialism	Ryle	1988
Eco-Socialism	Pepper	1991
GAIA Atlas of Green Economics	Ekins	
1992		
Getting There - Steps to a Green Society	Wall	1990
Green Lifestyle Handbook	Rifkin	1990
Green Political Theory	Goodin	1992
Green Politics -The Global Promise	Spretnak	1986
Home -Bioregional Reader	NSP	1990
On My Country And The World	Gorbachev	
1999		
Radical Ecology	Merchant	
1992		
Save the Earth	Porritt and Capra	1991
Seeing Green -Politics of Ecology	Porritt	1984
Sixteen Weeks with European Greens	Feinstein	1992
The Search For A New Beginning	Gorbachev	1995
The Second American Revolution	Rockefeller	1973
The Great New Wilderness Debate	Nelson	1998
The Greens and Politics of Tranformation	Resenbrink	1992
The Green Revolution	Sale	1993

The Green Alternatives	Toklar	1987
The Greening of America	Reich	1970
The Morning After Earth Day	Graham	1999
The Way -An Ecological World View	Goldsmith	1993
Toward a Transpersonal Ecology	Fox	1990
The Little Green Book	Lobell	1981
Voting Green	Rifkin	1992
	Grunewald and Barbier	

Eco-Spirituality

Goddess Mythology in Ecological Politics	Biehl	1989
Spiritual Dimension of Green Politics	Spretnak	1986
Greenspirit -Ecological Spirituality	LaChance	1991
How Deep is Deep Ecology	Bradford	1989
GAIA	Lovelock	1979
Deep Ecology and Anarchism	Bookchin and Others	1993
Spiritual Politics	McLaughlin and Davidson	1994
The Green Bible	Scharper and Cunningham	1993
Green Egg	Church of All Worlds	1993

Little Green Army

The Kids Guide to Social Action	Lewis	1991
Changing Our World Handbook Young Activists	Fleisher	1993
Captain Eco and the Fate of the Earth	Porritt	1991
Save the Earth -Created by Kids	Hirsh	1992
Earth Book for Kids	Schwartz	1990
The Kids Environmental Book	Pedersen	1991
Kid Heroes of the Environment	EarthWorks	1991
Wild, Wild Wolves	Milton	1992
Save the Earth -Action Handbook for Kids	Miles	1991
Dear World	Temple	1993
For the Love of Our Earth	Hallinan	1992
Hands Around the World	Milford	1992
Student Environmental Action Guide	EarthWorks	1991
Teaching Kids to Love the Earth	Herman and	
1991		

	Passineau	
This Planet is Mine	Metzger and Whittaker	1991
Going Green	Elkingoon Hailes Hill Makower	1990
Rethinking Columbus	Rethinking Schools	1991
Green Teacher Education for Planet Earth #34	Jun-Sept	1993
Radical Teacher Socialist & Feminist Journal #43	Fall	1993

Additional References

Title	Author	Year
Educating for the New World Order	Eakman	1991
Environmental Agenda for the Future	Island Press	1985
Unsettling of American Culture & Agriculture	Berry	1977
One World or None	Harris	1993
Biosphere Politics	Rifkin	1991
The Unfinished Agenda	Barney	1977
You Can Change America	EarthWorks	1993
Putting Power in Its Place	Plane	1992
Climate in Crisis	Bates	1989
The Way Ahead	Shapiro	1992
The Indian Way Communicate with Mother Earth	McLain	1990
Millennium-Winners & Losers in World Order	Attali	1991
Entropy -A New World Order	Rifkin	1980
Entropy -Revised Edition	Rifkin	1989
Earth	Ehrlich	1987
Earthwatch	Savan	1991
Seeds of Change	Ausubel	1994
Earth in the Balance	Gore	1992
1992 Earth Journal	Buzzworm	1992
The Turning Point	Capra	1982
Call to Action	Erickson	1990
Vote for the Earth	EarthWorks	1992
Psychopathic God	Waite	1977
Living Richly in an Age of Limits	Devall	1993
Last Refuge	Robbins	1994
The Rainforest Book	Lewis	1990
The End of Work	Rifkin	1995
Environmental Literacy	Dashefsky	1993
Avoiding Social and Eco Disaster	Bahro	1994
New Options for America	Satin	1991
Agenda 21 Earth Summit Strategy	Sitarz	1993

Planet Hood	Ferencz	1988
The Rediscovery of North America	Lopez	1992
Negotiating Survival	Gardner	1992
The Closing Circle	Commoner	1972
Voluntary Simplicity	Elgin	1981
Save the Animals	Newkirk	1990
Direct Action and Liberal Democracy	Carter	1973
Balancing on the Brink of Survival	Kohm	1991
Real Choices New Voices	Amy	1993
State of the Ark	Durrell	1986
Free Things for Teachers	Osborn	1990
Macrocosm USA	Brockway	1992
Working with Earth, Economy & Environment	Kraft	1993
	Mcleod and Wells	
Putting People First	Clinton Gore	1992
The Animal Rights Handbook	L P Press	1990
It's a Matter of Survival	Gordon and Suzuki	1990
Media and the Environment	LaMay and Dennis	1991
Moving Towards a New Society 1976	Gowan	
	Lakey Moyers and Taylor	
Forward Motion	Socialist Magazine	1989
Green Man	A magazine for Pagan men #2	1993

Bibliography

Books

Bates, Albert K., *Climate in Crisis*, The Book Publishing Company, Summertown, TN., 1990

Brockway, Sandi, *Macrocosm USA* (includes insert), Macrocosm U.S.A. Inc., Cambria, CA, 1992

Clinton, Bill and Gore, Al, *Putting People First*, Times Books, New York, 1992

Communist Party U.S.A., *The United States in Crisis*, New Outlook Publishers, New York, 1969

Cuddy, Dennis, *Now is the Dawning of the New Age, New World Order*, Hearthstone Publishing, Ltd. Oklahoma City, 1991

De Roussy de Sales, Raoul, *My New Order*, Reynal & Hitchcock, New York, 1941

Drakeford, John W., *Red Blueprint for the World*,Wm. B. Eerdmans Publishing Company, Grand Rapids, MI, 1962

Durrell, Lee, *State of the Ark*, Gaia Books Limited, Bodley Head Ltd, London, 1986

Eakman, B.K.,*Educating for the New World Order*, Halcyon House, Portland, OR, 1991

Earth Journal 1993, Editors, Buzzworm Magazine, Buzzworm Books,Boulder, CO, 1992

Ebon, Martin, *The Soviet Propaganda Machine*, McGraw-Hill Book Company, San Francisco, 1987

Ehrlich, Anne H. and Paul R., *Earth*, Franklin Watts Inc., New York, 1987

Flint, R. Warren and Houser, W.L., *Living a Sustainable Lifestyle for Our Children's Children*, Authors Choice Press, an imprint of iUniverse.com, Inc., Lincoln, NE, 2001

Golitsyn, Anatoliy, *New Lies For Old*, Clarion House, Atlanta, GA, 1984

Gore, Albert, *Earth in the Balance*, Houghton-Mifflin Company, New York, 1992

Hall, Gus, *Ecology*, International Publishers, New York, 1972

Heck, Alfons, *A Child of Hitler*, Renaissance House, Frederick, CO. 1985

Hitler, Adolf, *My Secret Book*, translated by Salvator Attanasio, Grove Press Inc., New York, 1961

Hitler, Adolf, Speech 1933, *The Rise and Fall of the Third Reich*, Chapter 8, Education in the Third Reich,1959

Johnsen, Julia E., *Should The Communist Party Be Outlawed?*, The H.W. Wilson Company, New York, 1949

Koenigsberg, Richard A., Hitler's Ideology, Library of Social Science, New York

Marx Karl, *Communist Manifesto,* Regnery Comany, Chicago, 1954Marx, Karl,*Critique of the Gotha Programme,* 1885, repr. Karl Marx, Selected Works, Vol.1, 1942

Miles, Betty, *Save the Earth, An Action Handbook for Kids,* Alfred A. Knopf, Inc., New York, 1974, 1991

Milord, Susan, *Hands Around the World,* Williamson Publishing, Charlotte, VT. 1992

Milton, Joyce, *Wild, Wild Wolves,* Random House, Inc., New York, 1992

Pearson, Michael, *The Sealed Train,* Putnam, New York, 1975

Porritt, Jonathon, *Save the Earth,* Turner Publishing Inc., Atlanta, GA, 1991

Porritt, Jonathon, *Captain Eco and the Fate of the Earth,* Dorling Kindersley, New York, London, 1991

Rensenbrink, John, *The Greens and the Politics of Transformation,* R.& E. Miles, CA, 1992

Rifkin, Jeremy, *Entropy,* Bantam Books, New York, 1980

Rifkin, Jeremy, *Entropy,* Revised Edition, Bantam Books, New York, 1989

Rifkin, Jeremy, Carol Grunewald Rifkin, *Voting Green,* Doubleday, 1992

Rifkin, Jeremy, *Biosphere Politics,* Harper, San Francisco, 1991

Rockefeller, John D., *The Second American Revolution,* Harper and Row, New York, 1973

Stormer, John A., *None Dare Call It Treason,* The Liberty Bell Press, Florissant, MO., 1964

Turner, Henry Ashby, Hitler, *Memoirs of a Confidant,* Yale University Press, New Haven, 1985

Tyson, James L., *Target America,* Regnery Gateway, Chicago, IL 1981

Waite, Robert G.L.,*Psychopathic God,* Basic Books, Inc. New York, 1977

Williams, Albert Rhys, *Journey Into Revolution,* Quadrangle Books, Chicago, 1969

Articles, Newspapers, Magazines and Newsletters

Brodine, Virginia Warner, *'The Environment: A Natural Terrain for Communists',* Political Affairs, January, 1989

Cohn, Bob and Turque, Bill, *'Clinton rescues the Mexican economy',* Time magazine, February 13, 1995.

Corliss, Richard, *'Princess of the Spirit',* Time magazine, June 9,1995

Crawford, Peter, *Common Future,* Premier Issue, No. 1, Prout Research Institute, 1995

Doder, Dusko, *Experiment That Failed, The Bolshevik Revolution,* National Geographic, Vol. 182, No. 4, October, 1992

Democratic Socialists Brochures, Democratic Socialists of America, New York

Earth First Journal, *Eco-Depth Guage*, March, 1991

Earth First, slogan, The Macmillan Dictionary of Political Quotations, Lewis Eigen and Jonathan Siegel, Macmillan Publishing Company, New York, 1993

Ecologist, Vol. 21, No.6, Nov.- Dec. 1991

Ecology, Anarchism and Green Politics, Youth Greens, Minneapolis, MN, Left Green Network, Burlington, VT. September, 1990

EcoSocialist Review, Chicago, Democratic Socialists of America, Summer 1990, Summer 1991, Spring 1994

Earth Times, Vol. VII, Number 4, June, 1994, Earth Times

Elliott, Michael,'*Why the Mexican Crisis Matters*', Time magazine, February 13, 1995.

EnviroScan, September, 1994, Biodiversity, Rik Scarce, Eco-Warriors

Evans, Harold, The Sunday Times, 1971, Political Quotations, Daniel Baker, Editor, Gale Research Inc., Detroit, London, 1990

Grassroots,'*Green Cross International*' and '*A Clear and Simple Message*',Volume 2, Issue 1, Grassroots Publishing, Ltd., Blaine, WA, 1995

Greens - *Green Party U.S.A. Program*, Prompt Press, Green Committees of Correspondence, Kansas City, MO. Camden, NJ, 1992

Hall, Gus,'*The World We Preserve Must Be Livable*', World Marxist Review, May, 1988

Hall, Gus, '*A Mass Party In The Making*', Political Affairs, June 25, 1994

Hall, Gus, '*The Caricature of Communism*', Political Affairs, January, 1989

Hershey, A. & H., *Communists Rules for Revolution*, Maxine Salade

Herzen, Alexander, Russian Journalist

In CONTEXT, '*Redefining Entertainment*', No. 24, Fall 1989

McAlvany Intelligence Advisor, Don McAlvany, March, 1995, May, June 1995, Phoenix, AZ

Marquart, Kathleen, Putting People First, From the Trenches, February, 1994, September 29, 1994, November 7, 1994

Medford Mail Tribune, , Multiple entries 1995-2002

Montaigne, Fen, *From Red to Green*, Audubon magazine, Nov.Dec. 1994

Parade Magazine, Multiple entries 1995-2001

Progressive, The Progressive Inc., Madison, WI, February, 1995

Rensenbrink, John, *A Green Strategy for the 90s*, E, The Environmental magazine, September-October, 1990

San Francisco Examiner, Richard Powelson, *Religious leaders see green, Agree to take up environmentalism*, June 16, 1991

San Joaquin County Citizens Land Alliance, Tracy, CA. Feb., June 1995

Sierra, the magazine of the Sierra Club, Sierra Club Bulletin, September, October 1995

Thatcher, Margaret, IMPRIMIS, March, 1995, Volume 24, No.3

Fedarko, Kevin, *From Russia With Venom*, Time magazine, July 11, 1994

Trilogy, Trilogy Publishing Inc., Winter 1991, Number 34, Lexington, KY

Utne Reader, *Voting Green*, Carol Gruenwald Rifkin, Sept. Oct. 1992, LENS Publishing Co. Inc., Minneapolis, MN

World Conservation Strategy, IUCN, International Union for Conservation of Nature and Natural Resources, UNEP, United Nations Environmental Programmme, WWF, World Wildlife Fund, in collaboration with FAO, Food and Agriculture Organizations of the United Nations and UNESCO, United Nations Educational Scientific and Cultural Organizations, Steps in a Strategy, 1980

Audio, Video Recordings

Elicker, Roy, Counsel, National Wildlife Federation, Pacific Northwest Resources Center, '*Public Lands Grazing*' Panel, Land, Air, Water Conference (LAW), University of Oregon, 1991

Liverman, Marc, Audubon Society Conservation Director, *Innovations in Endangered Species Protection Panel*, Land, Air, Water Conference (LAW), University of Oregon, 1991

Stahl, Andy, Sierra Club Legal Defense Club, Research Analyst, 'Allbrook Panel: *Old Growth's Last Stand*', Western Public Interest Law Conference, University of Oregon, 1988

Stossel, John, ABC News Special S010629-01, *Tampering With Nature*

Index

About the Author

Holly Swanson is an author and the founder of Operation Green Out! a campaign dedicated to citizen awareness and political action. The mission of Operation Green Out! is to get Green politics out in the open and out of America's schools.

Swanson wrote *Set Up & Sold Out* after initial investigation into the environmental movement triggered concerns about the undisclosed political agenda of the Greens. *Set Up & Sold Out* is the result of 10 years of extensive, independent research, into both sides of the environmental debate. Her goal is to interrupt the hypnotic mentality created by years of Green social conditioning and bring these issues to the forefront.

Order Form

Set Up & Sold Out (___) *Copies* at $20 each plus shipping

Name:_____

Address:_____

City:_____State_____Zip_____-_____

Telephone: (_____)_____-_____

Email Address: _____

☎   Telephone orders   **800-684-1992**

      Fax orders   **541-830-1448**

Payment   ☐ Visa ☐ Mastercard ☐ Discover ☐ Debit Card ☐ Check

Credit Card number_____-_____-_____-_____

Name on Card_____

Expiration Date_____ Billing address Zip Code_____

Postal orders: C.I.N., P.O. Box 2645, White City, OR 97503

Shipping: Check one:

☐ Book Rate @ $2.00 each   ☐ Priority Mail @ $6.00 each
(7-10 days delivery)   (2-3 days delivery)

(Call 541/830-1446 for quantity pricing or multiple copy shipping rate)

Make checks payable to: C.I.N. Publishing

Thank You

Operation Green Out! website: www.greenout.org
Campaign participation, please see next page.

Cut along dotted line and mail your contribution today!

Yes, I want to join Operation GREEN OUT! and help get Green politics out in the open and out of our schools.

OPERATION GREEN OUT! ™

Name: .... email: ....

Address ....

City: .... State. .... Zip: .... Phone: (..........)..............

I want to help build this grassroots movement. Here's my contribution:

☐ $500 ☐ $250 ☐ $100 ☐ $50 ☐ $35 ☐ $25 annual membership.

*With a contribution of $35 or more, you will receive a copy of the book *Set Up & Sold Out*.

☐ Visa ☐ MasterCard ☐ Discover

Credit Card Number:..

Expiration Date: .... Name on Card: ....

Please make checks payable to: **Operation Green Out!** (Contributions and dues are not tax deductible).
P.O. Box 2645 • **White City, OR 97503** • **Phone: 541-830-1446** • **Fax 541-830-1448**